Praise for David A. Morehouse

"There's a power that very few people know how to harness—David Morehouse knows the way. He can teach it to anyone with the will and desire to learn."

—ANTHONY ROBBINS
Awaken the Giant Within; Unlimited Power

"Through his pioneering work with Remote Viewing, David Morehouse is mapping the future of consciousness in the West, a merging of scientific rigor and spiritual possibility that anyone can access."

—DEEPAK CHOPRA
Ageless Body, Timeless Mind; How to Know God; The Seven Spiritual Laws of Success

"David has shown us how a tool made for war can become a path of spiritual transformation. He has shown the courage to walk in the way of peace."

—DON MIGUEL RUIZ
The Four Agreements

"It is my privilege to know David and experience the service that he is offering. He is putting into everyone's hands the tools for the expansion of their consciousness. David's presence and his teachings are very important in this moment of the New Sunrise."

—JORGE LUIS DELGADO
Andean Awakening: An Inca Guide to Mystical Peru

"Remote Viewing is real, David is real, and you should let both be a new beginning for you. Let your soul open up as broad as the night sky of the universe, and let it strengthen you. Trust what you hear from David Morehouse because he is living his life to transform this planet."

—DANNION BRINKLEY
Saved by the Light

REMOTE VIEWING

REMOTE VIEWING

THE COMPLETE USER'S MANUAL FOR COORDINATE REMOTE VIEWING

DAVID A. MOREHOUSE, PH.D.

SOUNDS TRUE

Sounds True, Inc.
Boulder, CO 80306

SOUNDS TRUE is a trademark of Sounds True, Inc.

Published 2008
Printed in Canada

10 9 8 7 6 5 4 3 2 1

Library of Congress Cataloging-in-Publication Data

Morehouse, David, 1954-
  Remote viewing : the complete user's manual for coordinate remote viewing
/ David A. Morehouse.
      p. cm.
  Includes bibliographical references (p. 371) and index.
  ISBN 978-1-59179-239-0 (hardcover)
  1. Remote viewing (Parapsychology) I. Title.

BF1389.R45M67 2007
133.8'4—dc22

2006101646

♻ This book is printed on paper recycled from 100% postconsumer-waste and processed
without chlorine.

One always learns of one's mystery,
at the price of one's innocence.

Robert Davies

This book is dedicated to all the students of Remote Viewing the world over. To those who braved their conditioning and made the journey inward to self-discovery and outward to the edge of knowledge. To the pioneers of this art and science, Russell Targ and Harold Puthoff, and all those who courageously worked with them to establish in science the credibility and viability of human potential. And most certainly to those monitors and Viewers who served their country in the mysterious and often controversial unit of psychic spies: Skip Atwater, Ed Dames, Paul Smith, Lyn Buchanan, Mel Riley, Joe McMoneagle, the late Gabrielle Pettingale, as well as Angela (last name omitted) and Robin (last name omitted). Further, this dedication extends to all who served or explored, and who, with valor, embraced the new battlefield of mind and dimension—and honored it.

Contents

List of Figures

List of Handouts

Acknowledgments

*When I find myself fading, I close my eyes
and realize my friends are my energy.*

Anonymous

In the movie *The Affair of the Necklace*, there's a line of dialogue that says, "Honor does not come from a name; it comes from what lives in the heart." I have never forgotten this, and I can never forget the following people, who, with their hearts, guided my work: Anthony Robbins, Deepak Chopra, Don Miguel Ruiz, Jorge Luis Delgado, and Dannion Brinkley.

My father, Virgil Morehouse, who passed away during the writing of this book—a career soldier, father, husband, and grandfather—his greatest life lesson to me was to "learn to forgive." My beautiful mother, Marba Morehouse, whose perseverance and attitude toward life inspire me still. Roger and Mary DeMartin, for bringing Patty into my life. My brother and sister, Dennis Morehouse and Jennie McCallum, who have been with me through life, with love and support. Glenn and Clydell Cox, Max and Rita Sones, Natha "Kitty" Davis, and all the family who have inspired perseverance.

My editor, Alice Karow, who tirelessly carved this work from a mountain of material. My publisher, Tami Simon, and the entire staff of Sounds True, for their vision of spirit and opportunity. My friends—I am blessed with far too many to name here—but especially those who played a role in this book:

David Hughes, Mark Waters, Craig and Laura Burness, Michael and Julie Nitty, Sam and Lynn Georges, and Colonel Robert Frank. Theron and Mary Ann Male, Ted and Mary Macy, Mimi Peak, Joanne Chrobot, Michael Craft, Jeff DeMartin, Jason Appleby, Jason Hooper, Joey Cassanova, Stan Evanson, Anne Haritatos, Rommel Lozano, Donn Hopkins, Randall Henderson, John Herlosky, and James O'Brian. Hundreds of other dear and close friends, and, of course, I must recognize the boundless inspiration of over twenty-three thousand students.

The soldiers I have served with, learned from, and been inspired by: GEN Dan McNeil, GEN Fred Woerner, LTG James Dubik, MG Kenneth Leuer, BG Joseph Stringham, BG Mick Bednarek, BG Tony Tata, COL Wesley Taylor, COL Tim Scully, COL Keith Nightingale, LTC Jim Reese, CSM Sam Spears, CSM Larry Allen, CSM David Dalton, COL Sid Head, Chaplain MAJ Tim Walls, SGM Scott Mitten, and CSM Mark Helton. And all those whose ranks I do not know, but for whom I carry the utmost respect: David Hart, Virgil Willoughby, Kevin Connel, Chris Pipes, Doc Donovan, Timothy Hayes, Tom Paschal, Gary Vorous, State Representative (and Ranger) Jack Hennessey, Jeff Greene, Troy VanBeek, and James Williams.

I could not have finished this work without the love and support of my wife, Patty. She was there by my side for six years of my life, watching me in the quiet moments, balancing life amidst the clash of time and being. She never faltered in her belief that I needed to write this book. She maintained that it was the need of humanity to have this work for its use, however significant or not. Patty helped me see through the fog of my existence and perceived obstacles—she is as much responsible for this book as I am.

My publisher, Tami Simon, also lovingly supported me, gently pressed me, and perceptively stood down when she knew I was straining against the tide. Her staff at Sounds True is a committed and focused gathering of purposeful, spirit-minded people, who make me welcome each day and thank God for their presence on this planet. To Nancy Smith, the engineer of all that I do with Sounds True, I give my thanks and respect in appreciation for her tireless devotion to excellence. Nancy's candor, her spirit, and her focus have made this work possible.

To my children, Michael, Mariah, and Danielle, and my grandson, Gavin; to my two beautiful stepchildren, Courtney and Jason—I thank you all for your love, your support, and your belief in me. There is greatness within you, already manifest and still more to come. If I were, in my youth, a fraction of what each of you are, I might have cured cancer or invented something extraordinary by now. I am grateful for your presence in my life, and what I learn from you is immeasurable. Your example makes me want to be a better man.

Foreword

Welcome to the realm of endless possibilities. Discovering this realm is like being three years old and seeing the ocean for the first time. It is exciting and a bit scary at the same time. The water seems endless on the horizon. Your entry into the water is filled with the new experiences of the feel of the salt water, the power of the waves, and the smell of the sea air. New sounds fill your ears, and you savor life in a new way. You will need all your senses, including your sense of adventure, and your ability to welcome new possibilities as you enter the world of David Morehouse and Remote Viewing.

Coordinate Remote Viewing starts with an ideogram, a quick expression of pen on paper that conveys the knowledge of the unconscious or "other" mind. This one short, intuited motion contains all the basic information of the target to be viewed. David, like an ideogram, contains all the basic information of how to live a purposeful, positive, creative, and loving life. When you have the privilege to know and study with David, you have begun to understand the man and his message. He presents all the necessary components to experience this reality of our modern life from a new, vastly expanded vantage point.

Nearly eight years ago, a close friend and mentor suggested that we take David's course in Remote Viewing. When we signed up for the course, we didn't have any idea of what to expect. We felt that we were having a bit of beginner's luck with our first ideograms and found the early exercises intriguing. By the second day of a five-day course, we felt like we were spending hours practicing scales when we wanted to play the piano. David insisted that we learn the basics, the scales, and promised that this time spent would be worth the effort. He said that we would need these skills and tools to facilitate our own talents in Remote Viewing. He said that everyone could accomplish Remote Viewing, but as with playing music, some have more natural talent. We weren't sure of how much talent we had; we just wanted to get to it. With each hour, we grew more restless, like horses at the starting gate ready to perform. Finally, late in the second day, we had a "target" and were off and running, or rather flying.

This first flight, or Viewing of a target, was for us a test of our newly learned skills. These skills and protocols were expertly taught by this former military officer, a teacher whose instruction left no doubt of his regimental background and his genuine caring that we each master our capacity to open to the endless possibilities that awaited us. Now it was up to us to allow it to happen. The first thought that races through the mind is "I won't be able to get it. Not me!"—a familiar belief from past school experiences. David told us to leave all doubt behind, and just trust and follow the protocols. It would just happen.

As the assignment ended, we were filled with a lot of doubt as well as curiosity. After coming out of a light trance experience, the "eureka" burst occurred when, to our amazement, our descriptions and sketches projected on the screen were very similar to the majority of other beginning students, and very similar to the target picture that had been in a sealed envelope. Our descriptions and especially our sketches of the "visited" target were too similar to write off as just chance. We no longer had doubt that we were not only on target, but also at the target, experiencing the target. It was in this experience of sharing our collected data that we came to accept and trust the vastness of what is.

This was just the beginning. As the course progressed, we had a growing appreciation of patiently learning the basic skills and just allowing the experience to unfold. Like a kaleidoscope being slowly turned, one's long-standing perspective is shattered as the mind adjusts to a novel, yet undefined, pattern that will forever be morphing with each Viewing journey. We instantly realized that we could and we did escape the shackles of what we were programmed to believe is our reality. An experience of excitement and awesome freeness seeps through the body, and this was just the beginning of what becomes more and more natural. We no longer perceive our lives, the planet, or the universe as separate, compartmentalized units, but as One—one living, breathing Being of which each of us is an aspect, a co-creator of our moment-to-moment reality, for which we are responsible and accountable.

At the end of the week, we were filled with many thoughts and emotions. The main lesson was realizing that the first person who ever misrepresents the truth to us is our self. It was all too evident that our minds can take what is real and filter it through our past experiences to misrepresent what is genuine. This was a fascinating discovery and is probably usual for most people. It highlights the realization that regardless of what we think is true, it is only a perspective based on individual experience. We know firsthand how the tower of a temple located in Asia that we have never seen can quickly morph into an ancient astronomical ruin that we did see in Central America. This has been a very valuable lesson, a lesson for life. It has allowed us to at least think beyond our own experiences and conditioning. Having learned Remote Viewing, we are more open to new concepts, varied points of view, and limitless possibilities. The universe is richer and more alive, with many new dimensions, experienced and yet to be experienced.

We continued to take courses with David. At each level, we learned more about the universe and the many talents we naturally possess. David was able to introduce us to many facets of our own abilities. The applications of Remote Viewing have increasingly unfolded in our lives. The benefits have been more than being able to "travel" to near and distant targets. Remote Viewing is a conduit to experience life more fully and to expand our intuitive awareness. It offers a more complete human experience, bringing the expansive capacity of our minds into focus. For us, Remote Viewing became more than an exercise of the mind; it ignited a personal journey inward and beyond that can take us across town or to another time and place. The main lesson is that there is a limitless capacity in how to experience all that is available to us. We can only live in the moment, but with David, we found that the moment can take us to previously uncharted targets, in and beyond space and time.

There are many times when we call upon the information learned and the experiences encountered in our forays into the "Matrix." It is still necessary for us to go back and play the scales, to practice the basics. We now live each day with heightened awareness, appreciation, and connectedness to the universe, in awe of the limitless possibilities for beneficial change in our quality of life on planet Earth.

It is our privilege and honor to know David and to travel with him on many journeys, beginning in a Coordinate Remote Viewing class at Omega Institute in New York, to places such as the Horse Head Nebulae and the Andes of Peru. We are honored to know David and would travel with him anyplace, anytime. We have been blessed to come to this moment in the company of our friend, teacher, mentor, and fellow traveler, David Morehouse.

We invite you to read this book and begin to travel with us.

Theron Male, Ph.D., and Mary Ann Male, Ph.D.

Introduction:
Welcome to the Journey Inward

One must desire something to be alive.

Margaret Deland, *O Magazine*

You need to know that something extraordinary is possible in your life. I need you to know that you are nothing but possibilities. In a world blatantly filled with screams of limitation, where others make every effort to define your reality and limit your promise, I need you to know through this work that you are omnipresent, omnipotent, omniscient, and eternal, a magnificent being existing in a finite condition. I need you to know that you can fill your life with love and compassion, with promise and possibility, and that you can live as an example to the world—and not as a warning. I need you to know that everything that is supposed to be for you—will be.

I learned, what seems a thousand years ago, that I have a blessed life and that what I need in this life also needs me. You and I are the same. If you seek all that is possible, then all that is possible will seek you. There are no unanswered prayers in the universe; however, I know that at times it may seem so. It may be clear to you now that what you want is not present in your life. You may be certain that your desires remain unfulfilled and that the glass of your life is half-empty, that your life is one of limited promise and possibility. Conversely, if you will learn to find the gift in any problem, you will deem your life one of infinite promise and possibility. You will feel secure that life is available, that excitement and passion await or are already present. The defining element is choice. Choice is a decision in the moment about your state—physical, emotional, and spiritual—how you will respond to your life situation. Choosing well implies you have a grasp of your needs and wants, how they differ, and how you will plan and live your life from a perspective of experience, learning, and mastery. If you realize that what you need in this life will always have priority over what you want, then you will begin now to manifest the life and destiny that is yours.

This book, my fourth, was the most difficult to write. I spent ten years gathering and objectifying my thoughts, fine-tuning my methods, and developing my materials, yet it has taken me two long years to assemble this material. Why? In large part, because I did not *need* to write it. I *wanted* to write it, and my needs overcame my desires.

I have lived a diverse and privileged life. I have trained well over twenty-three thousand students in the art and science of Remote Viewing. I have traveled the world teaching, lecturing, studying, and writing. I have lectured internationally—in the United Kingdom, Germany, Sweden, Norway, Peru, Canada, and the United States. I have lectured at the Mikhail Gorbachev State of the World Forum on issues concerning global peace and alternative methods of conflict resolution. I have presented at affiliate organizations of the United Nations on issues of global peace and the potential of spirit. I have lectured at the Alliance for a New Humanity, presenting concepts of and alternatives to human possibility in the entertainment industry. I am published in fourteen languages, endorsed by the most powerful peak-performance professionals and metaphysical and spiritual teachers in the world. I am ever grateful for my life.

When I served in the military, I was deemed by my superiors to be "destined to wear stars." I commanded an airborne infantry battalion for a short while, and I have commanded two rifle companies. I am deeply honored to have served with these men and to call them friends—I trust them with my life. When I served in the military Remote Viewing unit, the program manager, GS-15 Fernand Gauvin, declared in my written evaluations that I was:

> *considered the best candidate ever to have grasped expertise in the [Remote Viewing] collection technology. . . . He has not only consistently exceeded the training standards, but has completed the training program 30 percent*

faster than any other candidate in the history of the program. . . . He has trained new [Remote Viewing] candidates with a sense of conviction and excellence that permeates his own personal and professional success.

My senior rater, Dr. Jack Verona, the chief scientist of the Defense Intelligence Agency, evaluated my performance in this way:

He stands far above his peers and contemporaries in the mastering of this intelligence collection technology. . . . A superb officer, who has a keen intellect and an unusual ability to isolate the central issues of complex problems and solve them. Totally dedicated to the unit mission, he has improved training and facilitated the learning process of all soldiers and civilians assigned to the unit.

I share this with you to set the stage for what is to come. I know this technology, and I will teach it to you. I know it in my sleep; I know it backwards, inside out, and outside in. I know the science, the theory, the practice, the application, and the philosophy surrounding it. Often, I feel I know more about it than I want to know; however, it is my nature to be a trainer, to teach, to synthesize and quantify the learning process. It is one of my callings in this existence, and I honor this calling, writing the story of my life moment to moment with this awareness. It is my service, my honor, and my need.

As Dr. Verona indicated, this is a highly complex intelligence collection discipline, and you must be willing to commit the time and devotion necessary to learn it. Learning it will not be easy; nevertheless, make no mistake: you have the ability, right now, within you. Learn this discipline as though you were going to teach it and not just do it. With each chapter, think how you would explain it to another person; read with this in mind. This book is about the protocols of possibility, and the journey inward is a need; the path to it is a want. You may find you do not want to answer the need to know with this tool, the art and science of Remote Viewing. However, because you must never stop believing in the power of you, you owe yourself a level of devotion so that you might experience all that this path has to offer. Life is about patterns learned and adopted, patterns that sustain identities and manifest behaviors. Each time you commit to the need to explore inward, do so completely and without reservation. When you come to the end of this experience, mine what is positive from it, and take the next step forward. Follow the path to the edge of knowledge, if there is one, and then decide what the next step will be.

The next step may be another path, or it may be a version of the present path, whereby you carry forward all you have learned here, augmenting your next journey. Learn all this path offers, and master all that you learn; only then can you truly say, "This is not for me." Move from the place of not knowing what you know, to unconscious competence, mastery of tools, and self-work. Master what you learn here, taking it all the way to integration in your life—and then decide the next step.

I said that you need this journey, and you do. The desire to know if there is something beyond the physical in this existence is the most significant drive in all the human condition. The desire to know God, to believe in something, whatever the name or position, surpasses all other drives within us. Why else would young men and women give up their lives for what they believe exists beyond the physical? It surpasses even the drive to procreate, hence a marriage to God and celibacy within the ranks of humanity by those who choose that path. You need to know what exists on the other side of the veil; *how* you will make this discovery is a want. Many things—money, science, availability, you name it—may drive this want. Therefore, I will ask you to remember your need. Remember this need when you begin to feel lost, bogged down in the details of this structure.

Remember your need to know the unknown when you start believing you might want an easier way. Commit to being a hunter of excellence in yourself. I promise you I will lead and guide you through the process. You must master it and thereby transform; know that you cannot transform that which you have not experienced—and that is precisely the purpose of this journey.

The Roman historian and politician Gaius Sallustius Crispus (Sallust), circa 41 BCE, proclaimed, "Every man is the architect of his own fortune." Since I began teaching Remote Viewing in 1998, my dream, my want, has been for this book to manifest. Finally, here it is, and I am very excited for you and the journey you are about to begin. I assure you that this program of instruction will empower you with a new understanding and awareness of personal ability and tools you have always had available. Moreover, it will be through the understanding and application of these tools that you will design a new beginning for yourself, transforming, morphing, never looking back to what was, only existing in the moment with the knowledge that you are more than the physical world allows, and with this knowledge, you will manifest your destiny.

I say that these tools are already yours because you have always had the ability to see distantly in space-time. You may know this, or you may only suspect it. You may have supposed it all your life, or you may have recently experienced something that now calls you to explore this notion further. Regardless of your motivation, you are about to embark on one of the most fascinating and awakening journeys of your life—and I am honored to hold the teacher's chair for this experience.

I will say to you now the words that were spoken to me in 1987 when, as a young special operations soldier and a former U.S. Army Ranger company commander, I sat anxiously in a chair facing the program manager of a then top-secret military intelligence collection program code named Sun Streak. I listened to the outline of instruction that would give me the ability to transcend space and time to see persons, places, and things remote in space and time, and to gather and report intelligence information on the same. I remember that, as I listened, I heard the words "Your life will never be the same." I promise you now that if you will give this course of instruction all that you have in the way of desire, if you will commit to the field of knowledge contained herein, your life will never be the same again, in the most positive and beautiful manner. You will open a door that will change the way you see yourself, others, and this existence.

In this book, as you read for these few moments, swelling into days and weeks as you study at your own pace, you will explore human promise and possibility. It will be with this promise and possibility that you will live a life of courage and dignity, always aware of your eternal nature and of the great wisdom you are and have access to. Writer Fernando Pessoa once wrote:

> *This dawn is the first dawn of the world. Never did this pink color, yellowing to a warm white, tinge towards the West the face of the children of the world, whose brilliant eyes gaze upon the silence brought by the glowing light. There was never this hour, nor this light, nor this person that is me, nor this gathering who are this people of spirit and peace. What will be tomorrow, will be something else—and what we see will be seen by transformed eyes—eyes full of a new vision of the world—a vision of love, of compassion, of promise and possibility.*

What will be tomorrow will be something new—and what you will see in this life, in this world, will be seen through reconstructed eyes, through the nonphysical eyes of the Remote Viewer. Your eyes will be full of a new vision of the world—a vision of love, of joy, of compassion, of promise and possibility. Your silent stroll into the Matrix Field will soon be a continual conversation, and you will recognize that all of us—beings, buildings, stones, trees, sea, and sky—are a huge family elbowing each other with words in the great procession of destiny.

To feel everything as a Remote Viewer in fine, full detail makes you different; the sensations of your soul, known perhaps all too well by you alone, are still too embryonic for the world to grasp. As a Remote Viewer, you will experience life with behavior congruent with feeling things deeply, passions and emotions that are often lost among more visible kinds of achievement—you will begin meeting your needs at the highest of levels.

Understand that your needs and wants may indeed polarize from time to time. However, in the spectral analysis of your purpose in this life, if you recognize that your wants are in conflict with your needs, but your wants are the needs of those you serve, then they are your needs as well. Further, if you ignore the needs of others when it is your calling to serve, your life will stagnate; you will not be contributing on the level you need to contribute in order to feel alive and with purpose. And if you are not contributing, you are not growing, and any organism in this finite existence that is not growing is dying.

You are my hero, you are my dream, and you are the great clarity the world now needs. So much of the world is no longer able to give meaning to what it sees, though it sees clearly what is there. The world needs you to give it clarity—Remote Viewing will bring you clarity, and in so doing, you will transform self, and transformation of self will evolve into a transformation of the collective whole.

Your first task in this program will be to work to look inward, to find within yourself a place to begin. From this place, you will begin to work methodically to develop a language of purpose, of possibility and direction for yourself. Do not be afraid of the task! It will be difficult, and it will ultimately be imperfect. Personally, I will not weep over the imperfect pages in my life; I will only tell you where I feel I can do better. You will read this many times in the chapters and pages to follow: perfection is the lowest standard anyone can have, because it is never achieved. Even if you believe you have achieved it, your perspective is relative, and therefore imperfect in the assessment of another. Perfection never materializes; it is not your quest—only knowledge is your manna, and wisdom is your quest. At this level of experience, knowledge begins with self-assessment.

Enjoy the journey inward and beyond.

D. M.

1

What Is Remote Viewing?

DEFINITIONS

The original Department of Defense definition of Remote Viewing (RV) was "the learned ability to transcend space and time, to view persons, places, or things remote in space-time; to gather and report information on the same." It was a technique used to spy on the real or perceived enemies of our nation using a human ability to perceive and record information about a target that is far away from the person doing the Viewing.

Today, Remote Viewing is described in as many different ways as there are individuals teaching, talking, or writing about it. The above is an acceptable definition, but it is not an accurate definition of the actual mechanism of Coordinate Remote Viewing (CRV). To better illustrate this, I developed a more complete description several years ago. This version follows a scientific pattern of language used to describe the human interaction and interface taking place within the protocols of Remote Viewing. I teach that **Remote Viewing is the learned ability to use two inherent kinesthetic human activities to detect and decode eight-dimensional waveform expressions of target data into four-dimensional thought form (height, width, depth, time), and** to further objectify this data into two-dimensional media. I know that sounds like a mouthful, so let's break it down and understand it clearly.

I define Coordinate Remote Viewing as **the learned ability to use two inherent kinesthetic human activities to detect and decode eight-dimensional waveform data.** Detecting and decoding are the processes whereby Viewers in a relaxed alpha brain-wave state (an altered state) close their eyes and begin detecting (perceiving) data via one or more of the principal or nonprincipal modalities of perception, such as digital, tactile, visual, or auditory modalities, or possibly gustatory and olfactory modalities, of perception.

This **waveform data** is decoded by the conscious mind **into coherent four-dimensional thought form.** Using these modalities of perception, the Viewer's conscious mind, even the biological brain, develops coherent thought form around what is being perceived. Some Viewers hear words, while others see visual data; regardless of the modality of perception, the brain shapes the data into images, sounds, smells, tastes, and so on.

This **coherent four-dimensional thought form** is objectified **into two-dimensional media** via simple contours and texture sketches (visual data), and by writing the descriptors for sound, smell, taste, temperature, texture, and energetic and dimensional data (verbal data). So long as this data is held in the mind, it is considered conceptual illusion. In other words, it is not usable or real until it is objectified, meaning written down. In the mind, it can continue to morph, flex, grow, and shrink. This is what conceptual illusion does. Just try to think back to something traumatic in your life. The more you dwell on it, the more it shifts and redefines itself with each passing moment. It cannot and does not remain stagnant or fixed, hence the term *conceptual illusion*. It is a waveform expression of some event in past time, and it is not real; it is only an illusion. Therefore, you, the Viewer, are required to use your inherent tools of language and visual reconstruction (sketching) to objectify on paper what it is that you perceive.

In the world of quantum physics, everything is energy and energy is everything; therefore, on some level, everything can be expressed in waveform. It is this waveform data through which the Remote Viewer becomes aware of, or "perceives," information during the Remote Viewing session, the period during which data relevant to a distant target is acquired. It is this waveform expression of the target and all its components that the Viewer perceives and then records in the form of visual data (contour sketches and detailed renderings) and verbal data (using language to express color, texture, temperature, taste, sound, smell, energetic data, dimensional data, aesthetic data, emotional data, tangible data, intangible data, and other elements of information depending on the length and intention of the Viewing session).

In the protocols of Remote Viewing, detecting and decoding waveform data is the fundamental methodology. This may sound like something very odd, yet you are doing it constantly. You are, in fact, doing it right now. Virtually every instant of your waking life is filled with almost unconscious metronomic activity of detecting eight-dimensional waveform data and decoding it into coherent four-dimensional thought form. The four dimensions to which I am referring are defined by the three spatial dimensions of height, width, and depth, and the fourth dimension, a temporal one, of time.

Let's look at a relatively simple example. You are reading this description, either from a printed page or from a computer monitor. Light waves are moving from the monitor or the printed page to your eye. These "instruments" called *eyes* perform a critical function of detecting the light waves and transforming this waveform data into electrochemical responses that are sent to the brain. The brain detects these signals and decodes them into coherent four-dimensional thought form. Put another way, your brain recognizes the various patterns of ink on the page that constitute the letters in the written words of the language you comprehend. The decoding process in this example works through your ability to understand the language. Your appreciation of the words in the decoding process is then linked to your "experience Rolodex," which includes all that you have previously read about, witnessed, experienced, and so on.

If an artist looks across a landscape, a similar process to your reading of this page takes place. The difference is that the artist is *engaged* in the art and science of detecting the light waves and decoding them into coherent thought form. The completion of the decoding process involves objectification in a two-dimensional medium, such as placing paint on a two-dimensional canvas or dragging a pencil across a two-dimensional piece of paper. If the artist were to close his eyes, would the imagery stop? The answer is no. At first there would be what is called "persistence of vision," the electrochemical data flow to the brain from the imagery still impacting the retina of the eye. The older you are, the longer it takes for this to dissipate. However, once it subsides, is there more data available to the artist? Yes, there is. If the artist and canvas were taken inside, where the landscape could no longer be seen, could the artist still paint? The answer is, again, yes.

Would it be accurate? That depends on a number of conditions: the state of the instrument (the brain), anxiety levels, analytic processes or the ability to reconstruct from memory, and other variables that may alter the artist's ability to perceive purely in the moment. If the artist can relax, forget the name of what it is that he is looking at, if the artist can let go and just begin detecting the waveform expression of the landscape, with eyes closed or open, he can begin decoding the data into four-dimensional thought form and continue the objectification process by finishing the painting—this is a loose example of Remote Viewing.

To explore another Remote Viewing example, let us say I ask you to close your eyes, and I prompt you to go to a beach in your mind, a beach you have visited before. I can ask you to see the beach, smell the beach, hear it, and even taste it. I can direct you to explore the temperature of the water, the heat of the sun on your flesh, the texture of the sand beneath your feet, and all this sensory information would be available to you. You can smell the air, feel the cool water and the thermal energy of the sun. All this sensory data is coming from what? Your imagination? You are not physically at the beach, so where is the data stream coming from? If you decide it is the imagination, then what is the origin of imagination? Where does imaginary data come from? What constitutes imagination? Is this recall, is it a fabrication, or is it detecting and decoding waveform data that is relevant to the actual beach distant in space-time?

In fact, your ability to do this will rely upon all these elements. You will produce a certain amount of data from recall, remembering the last time you were there by sparking the neural network of the brain, prompting it to release subelements of data embedded holographically in the neurons and glial cells of the biological brain and beyond. You will fabricate a certain amount of this data, a construction of sensory data that will be as unique to the scenario as you are. And there will be elements of data that match the beach in real time: people on the beach right now, the weather conditions, smells, tastes, activity, emotions, and the like as they exist right now on planet Earth. The difficulty is that you will not be satisfied with this answer. You will want to know what is recall, what is fabricated, and what is "real," or in the lexicon of Remote Viewing, *raw viewing data.*

A Remote Viewing student in Stockholm, Sweden, announced to the class that he had lost his ability to smell as a child over three decades ago. At the age of eleven, he contracted a severe case of influenza, and the virus caused irreversible damage to the lining of his nose where the olfactory nerves have their endings. These nerve receptors occupy a very small area near the roof of the nose, and once damaged, result in either a diminished or a distorted sense of smell. The attending physician told him that without exception he could no longer smell, and that became his conditioning. For the next thirty-five years, he never questioned the physician's statement. He had accepted the belief that he could not smell anything at all, and any faint trace of aroma was quickly dismissed as an aberration, an errant idea, but certainly not a restoration of his sense of smell. However, in a Remote Viewing session, he smelled the scent of roses and other fragrant flowers. He felt a bit awkward describing this sensation to his fellow classmates, especially after making the definitive pronouncement of his inability to smell. He even laughed it off as an impossibility, suggesting that he had "made it all up in his head." That was until he saw the video feedback of the target site, which was the International Rose Test Garden in Portland, Oregon, home to over eight thousand roses and other flowers. He wept when he realized that he *could* smell, in fact that he had been able to smell all along—something in the Remote Viewing session triggered his brain to fire all the neural networks necessary to create the sense of smell. This is only one of hundreds of such cases. People who have lost the ability to walk can walk again in their mind's eye; those who have lost limbs can again feel through a tactile modality of perception in Remote Viewing. Those who have lost voice can again sing, and those who have lost sight or hearing can again experience the gift of sight and sound in their Remote Viewing sessions.

The more you study and understand the quantum perspective of the universe in which we exist, the more you will understand and perfect your ability to Remote View. Furthermore, those who seek to truly excel in this art and science will work diligently to understand the biology of the brain, the physiology of the body, the power of intention, how to achieve and sustain an altered state, how to analyze training progress—there will be hundreds of other variables that one can monitor and master in an effort to develop as a Remote Viewer.

So, what does this do for you? Well, that is another question, and the answer to that question could take up another chapter. Suffice it to say here that, in this existence, we all believe in something. All of us, and there are no exceptions to this rule, believe in something. Even if we believe in nothing, we believe in something. The human quest in this existence is for knowledge. We are on an eternal quest for knowledge that honors a timeless path toward wisdom. We each measure the attainment of this grail in our own way. Some measure it in financial abundance, some in spiritual awareness, others in personal power, others in quality of life, and the list goes on.

You may measure the story of your life, the purpose of this existence, in any way you desire. But think of this: How would your life be if you knew you are more than the physical and that you have access to the waveform expression of all life, of all thoughts, of all things in all dimensions? How different would your life be if you could see around the corner of time, just to the other side of the moment? How would you look at the people you love if you knew they are eternal, as are you? How would you guide your business if you could see beyond the surfaces of the competition, into their thoughts, their intentions? How would you guide your children in this existence if you knew that they are going to be responsible for ushering the human condition out of the next destructive phase of the global society or into the next rebuilding phase? How different would your life be if you knew that all you have to do is to close your eyes and look through the darkness, through the event horizon of time, to see the next great breakthrough in medicine, education, technology, science, and so forth?

Believing that this is possible is easy. It requires little from us in the long run. Because the belief is conceptual, it routinely alters itself, morphing from this to that based on superficial needs and desires. Beliefs are conveniences that can only become knowledge through the experience of doing. If you want to know more, if you are ready to move from believing to knowing, then Remote Viewing is for you.

The Remote Viewing ability is not unique to me or any other former military-trained Remote Viewers. We all have the ability. You have always had it; through every breath, every blink of the eye, you have been connected to something greater than yourself. Your conditioning has taught you to believe in the possibility of this but to doubt it could ever exist within you. Your conditioning has told you to doubt yourself. Remote Viewing is simply a manifest protocol designed to offer you irrefutable and undeniable evidence that you can see distantly in space-time with a variable, yet increasing, degree of accuracy. This evidence is what transforms your belief into awareness, a knowledge offering you a new perspective on a life filled with promise and possibility.

THE PROTOCOL

In each Remote Viewing session, you will follow the same principal protocol. You will be entrained through a cooldown CD into an altered state of consciousness (an alpha wave state, 32.9 to 14 Hz, or cycles per second, of brain-wave activity). Once in this condition, you will be given a series of coordinates, which are random numbers assigned to the concept of a target in the Matrix Field of the collective unconscious. I will explain this concept in detail later in the book; for now, just understand it as part of the process.

After you are given the coordinates, you will begin using one or more of the modalities of perception to follow two kinesthetic activities associated with the phenomenon of Coordinate Remote Viewing, that is, the "detecting and decoding" described earlier. You will detect eight-dimensional waveform data and decode it into coherent four-dimensional thought form, or conceptual illusion. In order to capture this conceptual illusion, you will further objectify your perceptions into two-dimensional media. You will sketch your visual and dimensional data—curves, arches, mass, density, and so forth—and you will write or record your verbal data in descriptions of color, texture, smells, tastes, sounds, energetic data, and so on. This objectification process allows you to take the fleeting conceptual illusion of what you are seeing in your mind's eye and lock it into a form of data that is usable and quantifiable.

When the session is completed, you will take all the quantifiable data you decoded during the session, and you will assemble it in accordance with a provided Session Summary Template, preparing a narrative record of your journey into the Matrix Field of the distant target. Once this task is completed, you will be given detailed visual feedback of the target you were supposed to be seeing. It is at this point that you will review your session and compare it with the actual target feedback. You will be able to measure what you thought you saw with what was there for you to see. What is perceived is gathered in the blind. In other words, you will do this without ever being told what the target is before or during your exercise; in Remote Viewing terminology, there is no *front loading* on the target. You begin the session with an empty glass, which you slowly fill through the process of detecting and decoding. What you produce, you produce through nonphysical eyes, the eyes of a Remote Viewer. When you review your session, you will see what was at the target that you did decode properly—this is called empirical knowledge through the mechanism of feedback.

THE THREE RULES OF REMOTE VIEWING

As you learn to become a Remote Viewer, and as you journey inward to seek knowledge, find truth, and become wisdom, you will constantly be asked to address the credibility of the art and science of this craft. Recognizing this, I long ago developed these three simple rules, which I ask that you learn and follow. Throughout this course of instruction, I will review why and how these are important to your training and practical application in Remote Viewing.

Rule #1: Remote Viewing Is Not 100 Percent Accurate.

Results from Remote Viewing can span the spectrum of accuracy from the zero point all the way to something in the area of 83 percent. These levels of accuracy will vary from person to person, from day to day, and from target session to target session. If someone tells you that he or she is always 100 percent correct, that person is being less than truthful. There is a reason you can never be completely accurate on any target session, and I will explain this later in this book. Again, remember to let go of the outcome. Your accuracy can only improve if you do.

Rule #2: You Can Never Trust the Results of One Remote Viewer Acting Independently of Other Remote Viewers.

Remote Viewing is a team effort, and all of us together are better than any one of us. Accurate results depend greatly on the ability of several Viewers to work the same target without corroboration, at various times, and with a single point of control. Never gamble the reputation of Remote Viewing on a single Viewer; to do so risks the future of Remote Viewing and the reputation of all credible Viewers.

Rule #3: Remote Viewing Is Not a Stand-Alone Endeavor.

Remote Viewing is a tool—not a be-all and end-all. Used properly, it provides answers or a piece of the puzzle that cannot or might not be gleaned by any other means. Despite the claims of some former members of the military RV team, Remote Viewing was not developed because the rest of the intelligence community was failing in its tasks. In truth, it was developed only to provide partial answers, fragments of information, to the analytic side of the U.S. intelligence community. It was brought into the intelligence community to augment existing collection methodologies. This is the calling of Remote Viewing in the future as well: to augment existing strategies in law enforcement, medicine, research and development, and more. Remote Viewing will never replace anything in conventional or nonconventional quests for information.

WHERE DID THE TERM "COORDINATE REMOTE VIEWING" COME FROM?

Latitude and Longitude

The concept of Coordinate Remote Viewing came from the early protocols for designating a target site for the Remote Viewers to view. Lacking any complete understanding of what was possible in this human ability, the scientists who developed the protocols assigned latitudinal and longitudinal coordinates to the target based on its actual location on the surface of the Earth. This two-dimensional plane had its limitations. Using latitude and longitude began to skew the data the Remote Viewers were able to produce. It did this for the simple reason that the more you work with latitude and longitude, the more you are prone to recognize where on the Earth you are working. For this reason, the use of latitude and longitude disrupted the scientific process adhered to by the Stanford Research Institute staff. The scientists performing the experiments on the Viewers began noticing that the Viewers' data was becoming highly accurate, perhaps too accurate, and they began searching for a flaw in the process. It was determined that the Viewers had begun memorizing the latitude and longitude coordinates and as a result were guessing at verbal and visual data that was supporting the target site. It was further determined that this was not intentional or by some sinister desire on the part of the Viewers to score well on the exercises. Quite the contrary, the Viewers were as disturbed by the difficulty as were the researchers. Something had to be done; other systems needed to be explored.

One such system was the Universal Transverse Mercator (UTM) Grid System. The UTM or Grid Mercator system divides the surface of the Earth into one hundred thousand-meter squares and further subdivides them into ten-meter squares, the size of a small home. Regardless of the level of division, this is still a system existing in an immovable template on the surface of the Earth, and it could potentially be memorized as well. Thus, it was abandoned as a possible replacement for the latitude and longitude system.

However, this was not the only reason the Grid Mercator system was abandoned. People were beginning to ask the questions that linked Remote Viewing to the exploration of other worlds, other civilizations, perhaps even those outside our solar system. If this application were developed, how would you assign coordinates to another planet in a general sense, or how would you segment using a UTM system what was potentially so far away that it could not be physically seen? You can see the problem. The UTM system is still only a two-dimensional Cartesian system, just like the latitude and longitude system is. Adopting it would solve nothing, and its inherent two-dimensional limitations would not serve any possible future use for off-planet work.

Random Numbers

Something had to be found that would permit the assignment of target coordinates anywhere on the Earth and beyond. The new system had to be without physical limitation and based on the concept of a target rather than on the actual physical location of the target. This opened vast new possibilities in what Remote Viewers would be able to see in the Matrix Field. The idea was codified in the use of random numbers that would be linked to the thought—the conceptual illusion, the concept—of the target that was held in the mind of the person assigning the numbers to the target. I will explain this further in the chapters that follow. For now, I would like you to grasp the notion of why this process was so necessary and ultimately so brilliant.

The assignment of random numbers meant flexibility. There would be no front loading, no witting or unwitting memorization on the part of the Remote Viewers. For the scientists involved, this meant no overt corruption of the data being developed by the Viewers. For the Viewers, it meant a complete release from the outcome, no attachment to the numbers, no struggling with the conscious mind or with the left brain that would try to make sense out of the coordinates. The numbers, in and of themselves, would mean nothing to anyone except the individual assigning them to the specific target. For this individual, the requirement was now a very serious one: the program managers, under normal protocol, must be capable of focusing their intention on the nature of the target, be it an object, person, place, or event in the past or the future. The Viewers' ability to do quality work hinged to a degree on this fact: the poorly focused assignment of the target concept would likely result in nonspecific target data by the Viewer. However, focused intention by a program manager would drive the Viewers deep into the intention of the target with far more accuracy than the broad latitude and longitude system could ever produce.

Theoretically, a program manager could steer the Viewers forward or backward in time, above the surface of the Earth, below it, or across the galaxy to something unseen yet existing in thought form. The system of assigning random numbers opened countless doors of possibility for the Remote Viewers, and it is the system you will be learning in this book.

HISTORY OF REMOTE VIEWING

Before you begin this Remote Viewing training program, I think it is imperative that you know the origins of what you are about to become involved in. Please know this from me: the phenomenon you are about to learn has nothing to do with the past, yet this phenomenon does have a past, and you should know it, or at least this version of it. Read this history to gather an awareness of how the Remote Viewing program began and who some of the critical players were. I feel this information is necessary to dispel any wild rumors you might hear about the origin and nature of this former Defense Intelligence Agency program. Again, what you are engaging in is the spiritual evolution of this former intelligence collection methodology, now a process of transformation with a deeply embedded spiritual focus, oriented toward the individual as well as the collective. As you progress through the book, this will become clearer; however, for now, use this information as a historical perspective.

For an even more in-depth historical perspective, you may want to roll up your sleeves and dig into the long list of books written by former Remote Viewers, monitors, program managers, and researchers. But understand this: they all have different perspectives, and they all believe theirs is the most accurate. Einstein said, "It is the theory that decides what we can observe." This is true in the recounting of any story or of any element of history. Napoleon once said that history is nothing more than fiction agreed upon. When it comes to the history of this unit, no statement has proven more accurate. Even if certain individuals collectively agree on a version of the history to be shared with the public, they routinely do not share the same version in private conversation. I could write an entire book on this contrast alone, but that is not my purpose. There is an inherent quest for truth in all of us; we want to know the past because we feel it gives us insight to the present and foresight to the future. Hindsight, however, in all its versions and interpretations, often fogs the moment and, in so doing, skews the right path of the future. Be satisfied with the moment, and seek the clarity of it. With that, let me begin by saying, clearly, that what follows is my version of the truth, nothing more.

In what seems a thousand years ago, in 1987, I stood on the desert floor of a long-forgotten valley in the Kingdom of Jordan. I was a warrior, doing what warriors do when they are not fighting wars: I was training for one. In one moment, I was commanding 235 United States Army Rangers, and in the next, I was wounded in the head by a stray Jordanian machine-gun bullet. The wound ushered darkness over me that became the brightest awakening of my spirit, leading me out of the condition of being lost in the unconsciousness of consciousness. Within a few short months, I was recruited into one of the most bizarre and controversial intelligence collection programs known to the Western world—I was recruited into America's top-secret clan of psychic spies known as Remote Viewers, a unit given the code name Sun Streak.

Here I was trained not in the art and science of war, but, rather, I was given a tool, a protocol, a system, a structure, that unlocked the inherent ability that lies within each of us to transcend space and time, to view persons, places, or things remote in space and time, to gather and report intelligence information on the same. I was trained to be a time traveler, a new breed of warrior utilizing a technique developed by science that called upon and synthesized the ancient wisdoms of this and other worlds. This technique is now instrumental in illuminating a new paradigm that is transforming the way thousands see themselves and relate to this present existence.

The Government Explores an Ancient Truth

Remote Viewing is not a new phenomenon; the ability has been ours since the beginning of time. The formulation and systemization of theological doctrine as set forth in ancient records present us with countless examples of humanity's learned and inherent abilities to transcend the physical, to see in the mind's eye people, places, and events separate from their physical reality. From the ancient hieroglyphics carved into the walls of forgotten Egyptian tombs, to *The Emerald Tablets of Thoth the Atlantean, The Urantia Book, A Course in Miracles,* the Koran, the Torah, the Talmud, and the Old and New Testaments—to name but a few—all give accounts of journeys out of the physical body, night flights of soul, projections of consciousness, and more. However, the most recent history began circa 1972 when the Central Intelligence Agency learned through various human intelligence sources that the Czechs, Chinese, Soviets, Germans, Israelis, and even the British were all heavily involved in the study of various aspects of what would be called paranormal.

These investigations were, in many ways, the spawn of very bizarre programs initiated by the Nazis during World War II. While exact details are a matter of historical debate, it is widely held that after the fall of the Third Reich, the Russians captured numerous documents and records held by Adolf Hitler's infamous Nazi

Occult Bureau. Other documents, partial and complete, became the property of various Allied intelligence services, who elected to study them further in the ensuing years or, in some cases, to totally ignore their potential.

When the CIA learned of these studies, the obvious question was, "Do we have such a potential?" At this juncture, the United States did not have such a capability, nor had it ever really considered it—until now. If all these other agencies were involved in studying the paranormal, then why were we not involved? It was clear that the nation's principal intelligence agency needed to catch up to the intelligence collection efforts of the others—at least in this alternative method of gathering intelligence.

In late 1972, CIA scientist Sidney Gottlieb, chief of the technical services division, procured a rather large monetary endowment to initiate the research project that began U.S. involvement in the study of Remote Viewing. If the Soviets and others were as heavily involved in this research as was being reported, the national security of the United States could be in jeopardy. The simple notion that this eerie capability might really be out there, and the possibility that we could do it, as well, almost certainly drove the CIA's decision process. You have to admit—it does pique one's curiosity.

Stanford Research Institute International (SRI) in Palo Alto, California, ultimately became the proving ground for what was to eventually be one of the intelligence services' most controversial, misunderstood, and often feared special access programs. The two men initially charged with the responsibility of overseeing this testing and evaluation program were Russell Targ and Harold Puthoff, Ph.D., both laser physicists working at SRI.

In my opinion, it is Targ and Puthoff who are clearly the early heroes in all of this. These two men (with others) risked their professional reputations to test and evaluate the possibility that human beings can transcend space and time for the purpose of "viewing" persons, places, and things remote in space and time, and can collect usable intelligence information on the same. Certainly, the vast majority of their colleagues would have loved it if this federally sponsored project had consumed its funding and six years of study only to conclude that there was nothing to it—that it was all worthless and the project should be abandoned. However, this was not the case. Instead, the answer was quite the opposite: there was something to this. This phenomenon was credible; it was measurable and definable and trainable. It was certainly not 100 percent accurate, but then again, neither was anything else in the intelligence collection assets; they all had their limitations. As long as one understood the limits of the technology, then the technology could be employed as another collector of information, another provider of pieces of the jigsaw puzzle that was truth in the espionage game. In short, the CIA was handed a new intelligence collection methodology: psychic spies.

To digress briefly, a New York City artist, author, and gifted natural psychic, Ingo Swann, became one of Dr. Puthoff's first test subjects. According to Mr. Swann, he initially participated in a number of pioneering experiments performed under the auspices of the American Society for Psychical Research. Upon being recruited into the project, Mr. Swann worked with Dr. Puthoff at SRI's Radio Physics Laboratory in Menlo Park, California. It was here that Puthoff and Swann—and a number of others—conducted a series of ever more sophisticated experiments, developing the protocol or structure they ultimately christened "Remote Viewing," opting for this term over the much-debated label of "Remote Sensing."

According to Mr. Swann, he was asked by the CIA to train other men in the art and science of Remote Viewing, men who he claimed were bizarre in their manner, mechanistic and cold in their approach to learning Remote Viewing. Seemingly, they were there for the training, and then they were gone, never to be seen or heard of again. I use this as one piece of evidence that other Remote Viewing elements existed in the government intelligence agencies. I cannot accept the notion that only one Remote Viewing program existed; this would go against all philosophies and practices within the military and government intelligence agencies to never put all their eggs in one basket. Who would spend tens of millions of dollars on a program that existed in one place and had only one life to live? I assure you, nobody in the intelligence community would. Recognizing the potential for controversy and public ridicule if ever discovered, the CIA did what it has always done—distanced itself in word and deed from the project. There is an old adage in the intelligence community: "Always keep someone between you and the potential problem." The project was handed off to the Defense Intelligence Agency (DIA) under the program code name Grill Flame. It is assumed that other programs continued to thrive under the oversight and administration of other military services and intelligence agencies. However, the Army's program, which had originally begun as a counterintelligence effort, was doing so well that its mission was destined to morph into something else.

The original mission was to evaluate through reverse engineering how vulnerable the U.S. intelligence agencies and their secrets were to psychic spying. This was done to such a degree of accuracy that Department of Defense and Army officials decided to change the emphasis from assessing friendly vulnerabilities to actively collecting intelligence information against America's Cold War adversaries. Unfortunately, but expectedly, the Remote Viewers had their detractors, such as Major General Bill Odom, Lieutenant General Harry Soyster, upper-level bureaucrats in the Department of Defense and the CIA, and politicians within the White House and Congress.

By 1980, all the Remote Viewing programs were suffering from a lack of popular support. The Army program lost all its funding, lacked any permanent home, and was destined for extinction. Several sources within the intelligence community, third parties who either knew of the Remote Viewing programs or had some level of oversight relative to them, have indicated to me that Remote Viewing was not the target of these cutbacks; rather, it was the entire direction some elements of the intelligence services were taking. During this time, 1978 to 1980, the military was in pursuit of such things as the Golden Sphere Concept, the quest for advanced human performance potentials; the Task Force Delta Concept Paper; the First Earth Battalion; and the Warrior Monk's Vision, sponsored by Lieutenant Colonel James B. Channon, Colonel Mike Malone, and a host of others. Again, not to impugn the work of these men and others, but it was simply becoming too far out on the fringe for the comfort of a large number of people. It could be said that the envelope was being pushed too far, too fast, especially for people who felt that careers would be lost over these kinds of projects. It didn't really matter how you expressed it or explained it—it was the application of what the larger percentage of the military and civilian population would call the *paranormal*. As a sort of knee-jerk response to it all, many sought to squash anything that resembled unconventional approaches to leadership, tactics, strategy, intelligence collection, and the like. Remote Viewing would become collateral damage in the quest to trim the fringe efforts.

Despite everyone's sudden interest in burning witches, Major General Bert Stubblebine, Commander of the U.S. Army's Intelligence and Security Command (INSCOM), took a personal and active interest in the Remote Viewing program. INSCOM was a Washington, D.C.-based unit. At the time, it existed in an old building complex near the headquarters of the Third Army (the Ceremonial Old Guard) and eventually ended up in a new location at Fort Belvoir, Virginia. In 1983, General Stubblebine directed that the Remote Viewing program be redesigned under a new code name, Center Lane, and be called the INSCOM Center Lane Program. Under this umbrella, General Stubblebine could fund the program directly from INSCOM's budget without the requirement to justify a budget from any outside agencies or through the Deputy Chief of Staff for Intelligence, the Army's ranking intelligence officer. Funding the Remote Viewing project in this way also meant that other units and projects within INSCOM would have to pay the bill—not a good thing when funding is tight across the board in the military. Most command-ers would willingly cut something as controversial as Remote Viewing in favor of having more to spend on other, more overt and successful projects. This approach sowed the seeds of discontent throughout INSCOM and met with opposition within Stubblebine's command at the subordinate level, as well as from many of his colleagues and superiors.

I have to say that General Stubblebine is another of the unsung heroes of Remote Viewing. You hear little of him now. He is a man who trusted much, believed in human possibility and potential, and was willing to sacrifice himself to promote the notion that we are indeed more than the physical. Had it not been for him, Remote Viewing might not have lived long enough for the rest of us to be writing about, discussing, or teaching it at all.

What About the Skeptics?

Most of us never practice science—we merely become compilers and communi-cators of it. Most in this genre of work like to call themselves parapsychologists, and that is a grave mistake. In the quest for truth in Remote Viewing, there are no real parapsychologists—they are nothing more than individuals masquer-ading as scientists, alleging they can prove Remote Viewing, mind-reading, telekinesis, psychokinesis, and a host of other paranormal mysteries. Many reputable authors, scientists, and certainly skeptics refer to parapsychologists as pseudoscientists, meaning they espouse a system of methods and assump-tions they erroneously regard as scientific. I am very pleased to say this was not the case at SRI. Had SRI and those scientists affiliated with the project not worked completely and thoroughly under the protocols of their field, the door for skeptical criticism would have been left wide open. It is the scientific procedure used to develop and evaluate the protocol of Remote Viewing that has kept it from the pseudoscientific wolves all these years.

I include a note on skeptics at this point because I feel it is critical that you have a clear understanding of who is debunking this work, exactly what their scientific background is or is not, and what motivates their skepticism. I have been interviewed several hundred times on radio and probably fifty times on television all over the world. In about 20 percent of those interviews and appearances, I have had the distinct pleasure of having a counter-position representative from the Committee for the Scientific Investigation of Claims of the Paranormal (CSICOP) or some other skeptical committee. I agree with Dr. Raymond Moody's description of these representatives, likening them to the hecklers of nightclub comedians—that is to say, what they really crave is not excellence in science but more attention for themselves.

Most self-proclaimed skeptics are not true skeptics at all. In one sense, they are simply "professional skeptics," earning a living through the proclamation that there is nothing beyond the physical in human ability. In another sense, they are ideologists who think they have the answers. The ideology they espouse is known as *scientism*, the belief that the methods and assumptions of the natural sciences are the only ones appropriate for the pursuit of knowledge. Scientism is an open value judgment that other disciplines ought to conform their techniques of investigation to those of the physical and biological sciences. These skeptics are in fact not interested in science; rather, they are fueling some sort of social movement against the possibility and promise of humanity. Knowing what they espouse, consider this premise: If Remote Viewing cannot be explained by science (their science), then it cannot exist at all; it must be a hoax or, at best, wishful thinking, certainly a waste of taxpayers' money. Yet these skeptics openly use electricity when there is not a physicist on the planet who can explain in anything but theoretical terms how electricity travels along a copper wire. If one adheres rigidly to the criterion that everything must be explained unconditionally, then we should not be reading by the light of incandescent lamps, since we only theoretically understand the power behind them. We should not be using aspirin, since we do not fully understand how it works in the human body. We should not be using approximately 36 percent of the pharmaceutical contents of the *Physicians' Desk Reference*, since we do not fully understand the pharmacology of the drugs in the human body—we only observe the results. The scientists at SRI could not tell you how Remote Viewing works—not really. They can only theorize, and that has been the sole grounds for skeptics to discredit Remote Viewing—the same people who accept the unexplained movement of electricity because it is convenient for them.

The Birth of Star Gate

Around the time of Center Lane's debut, the Army and SRI signed a training contract, which led to five military and Department of Defense civilian personnel being trained in the new Coordinate Remote Viewing technique at SRI facilities. In 1986, INSCOM transferred the unit to the DIA, under the Directorate of Science and Technology (DS&T), and changed its code name to Sun Streak. Early in the 1990s, it went through yet another code name change—this time to Star Gate, the name by which it became known to the world when the program was declassified in 1995.

During its lifetime, the Remote Viewing unit collected intelligence against a broad range of targets: strategic missile forces, political leaders (theirs and ours), counternarcotics operations, research and development facilities, hostage situations, military weapons systems, secret installations, technology developments, terrorist groups. The list was staggering, and the successes were many—as were the failures. Yes, failures—meaning sometimes producing limited usable results. Nevertheless, consider what we are talking about. Even on a bad day, this innate ability within each of us is nothing but spectacular!

Damage Control at the CIA

In 1995, Congress directed that the CIA take back responsibility for the program from DIA, DS&T. This was principally due to the fact that my book *Psychic Warrior: Inside the CIA's Star Gate Program* was being printed by St. Martin's Press, despite the efforts of some former members of the unit, who later published their own versions of the unit history using the platform offered by the very book they were attempting to disqualify. The CIA was concerned; a book is considered durable media, meaning it will be around for a long time, and even though this was not the first book on Remote Viewing, it was the first book written by a former "psychic spy" who was linking Remote Viewing to the military and to the CIA—now, that was cause for concern. Let me be perfectly clear on this: it was never the official effort of the DIA or the CIA to stop the publication of any book about Remote Viewing. In fact, the technology was so controversial, one might imagine they were hoping the cat would be let out of the bag so they could justify shutting the program down—but that is just speculation. No, every nasty thing done or said about Remote Viewing, or Remote Viewers, came from other Remote Viewers. The CIA knew it was going to be spread all over the media—even more than it already was.

Historically, when there is controversy in the wind, the agency exercises its right to opt out at the most opportune moment. When this option fails, usually due to a timing error, then the only thing to do is to tell your version of the story first. What followed was an extremely well-executed media blitz, which included Ted Koppel, Larry King, and a variety of major newspapers across the country and in Europe. What Americans should be asking themselves at this point is: Why would the CIA make a decision to tell the people of the world about this program? What purpose did it serve? Were they suddenly afraid that the autobiographical *Psychic Warrior* was going to steer you in the wrong direction? Did they feel that they needed to make sure you knew the truth first, from them? Let the reader be the judge.

Later that year, under the guise of being an objective study by the American Institutes for Research (AIR), a reputable Washington, D.C., think tank, the CIA commissioned the services of one of the most well-known scientific skeptics in the country. The final report was designed to skew the assessment of the accuracy and usability of intelligence from the Remote Viewing program to such a degree that the program, after twenty-plus years of use, would be deemed totally useless as an intelligence collection resource.

In mid-1995, the program was canceled, and, two weeks before *Psychic Warrior* hit the bookshelves, the program was disbanded and the buildings were bulldozed and hauled away. Coincidence? I don't think so. The impact of a writer's work often exceeds his intention. However, the CIA did conveniently keep for itself all the personnel spaces that were transferred from DIA, DS&T, which is additional evidence to fuel the suspicion that the program lives on in all its original service variations. As I said early in this history, the intelligence community does not place all its eggs in one basket. The CIA would never have left an entire collection methodology open to the potential destruction of one rogue who might write a book about it. Rather, they would keep the technology safe via a standard process of compartmentalization. The government would never abandon Remote Viewing—it proved far too valuable for the money it cost. What they will do is ensure that they never make the mistake again of letting such a controversial and potentially far-reaching technology rise to the surface. They will watch it more closely and watch those whom they train to do it.

There ends the history. What is truly important here is that you move past all of this and discover what Remote Viewing is now and what it can be in the future. There are many variations of this story, and there always will be. I am reminded of Kant's intuition and scientific reliance on the senses he called *Gestalt theory* or *isomorphism.* This theory prompted him to maintain that "truth is whatever makes you live your life better. Only the truth which edifies is truth." Remote Viewing is truth! It is an empowering art and science that will open the possibilities within you, creating doorways to levels of understanding never before thought attainable.

2

Something Extraordinary
Is Possible in Your Life

Only someone who is ready for everything,
who doesn't exclude any experience,
even the most incomprehensible, will live the relationship
with another person as something alive . . .
and will himself sound the depths of his own being.

Rainer Maria Rilke, *Letters to a Young Poet*

AM I IN THE RIGHT PLACE?

You are in the right place to learn this phenomenon, to become a Remote Viewer, as long as you are entering the process with the correct state of mind. I define
having the correct state of mind as having an honest and open perspective on
the possibility that you are more than the physical. On the other hand, if you are
coming from a perspective that says, "I do not believe in this human ability, but I
am willing to put some time in, regardless," I can promise you that this program
will do nothing for you. You are essentially presupposing there is nothing to this
ability, and that is an unsuitable perspective of limited promise and possibility—
and you may be surprised to know that it is indeed a minority position.

According to polls taken by various sources at the approach of the new millennium, approximately 98 percent of the population of this planet believe there
is something more than the physical. This percentage can be fractured into various groups and belief structures spanning the cultures and religions of the world,
but it remains that the largest percentage of us, regardless of the name we give it
or the face we place upon it, believe in something more than that which we can
simply see, touch, smell, taste, or hear.

The other 2 percent of the population believe there is nothing more than the physical. They do not, in fact, know there is nothing—they only believe. Therefore, their position is no more powerful than yours; in fact, in sheer number alone, they are deeply in the minority.

The question remains: Where are you in this equation? Do you believe there is something more than the physical, and are you simply looking for further proof? Or do you believe there is nothing beyond the physical (and here, too, are simply looking for further proof)? If your position arises from the latter, you should go no further in this program; you will be wasting your time and money. It is not the objective of this book, nor is it within its scope, to rip you from your belief structure and prove to you that the phenomenon of Remote Viewing is possible. For you, it will not be possible, because your intention would prevent it from being possible.

This book is designed to walk you through a process, protocol, and structure that will, without fail, cause you to extract usable visual and verbal data relevant to a target distant in space-time. The process is infallible, and the results are undeniable, but your intention is key in this process, just as it is key in any process you engage in. For example, if you begin a mathematics class at any grade level with the conviction "I cannot do math," or "I'm not any good with numbers," then that is exactly what you will reap. Your intention is a statement of your own identity, and this intention creates a manifest behavior that in turn reinforces the identity all over again. You can either unleash your personal ability, or you can, by your own intention, limit your ability to do anything of value in this life. It is all a matter of choice on your part. You may choose possibility, or you may choose limits. This said, where are you now? Which segment of the human population do you stand in?

I will assume, if you are continuing to read, that you consider yourself to be a member of the 98 percent who believe there is something more than the physical. Perhaps you do not even have a name for it, but you suspect it is there. Do you believe in something beyond the physical but see your life situation as one of limits, of emptiness, of impossibility, and of boundless obstacles? Is your glass always half-empty? Do you find yourself in constant evaluation of yourself from a perspective of "I should have, if only I would have, if only my life had been different"? If you do, then you are looking backward into the conceptual illusion of yesterday. You are living in the energetic representation of the past, and as such, you are missing your life—and you will miss the object of this training, as well. Just as you choose to live your life, you will choose to engage in any journey along your life's path in the same manner. You cannot expect that any path by itself will be the catalyst for your transformation—you, and you alone, are that catalyst, and you must be willing to take responsibility for your choices, your outlook, and your intentions. If you step into this book masking your intentions, then you are simply waiting for the failure you already believe is coming—and in that case, it will manifest for you.

If you are able to look carefully within yourself and give yourself an honest and open evaluation—an assessment of where you now stand in your beliefs— then you will have an honest and secure place in which to begin this training. Gradually, line upon line and precept upon precept, you will, through the experience of choice, shift your awareness into the intention of possibility. When this happens, the rate of return in the physical, emotional, and spiritual experience of any endeavor, of any path, will increase exponentially. It begins with self-evaluation; it begins with a statement of intention; it begins with a desire to see and live your life in a new manner of seeing—a wakefulness that is the eternal right of us all.

THE OBSERVER AND THE EVALUATOR

I am providing you with a model that I know will help you in your preparation for transformation (see Figure 2.1). In this model, you can see two different cycles: the observer cycle, which is considered a positive cycle of intention, and

FIGURE 2.1 **The Power of Intention: Your Manifest Behavior**

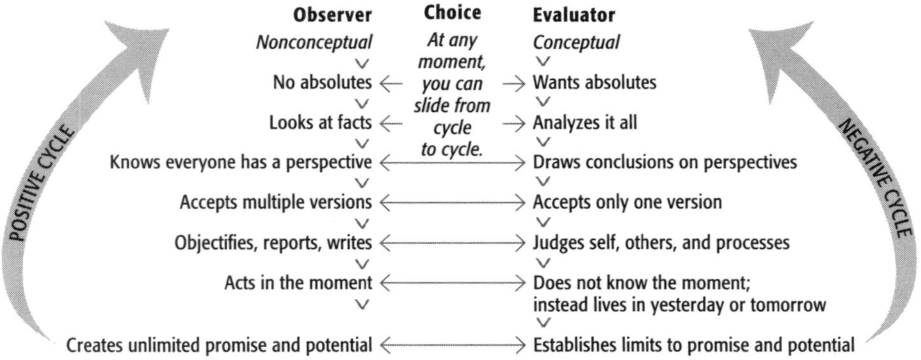

the evaluator cycle, which is considered a negative cycle of intention. I encourage you to constantly make it your intention to be an observer in life and not an evaluator. If you follow the model down the evaluator cycle, you will possibly find many similarities to how you live your life. You can see that evaluators quickly drop into the conclusion element of the cycle, drawing conclusions about self, others, and process. These conclusions always lead to judgments of self, others, and process, and judgments narrow the spectrum of possibility in life.

On the other hand, if you choose to live within the observer cycle, you can see that observers do not draw conclusions; rather, they are open to and accepting of what exists within the moment. Observers do not struggle with the negativity of conceptual illusion; instead, they exist by choice outside of conceptual illusion and drink only from the moment, which in turn manifests a life of courage and dignity with no limits to promise and possibility. You will also notice that the lateral arrows in the model indicate that you can, through the mechanism of choice, jump from cycle to cycle at any given moment. Therefore, you should never consider yourself locked into a pattern; you may choose at any time to enter a positive cycle or remain in a negative cycle—you always have a choice.

I would like you to commit to being an observer throughout this book. In fact, commit to being an observer in your life. By doing so, you will open doors to learning you never thought possible. In addition, you will open to levels of understanding in your life, in your relationships, in your career, and, of course, in your Remote Viewing that will empower you beyond previous comprehension.

DO I HAVE WHAT IT TAKES TO DO THIS?

At this point, you are probably asking yourself this very question: "Do I have what it takes to do this?" It is a common question, and I consider it completely fair at this juncture. You are probably reeling with the concepts of conceptual illusion, observer or evaluator, half-full or half-empty, choice and intention—but do not get overwhelmed by these concepts. They will become clearer as you progress through this program. So, the question remains: Do you have what it takes to do this?

I assure you that you do have what it takes. You see, the military intelligence community and the Central Intelligence Agency spent tens of millions of tax dollars developing the protocols of the program you are about to engage in. As such, one of the very first questions posed by the intelligence community was,

"How do we know who will be good at this?" What is more, "Can anyone do it, or will we have to develop some selection process to identify the necessary psychological profile that would indicate a certain level of ability in this field?"

The answer was astounding. There was indeed a necessary psychological profile, and it was simply that whoever was to attempt this formal training process must have a belief, a desire, a hope, a wish, or a prayer to know that there is something more than the physical. Therefore, if you are in one of these categories, then you have what it takes to do this. The protocols of Coordinate Remote Viewing will take you from this place of belief or prayer or hope and present to you irrefutable evidence that you are more than the physical.

For that matter, how can you not learn what you already have the ability to do? Any intelligent human being with a willingness to learn has the ability to become a successful Remote Viewer, given the proper training and guidance. The information contained in this book will certainly assist you toward that end, but you will not learn how to Remote View by simply reading this book. Remote Viewing is a learned skill, which unlocks and fine-tunes your own innate abilities—and like any learned skill, it requires careful training via a disciplined regimen of lecture, illustration, practical exercise, feedback, follow-up training, and practice, practice, practice!

You may, on occasion, hear some former military-trained Remote Viewers and even some of the mid-level researchers affiliated with the Remote Viewing program maintain that only a small percentage of the population can actually learn to Remote View. I want you to know that this is absolute rubbish. You already have the ability. All this program is designed to do is to unlock an existing ability in a manner that will provide an understandable, reliable, and consistent protocol. Some of you have already discovered it naturally, while others may have discovered it through some physical, emotional, or spiritual trauma, and still others have yet to unleash this intrinsic ability—which may be why you are here now. If you want to become a Remote Viewer, this book will transform you.

YOU ARE NOT ALONE IN THIS

More than twenty-three thousand students have already made the journey inward to know they are more than the physical. In that number, there have only been two failures. Before I address the two failures, I would like to give you a brief demographic profile of those who have come before you.

To begin with, the age spectrum extends from the youngest Remote Viewing student at age eleven to the oldest at ninety-three. The twenty-five-to-fifty age bracket constitutes the largest number of students. Not surprisingly, more females than males have learned to Remote View, at a ratio of about 3:2. I have trained students from forty-two countries, with the largest concentrations being in the United States, Canada, Great Britain, Sweden, and Norway. The largest professional demographic of Remote Viewing students is in the engineering fields. Roughly 3,800 engineers from various disciplines have learned to Remote View in the past six years. These are electrical, mechanical, and chemical engineers; an aerospace engineer and even a NASA engineer have taken this class. The next largest profession is physicians, about 2,900, from researchers to surgeons and from osteopathy to general medicine. This demographic also includes various elements of the nursing and medical technical professions. Well over 2,000 law-enforcement personnel have taken this course. Finally, there have been 1,800 educators from kindergarten to the university level. The rest of the student population is spread across the spectrum of human endeavor and interest.

This phenomenon is embraced by those with a genuine interest in what lies beyond the physical, and ultimately draws those seeking to better know their inner voice, to develop their intuition, to create vision in their life and work, to know God . . . indeed to develop a relationship with God, deep within the realm of the Creator. All are on a quest to seek truth, find knowledge, and become wisdom. Therefore, you can clearly see that you are in magnificent company—you are not alone in your quest.

So, can you fail at this endeavor? Yes, but it will be your choice to fail. Both of the students who failed in this process decided early on that they were going to fail. They stood constantly in the role of evaluator, and as evaluators they drew conclusions about themselves and the process, and finally succumbed to their own judgments. If you will listen to me, step out of the role of evaluator, and follow the protocols as they are taught, you will be successful as a Remote Viewer.

You may not be satisfied with your performance at first, but practice will make you better. You have had a lifetime to suppress your understanding of what it means to see beyond the physical; why would you expect that in a matter of days you can restore what decades have consumed? You cannot. You must work very hard to become good at this, but I know that you have it in you, or you would not have come this far.

WHAT IS BELIEVING, AND HOW DOES IT DIFFER FROM KNOWING?

We have already established the fact that a good deal of the population of this planet is honoring some path, some belief structure. Most, if not all, are content with believing the story or version of the story that is delivered to them, meaning much of humanity is happy to accept someone else's version of what is, what should be, and what might be. I would not place you in this category, by virtue of the fact that you are here now to explore what is beyond the physical. Put another way, you are unwilling to accept another's version of what is on the other side of the moment, of what is beyond the veil—you want to know for yourself.

So then, how does one come from belief to knowing? It is by the firsthand experience of functioning consciously in both the physical and the nonphysical worlds. As long as you accept or reject my interpretation of what it is like to be a Remote Viewer, then you will never know what truth is. Ultimately, there is only one way to know: make the journey inward and seek your own truth. It will be your version of the truth, and that will be the most valuable. Any version accepted without your own personal experience is a resignation to endure the vision of another.

Through a process of gradual evolution spanning millennia, the mystery of your being has manifested itself in the physical world as a growing understanding of your omnipotence, omniscience, and omnipresent nature. Your cosmic-terrestrial biography has been woven into the dark Matrix that is your unconscious mind, and despite your best efforts to ignore the voice of soul, on some level, you sense that you are eternal. This aspect of yourself has been called various things by the many ethereal travelers peering into the unconscious: the global mind, the Akashic Record, the Matrix Field, the holographic universe, the collective unconscious, the implicit order, nirvana—God. There is no shortage of interpretations of this sense, or of those who accept them as absolutes, self-manifested as beliefs.

The paradox is simply that beliefs are thieves of freedom, anxieties to affect reality that only further distort it. Embracing a belief is easy—seeking knowledge is not. Georg Christoph Lichtenberg stated, "With most men, unbelief in one thing springs from blind belief in another." Beliefs service the desire for truth, while knowledge nourishes the reverence of it. In this evolutionary millennium, beliefs masking truth serve only to retard your scientific and spiritual development; this unconsciousness of consciousness has become a vehicle of retrogression. This condition blinds you to your possibilities—limiting you to a global society, which is a conditioned existence within the infinite and multidimensional—as a member of a species.

Perhaps the greatest problem facing all humanity in this existence is to hear and recognize the voices that know truth, as truth establishes reality. In the struggle for truth, so much is lost between accepting that which is delivered to you through the interpretation of others and that which you seek in earnest through the journey inward. It is there, in the vast Matrix of the unconscious mind, that truth is found, devoid of conscious analysis and imagination; it is there that truth seen through the eyes of the observer is manifest.

As a Remote Viewer, you must constantly struggle to transcend your present position on your understanding of reality, perhaps even contradict your understanding in order to honor truth. Employing this book, you will grow in scope and depth of insight through experience in the physical and nonphysical worlds. Remote Viewing is one path into the Matrix of all creation, that brings your version of this truth, truth through experience, to define reality and hone your understanding that you are on an eternal path toward wisdom.

HOW DO I KNOW THAT I KNOW SOMETHING?

There are three mechanisms that can be applied to the analysis of knowing: spiritual knowledge, intuitive knowledge, and empirical knowledge. It is the last that is most critical to the learning and application of Remote Viewing, but I will discuss the other two first.

Spiritual knowledge is a rare form of knowing, and it is a form of knowing that is easily confusing to the person searching for it. This knowledge exists in a state of flux between a nondualistic awareness and a dualistic awareness, and is often described simply as "inexpressible." The term "inexpressible" refers to our human inability to assign language to what it is that we have experienced. In another sense, it also addresses the fact that we cannot have an objectified spiritual knowing in a nondualistic awareness.

Allow me to explain it this way: We exist in a dualistic realm. For there to be darkness, we must have a recognition of the presence of light, in order to contrast the one against the other. We must have an awareness of goodness if we are to point out the existence of evil. In our normal waking state, we exist in a four-dimensional (three dimensions of space and one of time) dualistic realm, and whether we are in the evaluator role or the observer role, we are able to compare and contrast what we see, using any number of principal or nonprincipal modalities of perception. That is, we perceive data primarily via digital, tactile, visual, or auditory modalities, and we are aware of these perceptions. I will discuss these modalities in more detail later in the book.

However, if we are in a position to spiritually experience something in the absolute, then we can say that, for a moment, we are in a nondualistic existence, comparing nothing—no analysis, no contrasts. There is only the experience. In the instant we become aware of our experience, we flip to the dualistic mode of interpretation, and there, at the speed of thought, we become dualistically aware of our condition, our experience. In this moment, we are paradoxically outside of the knowing of the nondualistic experience and suddenly find ourselves struggling to sketch or express in words relevant to the spiritual experience, because we are back in a dualistic modality.

It is this effort, this struggle, that drives us further back from our initial point of awareness. Thus, a spiritual awareness is, by its very nature, impossible to define; it can and must be relegated to a simple agreement between those who have experienced it, and it must rest in the cradle of the verbal expression "I know." This level of awareness is outside the scope and focus of the beginning Coordinate Remote Viewer, but it is well within the focus of the more advanced practitioners of the phenomenon, for example, the Extended Remote Viewer, the Master Extended Remote Viewer, and those participating in Phase V of the training at the Explorer Group level.

The second way through which you may know how you know is intuitive knowing. Intuitive knowing is all around us; we see versions of it every day and give these examples little, if any, attention. An example of intuitive knowing is when you decide not to go on a trip for some unknown reason—you "just know" that you do not feel good about it. A day or two later, you find that something terrible happened at the hotel you would have been staying at. Another example of intuitive knowing is when your mother calls you unexpectedly to ask if something is wrong. You may be in some sort of financial trouble, or perhaps you or your child is seriously ill. You did not want to bother your mother with anything so you didn't call her, but she "just knew" something was amiss and called you. It can also be described as "mother's intuition" or "women's intuition" or a "gut instinct" or perhaps even by the comment "I followed my heart." All are excellent examples of intuitive knowing.

Intuitive knowing is probably what brought you to this book. In many other examples, it was intuitive knowing that brought a physician to class or an engineer to class. The great Einstein knew intuitively that the wisdom necessary to move humanity forward in the realm of physics did not come from a textbook. Textbook knowledge was simply the listing or compilation of empirical knowledge. Einstein knew that intuitive knowledge was derived from mastering the unseen and mystical places of human awareness that exist outside of the physical. It is intuitive knowing that will be one of your ultimate goals in Remote Viewing. Essentially, you are learning to walk in both worlds, the physical and the nonphysical, simultaneously and without cause to step out of one to compare the other. This will be your life "on purpose," knowing that Remote Viewing is a tool, just a tool, that will one day be put away when the ability to walk in both worlds is mastered.

The final manner of knowing is empirical knowledge, which comes from a measurement of quantifiable attributes in the summary and analysis of your Remote Viewing sessions. You will learn the process from this book. If I am to take you beyond your beliefs to a place of knowing, I must use this protocol. I must be able to measure what you think you saw in the session with what you were supposed to see; this is how learning will take place.

YOU WILL BE TRANSFORMED

By now, you may have sensed that I am using Remote Viewing as a vehicle to teach you more than just the ability to see distantly in space-time. It is not some hidden plot; it is by design, and it is always what I use Remote Viewing for. I want you to know that Remote Viewing is a tool; it is just a tool. The tool is not what is important. What is important is that the tool demonstrates to you that you, in fact, are endowed with very powerful and wonderful gifts in this life. What is critical is what you choose to do with these gifts, once recognized.

The wisdom gained from accepting the existence of this phenomenon will most assuredly confirm your understanding of your place in the universe, on our planet, and in the course of global societal evolution. Think long and hard about this process. Look deep within yourself, and seek the answer to important questions: "What is my purpose in learning to use this gift, to tap into this godlike ability? How can I use it to make a difference in this world? How will it change my life for the better?" These questions are critical to your acceptance of this ability. It is not simply a hobby or a way to pass the time pleasantly—it will affect us all. The question is, how will it affect you?

The tool of Remote Viewing is presented to you so that you might know you are more than the physical. Knowing supplants believing on virtually every energy level, and the beauty of Remote Viewing is that the evidence of this ability is irrefutable and undeniable. Evidence of this quality is rare and it is powerful. When you know you are more than the physical, you must then know you are part of something larger than yourself, and you are connected to it and always have been. In the lexicon of the Remote Viewer, this point of connection is called the *Source*. You may consider the Source to be the energetic representation of God, if you wish. Just do not look for it to be a place within the physical universe. It is a state of being. I even hesitate to use the term "connection" because it implies there may have been some disconnection, and there never has been, nor can there ever be. You have always been a part of the Source, and the Source is you. You have always been able to access the Source; it is just because of your conditioning that you have stopped listening to, looking at, and feeling the infinite.

Opening the conduits into the unconscious mind, which is what Remote Viewing does, will bring you to a place of effortless perfection in the knowing of who and what you are in this existence. In other words, you will recognize your calling in this existence and elect to honor that calling, whatever it may be. In so honoring this calling, you must live your life in such a way as to define your personal mythology, to write the story of your life with the gifts you have been given. Remote Viewing is just a tool to help you recognize those gifts in a very powerful and sure way. As you live life defining your mythology, you will be living your life on purpose, making a positive difference in the human condition. Living life on purpose is walking your life's path.

You may wonder: "Which path should I be on? What has this path to do with my existing path? Which do I choose? Do I have to choose one or the other?" In Figure 2.2, I have presented a model to illustrate a number of paths, each with the purpose of facilitating our individual or collective passage out of the consciousness of the physical world and into the unconsciousness of the Matrix Field. I'll define the Matrix Field for you in Chapter 4, but for now, you may consider it the Akashic Record, nirvana, the Gap, the realm of the unmanifested, the mind of God—all may be used synonymously. If all paths are focused on the support of their belief structure, then all paths serve similar purposes, facilitated by different practices.

Remote Viewing is just another path. It is not an end-all, be-all path, it is not the only path, and on many levels, it may not be the best path—but it is

FIGURE 2.2 **Which Path Do I Follow?**

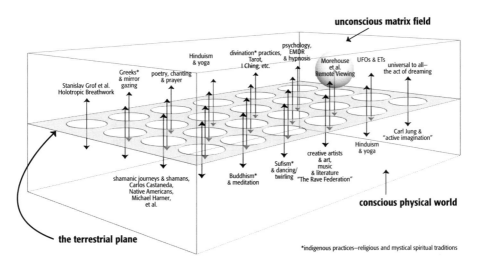

a very effective, scientifically supported, and evidentiary path. It is a powerful teaching path due to its ability to produce irrefutable evidence that you are more than the physical. And it is for this reason that I teach it and use it as a tool of transformation.

On the subject of paths, I only ask that you leave your veneration of any particular path outside of the learning process for this program. You cannot learn at the maximum evolution if you are constantly pushing what you are learning through the filters of your present path. You are not asked to forsake the present path, only to remove it from your view while you ingest new material. Ultimately, you will find that Remote Viewing will effectively augment your present path, or you may find that your present path augments Remote Viewing. You are encouraged to leave your academic and intellectual egos outside of the process of learning. Yogi Berra once said, "It isn't what we know that causes us problems; it is what we know that just isn't so that stops all progress." Let go of the path for a moment, and allow the information to be presented while you are in the observer role. Once you have concluded your practice for the day, resume your path, and process what you have learned accordingly.

3

How to Use This Book

Every passing moment is a chance to turn it all around.

Cameron Crowe, *Vanilla Sky*

WHAT YOU WILL LEARN FROM THIS BOOK

There are six stages in the Coordinate Remote Viewing protocol. When teaching the program in a classroom, I divide it into two phases of training. Phase I of the training program constitutes learning Stages I, II, and III of the protocol, which takes approximately thirty-five hours of training time in three days. Phase II of the program—Stages IV, V, and VI of the protocol—is another thirty-five hours of training time spread over three days. I also teach, in many parts of the world, a Phase I-and-II-combined course that is approximately seventy total hours of training time formatted to fit into a five- or seven-day class, depending on where I am and whom I am teaching.

Clearly, you can invest a good deal of time in the classroom environment, and this is where the major portion of the training takes place. Learning Remote Viewing in a residential training course has its advantages and disadvantages. In a residential course, you are completely immersed in the learning and work environment I provide for you; you do not have to think about creating any space; all you have to do is show up for class, and my staff and I do the rest. The major drawback to this format is the cost to you, which easily tops $1,350 and is constantly rising due to the cost of venue, travel, materials, lodging, and food for a large training staff. Another drawback is that you are required to devote up to a week of your time, plus cover your travel and lodging expenses. Many people simply cannot afford to do this, yet they want to learn Remote Viewing. For this reason, Sounds True and I decided to bring together all the essential training elements of Coordinate Remote Viewing into an affordable, portable, and self-paced home-study training program, which I know will get you to the same level of proficiency as the resident training course, if you apply yourself.

This book will teach you everything you need to know to become a Coordinate Remote Viewer, learning Phase I (Stages I, II, and III) and Phase II (Stages IV, V, and VI), at which point you will be considered an intermediate-level Remote Viewer (there are also three advanced levels of training you may pursue). Your initial focus will be on learning the theory, the dynamics, the science, the philosophy, and the protocols necessary to get you beyond that simple place of believing there is something beyond the physical, to a place of knowing there is.

Once you understand the theory behind the art and science of Coordinate Remote Viewing, you will be given instruction on the protocol of CRV, meaning the actual system of detecting, decoding, and categorizing data relevant to a target distant in space-time. In this program, you will be taught how to create the optimum learning environment; how to create the optimum CRV work environment; how to descend into and sustain an altered state of consciousness; how to work within the protocol; how to prepare a narrative session summary; and finally, how to evaluate your session data and compare it with the target feedback provided. From here, you will be given training tips and techniques that will help you improve your performance by increasing your skill and experience levels. You will have access to a Sample Session, included as a separate chapter in this book, to support your training efforts.

What you will learn right away is that this is an absolutely structured process that has little if any room for interpretation. The more you follow the structure of CRV, the better you will do. Consequently, the more you deviate from this system and my instructions for working within the protocol, the poorer will be your performance. This is not a simple process to learn; it is not a subjective magic carpet ride that allows you to just let happen whatever happens. It is an absolute dogma, a discipline designed to teach you to see distantly in space-time.

CREATING THE OPTIMUM LEARNING ENVIRONMENT

Optimum learning begins with you and your intention. If your intention is to do well with this course, to focus and study intently, then you will succeed. This course is designed to get you where you want to be, and if you follow the program, you will become a well-trained basic-level to intermediate-level Remote Viewer. This said, nothing is a given if you do not do all that you can to facilitate the learning environment. Here are a few things I recommend to help you do your best in this course.

Establish a Suitable Work Space in Which to Study

Consider this space to be a sacred and quiet place that you will create. Find a place in your home, your office, the public library, anywhere you can be left alone for a period of two hours. This work space should provide you with a desk for taking notes, practicing structure, sketching, and so on. The space should have a suitable light for reading and ample room for your compact disc player and headphones.

Once you are ready to begin the actual practice of working a Coordinate Remote Viewing target, you'll need a work environment that allows you to sit in an upright and relaxed posture at a desktop surface free of clutter and distracting colors, sounds, or smells. Be sure to turn off the phones, and tell anyone in your work environment not to disturb you for ninety minutes.

What You Will Need

A stack of 8½-x-11-inch plain white paper. This paper can be three-hole-punched so that you can place it in a notebook for future reference and review. The paper must be unlined, white paper to minimize any effect of persistence of vision during the session. I will later address in detail why the paper must be unlined and why you must use a black pen.

A black ballpoint pen. Look for a pen whose ink does not bleed through the paper each time you place the tip of the pen on the page to probe for data. Try different paper-and-pen combinations until you find what works for you. It is impossible for me to specify a particular style of pen and paper since there are so many variables worldwide.

A CRV cooldown eye mask. This eye mask is primarily used in Extended Remote Viewing training; however, in recent years, many Coordinate Remote Viewers have begun using it during the cooldown process. When you wear it during the cooldown, it will help keep you from being distracted by light or other interruptions that may cause you to reflexively open your eyes. Some Viewers keep it handy and pull it back down over their eyes at any time during the session when they feel it is necessary to take a break from the signal line.

Your CRV cooldown CD. The cooldown process is your preparation for the Remote Viewing session, taking you from the wakeful beta brain-wave state into the relaxed and focused alpha brain-wave state, much like a deep meditative state.

A CD player. A portable CD player is best for this kind of work because it provides you with more flexibility. You can carry it from room to room or to the library or other study area as needed. These players are very affordable and are readily available from most department stores.

While it is important to have a comfortable and optimum work environment, do not become obsessed with making it perfect. Remember that this process was designed for soldiers to use on the battlefield and that a less-than-perfect environment will balance out in the retention curve. Thus, your work atmosphere need not be perfect nor entirely free of distractions. What matters most are your attitude and your intention!

Schedule Focused Study Time

Schedule a time to study this course material when you will not be disturbed by phone calls, visitors, children, friends, meals to cook, or errands to run. You will need this time to focus on the material, to absorb the lectures, and to become familiar with the book's contents. If you miss an element and move on, you will have serious problems and questions later. Each piece of the instruction is essential for what comes later; even the anecdotes will prove useful to you as you progress.

Schedule Your Training Program

What you write down will happen. Establish a system for learning the material right now. I recommend that you schedule each chapter, and then do your very best to adhere to the schedule. Try to schedule one chapter per week. If you do not develop a plan, then you will likely skip around in the sessions or read the book at odd and inconvenient times when you cannot take notes or work the exercises. Set realistic goals for the course, and by that I mean do not try to get through all of it in a week and think you will master the material or maximize your results.

If you feel you can handle the workload and still maintain a level of quality, then speed up the scheduling by increasing the number of chapters per week to a level you are comfortable with. This is a self-paced learning process, and I do not want you to think I am holding you back. I have trained thousands of individuals to do this, so I am speaking from a teaching perspective that I know will work. That said, you will have to determine how fast you will run or how slowly you will walk through this program. The choice is yours—the most important thing is to have fun while you are learning. Take your time; be sure you are comfortable with the concepts in each segment before you move on to the next chapter.

Do Not Shy Away from a Less-Than-Perfect Learning Environment

Let's face it, working from home with all the possible distractions and environmental conditions is far less desirable than learning these protocols in a controlled environment of light and sound with a one-to-one instructor-student ratio. The compensation for learning in a less-than-perfect environment is that it adds a welcome element to the process. It is true that increases in stressors due to less-than-optimum training environments result in a decreased performance curve. Figure 3.1 shows what happens to the performance curve when the student is working in an optimum learning environment. You can see that the performance curve increases across the duration of the session. This means that the ability to accurately work within the session structure to detect and decode usable data will likely be at a consistently higher level than if the environment were less than optimum. However, you can also see that the retention curve, your ability to recall the convoluted protocols and keep track of all the necessary details within the session, decreases in proportion to the performance curve. Essentially, in a near-perfect environment, you may perform better but you will remember less about what you are supposed to be doing the next time. Initially, working in a less-than-perfect environment may actually help you learn the structure of the process.

In Figure 3.2, which depicts a less-than-optimum learning environment, you can see that while your performance curve will decrease, your retention curve increases proportionally. Hence, you may not produce as much usable session data about the target, but you will know the concepts and you will know the structure of Coordinate Remote Viewing, which is highly desirable. There were two signs that hung in the military Remote Viewing unit. One read, "If you don't write it down, it doesn't count," and the other read, "Content be damned, structure is everything." The latter of these statements is supported by the less-than-perfect learning environment.

FIGURE 3.1 **The Optimum Learning Environment**

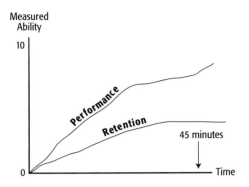

FIGURE 3.2 **Less-Than-Optimum Learning Environment**

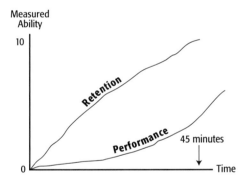

STRUCTURE IS EVERYTHING

The Sample Session is provided as a separate chapter in this book as a reference to illustrate how to progress through the stages of Coordinate Remote Viewing. It is also an excellent example of the "structure" of the CRV process. I do not care how much usable data you produce as a new Remote Viewing student. What I care most about is your ability to know the structure of CRV. The sign "Content be damned" meant that you should always let go of the outcome of the session and that you should never be tied to what you produce. You will have good days and not-so-good days as a Viewer, and that is a fact. However, the finest Remote Viewers care little about the output; they care only about their adherence to the structure. "Structure is everything" means that if you learn the structure, the content will come. Remember what we have already discussed: being an observer means letting go of the outcome and focusing on the structure, knowing that the content will come. If you slip into the role of evaluator, you will begin a cycle of conclusions and judgments that will attach you to the outcome—a very fragile perch indeed. Limited performance will speed up the evaluator cycle until all you are doing is judging yourself, your ability to do this, the process itself, and so on. You will learn nothing under these conditions; therefore, you must choose to step out of the evaluator cycle and get back into the observer cycle as fast as you can. It is always a choice you must be aware of.

ONE FINAL NOTE ON TRAINING ENVIRONMENTS

Remote Viewing was originally designed to be used on the battlefield during combat operations, potentially as a tool of special operations forces, such as the Rangers or Special Forces. It was never used in this manner due only to the controversial nature of the protocol. But what you should take from this notion is that if Remote Viewing could be employed effectively in battle, then just about any environment you select in which to study or apply this technology will be suitable. Thus, you can do this!

WORKING WITH YOUR BIGGEST OBSTACLE—YOURSELF

Success as a Remote Viewer depends not only on your technical ability, following the session structure as taught in this book, but also on your ability to direct your mind to remain the observer. The biggest obstacle in learning Remote Viewing is your own self-judgment. The greatest distraction to the Remote Viewing process is frankly your hardheaded and analytic conscious mind—that 6 to 8 percent of your brain that predominantly operates within a comfortable beta frequency as it goes about its business of constantly analyzing the physical world around you. Do not let it get the better of you; remember the model of intentions we just discussed. Keep your focus, keep your training schedule, keep your sense of humor, and most important of all, remain the observer. A large part of becoming a successful Remote Viewer will be developing your ability to quiet the inner dialogue, let go of ego, let go of self-doubt, and let go of the outcome.

You should approach this process of learning the art and science of Coordinate Remote Viewing in total humility, understanding both your significance and your insignificance to the Matrix of all creation. If you are willing to do this, it is certain that you will see your target. Your individual degree of accuracy can and will fluctuate from session to session and day to day, which is again why you should never trust the results of one Viewer operating independently of other Viewers. But if you will maintain a sense of commitment to yourself and to this process, you will improve. You can be as good as you desire in this; there is no inherent limit to your ability, only that which you set for yourself.

Quiet the Inner Dialogue

The inner dialogue is that nagging voice inside you that speaks to limits. It is not the voice of your higher self or of the unconscious mind. It is the voice of your conditioning, the voice that speaks in conclusive and judgmental phrases. This voice can be your greatest obstacle if you let it, but with training, you can turn this voice into a fierce passion for your work—it is all a choice. As you prepare for your session, spend a few moments doing those things that surround you with peace and calm. Look at art that inspires you; listen to music that sets you free, that lets you fly. In the residential courses, this is called *mission music;* we play music from the motion pictures *Braveheart, Titanic, Apollo 13,* and the like. The music lets the students soar within themselves, and they are then more than ready to engage in the cooldown process and work the session. Do not watch the news or check your e-mail or conduct business—do what settles your soul and quiets the inner dialogue. Movies like *Powder, Hoosiers,* and *Phenomenon* are great for turning off the chatter of "cannot" and stirring a dialogue of "can."

Let Go of Ego

Your ego can be defined as many things, but for the purpose of this program, I would like you to understand it as follows: Ego is who I am, it is what I do, it is my accepted identity, and it is my manifest behavior. The Old Testament states, "As a man thinks, so is he." Most people believe ego is that which protects, that which allows your unbridled belief in what is possible for you. Unfortunately, the condition most people encounter in life presents the exact opposite kind of ego. Most of us have egos that set hard beliefs in shortages, shortages we fulfill with self-talk such as "I can't do that," "I can't find abundance," "I can't find love," "It is too hard," and so on.

Throughout your life, you have encountered any number of events. Each of these events created a situation to which you assigned an emotion. This emotion cannot exist alone. It must be supported by a belief, and it is this belief that you accept as an identity, your ego. As you live your life supporting this ego, you attract into your life all that the ego needs—you have created a manifest behavior. Behavior attracts like behavior, and it is a continuing cycle that can only be broken by choice. You must choose to step out of it, to amend it, to establish another, more positive and loving identity.

Thoreau said, "If one advances confidently in the direction of his dreams, and endeavors to live the life which he has imagined, one will meet with a success unexpected in common hours." Let go of the ego that sets limits for you, that limits your promise and possibility. As you progress through this program, do not think about what is missing; rather, focus on what is present, on how much you are learning. What you do not presently understand will come to you if you see it for yourself. See yourself in the observer role, feeling how you will feel when you realize all that is possible for you. See yourself surrounded by the conditions you want to see, and any time you find yourself not in this cycle, know immediately that you are in the resistance of the evaluator role, and step out of it by choice. This is quieting the negative inner dialogue of the ego.

On the other end of this spectrum, you have to contend with your ego's tendency to inflate your own ideas of who you are and what you should be capable of doing. Be humble and appreciative of this great gift that has always been yours, this scientifically driven protocol that will enable you to see distantly in space-time. See yourself in a condition of success, but do not engage in any practice from a perspective of ego that says, "I don't need this protocol; I can do this on my own," or "This structure is too cumbersome; I have always been able to do this . . . this is just getting in my way." These are manifestations of ego that create obstacles of another sort; they are not positive, they are likely fear-based, and they are again from the resistance of the evaluator cycle.

Your ego in this condition can present obstacles—resistance to the idea, the imagination, the vision, that you can be all that you desire to be. It is a very fine line, this way of thinking, of being. On the one hand, your ego can create an evaluator obstacle of "I can't," while on the other hand, it may create the resistance of "I am beyond all of this." Both are limiting beliefs, and you are responsible for correcting them. Be aware of the potential for resistance, but think good thoughts, and decide each day to be happy, to fill your life with joy, and to learn.

Let Go of Self-Doubt

Self-doubt is just another manifestation of ego. It is still based on the catalytic marriage of emotions and beliefs coming from moments in your life. It is still an identity, which you use to create a manifest behavior. It is still a self-inoculating cycle that is controlled by choice. Living at this end of the spectrum is just as hazardous and limiting for you. If you indulge in self-doubt, you will constantly criticize your own work and results (which is analysis), doubting any perceivable information or session data that you develop.

In this cycle of resistance, your sessions become unusable due to the tremendous amount of information that you omitted because you felt you were just not "on" this time. You will begin to use language such as "I can't remember everything I am supposed to be doing here," "The CRV structure is way too hard for me," "I am stupid; I don't know why I spent the money on this; I should have known that I could not do something like this," or "I knew I didn't have any ability." This is all the self-talk of the doubter in the evaluator role, passing judgment on self and process. You already know how to step out of it. It is a choice to be in it. You must take responsibility for it and choose to step out of it. If you say, "Well, this is who I am," then you are choosing to exist in the evaluator role, to accept this limiting identity and surround yourself with the energy of resistance.

Let Go of the Outcome

Nonattachment is an ancient teaching. Letting go of attachment is a lifelong practice, a practice that absolutely applies to the process of learning Remote Viewing. The most important thing you will do in this book is to learn the structure and protocols of the Remote Viewing process—all else is secondary. Your skill and ability will come through knowing the structure and then committing to a life of practice and the pursuit of a path.

Nothing of value and quality in life comes without a humble devotion to what manifests it in your life. Create energy around yourself of surrendering to the process. Create a life of practice, of discipline, and of study. Seek truth (your version of it), find knowledge, and become wisdom. Let go of your desire to win, and be content with the assurance that you have this ability and that in time you will master it. Surround yourself with this image, this dream, this vision, and then let go of the outcome. If you keep looking into the conceptual illusion of the future, of what has not yet happened, and place all your energy there, then you are missing the moment—and it is how you live in the moment that will create the space for all that you desire to manifest.

THE PRACTICE: MAXIMIZING YOUR RESULTS

The process of learning Remote Viewing contains two elements: lecture and practice. You are already engaged in the lecture element contained in the book. Now I would like to briefly address what you should do in order to maximize your result in the actual practice of Remote Viewing.

The Method for Successful Performance

There are some practices you can engage in that will help you maximize your performance ability in the practical exercises. You will hear me say repeatedly that everything is energy and energy is everything, and you will come to know the physics of this in Chapter 4, "The Physics of the Metaphysics." Life is energy, and everything in life is energy. Your very physical existence is defined and guided by energy. Nothing you do, say, think, watch, eat, or drink is devoid of energy; to the contrary, it is all energy.

All energy has the ability to affect other energy. You, as energy, are affected by countless forms of other energy. You can empower yourself and master your energy, creating an environment, a life, a knowing, filled with illuminated and powerful loving, positive energy. Alternatively, you can choose another energy. Choice is always part of the equation. If you feel you are in the presence of others who are taking your energy and bringing you down, remember that it is your surrender of power, your choice to give away energy. It cannot be taken by force from you. Choose to attract and build your energy in positive ways; do not look for ways to be offended, but instead look for ways to serve and empower others.

Positive energy in your life creates possibility; thus, you must constantly seek forms and sources of energy that sustain the possible for you. Avoid images, music, gossip, and other forms of negative energy that displace the positive in you. Do not place in your body substances that are incompatible with the positive energy of the body. I make these recommendations without any moral agenda. My purpose here is to give you as much information as is possible— then you must decide what advice to follow. This advice or information is not intended to be medical advice; I provide it as educational information only.

Food

What you eat is energy, and it will affect your body's energy. However, diet regimens, such as vegan, have not been proven empirically to have any marked effect on the Remote Viewing session. In fact, a vegetarian diet versus an omnivorous diet seems to be of little or no consequence. Therefore, one can assume that any diet of moderation would be adequate—and this is my view. However, I believe you should follow a practice that you are comfortable with, one that contributes to overall health and a sense of well-being. For some, this may include the consumption of meat; for others, not—it is very much a personal choice.

That said, know that you should limit the amount of meat you consume, especially before engaging in a Remote Viewing session. All meat carries an element of energy that is positive and nutritious, but there is also an energy of death carried with it. If you think this sounds a bit weird, think about it again for a moment. The animal was killed so that you could consume it, so there is an energetic imprint carried with the flesh you consume.

When you are trying to condition yourself energetically to detect and decode the subtle nuances of target data derived from the Matrix Field, it is conceivable that the energetic imprint of the animal, which will be negative to a degree, can influence or skew the session data. Most often, this is described by Remote Viewers as just a sense of unrest or an inability to be at peace. In the conscious mind, the mind driving you through the physical world, the effect of eating meat probably goes unnoticed, but to some Remote Viewers, it is absolutely noticeable, and it is considered by those experiencing it to be a deterrent to a good session. Again, the choice is yours; I am simply providing the information.

Water, Exercise, and Sleep

One of the most important things you can do is to keep hydrated. The body and mind function at peak performance when the body is hydrated, well rested, and well exercised.

Stimulants

Although the regular use of stimulants such as coffee or tea has minimal effect on the Remote Viewer, it is highly suggested that you refrain from using stimulants before doing a session. If you must imbibe, try to use plain water or perhaps green tea. Heavy use of coffee or tea, or ephedrine or other weight-loss drugs, whether over-the-counter or by prescription, will not help you do your best Remote Viewing work.

You want to be relaxed and focused in your sessions. Stimulants constrict the vascular system of the brain and produce a sort of masked or insulated feeling in the Remote Viewer. It is difficult to perceive data once inside a figurative chemical drum, so refrain from the use of these drugs during your Remote Viewing session, and be sure to begin eliminating their use several days before you conduct a session.

Alcohol

An excessive use of alcohol will impair one's ability to Remote View. Used during or before a session, alcohol will degrade the Viewer's ability to unacceptable levels. The session will invariably be useless within any practical model. Hangovers or degraded cognitive ability extending from prolonged abuse of alcohol will obviously degrade the quality of the Remote Viewer's neural tissue and directly affect the session product. If you must drink, follow an old rule: Do it in moderation. There is ample medical research available on amounts considered medicinal and healthful, as well as consumption levels known to be dangerous or harmful. Educate yourself if you do not know the limits, and if you can, refrain from use altogether, as alcohol will not help you do your best work.

Illicit Drugs

The use of illicit drugs will never enhance the Remote Viewing session or product. It is believed by many that the use of cannabis enhances creativity. There is little dispute that marijuana can influence creativity, and it is frequently endorsed by artists for this function. However, it is a commonly held belief within circles of very skilled and experienced Remote Viewers that *any* drug used during the session will be "in charge" of the session. If the drug is in control of the session, then you are not, and Remote Viewing is all about doing your own work and providing your own version of what is perceived. We have too many opportunities in life to give power away; do not give it away to a substance you believe will enhance the Remote Viewing experience, because, I assure you, it will not.

The use of natural or synthetic psychedelics, depressants, painkillers, or anything of this ilk will most certainly affect the session as well as the Viewer. You are always better served when you enter an altered state of consciousness via the power of your own mind and not through the influence of some external agent.

Use of illicit drugs, such as crack cocaine, cocaine, methamphetamines, or any chemical in this spectrum, for example, Ecstasy and similar synthetics, has been medically proven to have degenerative effects on the human brain's ability to think. Remote Viewing is difficult enough without making the mistake of adopting the philosophy that drug-induced or drug-assisted Remote Viewing will work—it will not.

Remember that the government of the United States spent tens of millions of dollars developing this technology for use in the intelligence world, a world with few if any limits, moral or ethical. If the use of drugs of any kind had been shown to enhance the intelligence collection efforts of Remote Viewers, we would have been using them in great abundance. Be assured, we used nothing but our own inherent abilities.

Antidepressant and Antipsychotic Drugs

In every residential class I teach, students are asked to sign an agreement indicating they will take full responsibility for their experience and their actions during the course. This form also requires every student to list any and all medications they are taking, including antipsychotic medications, antidepressants, psychotropic medications, and other related medications. The use of these medications does not prevent the student from attending the class; however, it does indicate to the staff those students who may have difficulty detecting and decoding certain levels of information.

If you are taking prescribed medications, you should not stop taking them unless you are under the supervision of a physician. It has been found that the awareness that comes from the Remote Viewing experience helps the Viewer take back control of his or her emotions and feelings, and this has countless times facilitated the Viewer's elimination of the medications—but such is not always the case, nor should it be an expectation. If it happens, great; coordinate with your physician to begin discontinuing use of the medication in a controlled manner. Do not stop taking the medications on your own, because abrupt discontinuance of any medications may have very serious side effects. Use common sense, and consult your physician.

All of that said, these medications will absolutely degrade your ability to use the various modalities of perception and to detect and decode the waveform data. If you think about it, this is exactly what the medications are designed to do: provide a chemical buffer to what you perceive. The medications are designed to control the conceptual illusion you experience, to help keep it all in perspective. Coordinate Remote Viewing is the process of detecting and decoding eight-dimensional waveform information into coherent four-dimensional thought form, also called conceptual illusion. If you have an abundance of a medication in your system that is designed to limit the effect of conceptual illusion, your ability to form large packages of verbal and visual data will be reduced.

What do you do if you are someone who must take such medications? You just do it. You will have to work harder than the person who is not taking the medications, but so what? Work harder. Do not look for an occasion to be offended. Look for the positive in the situation. You are well; you have people who love you and a physician who cares for you. If the medications are necessary, you keep taking them until you and your physician feel you no longer need them. Often, changing the energy of your life by recognizing that you are omnipotent, omniscient, and omnipresent in the unconscious will be the inspiration you need to work your way out of depression or any other need for medication. You are infinite, and you have infinite healing energy within you and from the Source. As you reconstruct yourself in a new manner of being, use your power to heal and to balance your life—I promise you, you can do this.

MORPHIC RESONANCE

You have probably heard about the "hundredth-monkey effect" or Sheldrake and Young's theories on the global mind or the collective unconscious. Morphic resonance is the phenomenon supporting these theories and, in this case, concepts involving experience and learning. If everything is energy and energy is everything, then every experience, every thought, carries with it an energy, a frequency that never dies, never goes away, but exists in an eternal and infinite realm. This realm has many names, several of which I have already shared with you. You can think of this realm as a collective pool of energy, of the energy of human experience, in this case. Therefore, every experience is energetically recorded in this field or pool, and everyone has access to the record.

What we know in education is that students are learning faster than ever before. We know that physics and mathematics are ingested faster than they were fifty years ago, that humankind is not moving backward intellectually, but is always moving forward. In terms of Remote Viewers, it means that those of you learning this now are potentially going to begin where those of us who learned it years ago left off. Thus, you are better Remote Viewers than we were. Why? Because of morphic resonance. You begin with the ability to drink from a pool of wisdom that has the energetic experience of more than twenty-three thousand other Remote Viewing students recorded in it.

So, let go of any fear of failure—you are already better than I ever was, simply because you begin your journey with my experience. Quiet the inner dialogue, let go of ego, and let go of self-doubt. Move forward in a balanced, humble manner, creating a sacred space within. Engage the ritual of Coordinate Remote Viewing with effortless perfection, connected to the Source from which you came. Know that you are eternal and omnipresent at the unconscious level of existence; know that you are more than the physical. Your journey inward begins . . .

4

The Physics of the Metaphysics

THE MARRIAGE OF SCIENCE AND SPIRIT

We can run into difficulty any time we begin to apply scientific and mathematical definitions to metaphysical concepts, which are inherently nonmathematical and nonscientific. Nevertheless, those of us teaching metaphysical concepts, as well as those of us within the scientific community, have an inherent responsibility to the human condition to find some common language between the metaphysical and scientific communities. What is clear is that the synergy as well as the clashing between the two communities will never disappear. The marriage between science and spirit has existed since humanity became aware of the obligation to explain this existence. This on-again, off-again relationship will continue until the two merge in some new coexistence that mandates a mutually supportive path. Countless times in human history, this relationship has come to a point of new potential and possibility. For various reasons, the relationship has fallen apart; one undermines the other, or one oversteps the boundaries of the other. Regardless, science and spirit are constantly drawn together in the hope that some accord will manifest, and all humanity will benefit from the collective wisdom.

The greatest scientific minds of our time have always recognized the need for this relationship. The greatest scientific minds of our time have not negated the existence of spirit. To the contrary, those who spend a lifetime unraveling the mystery of life know firsthand the human need for the spiritual. They understand this perhaps better than those who spend a lifetime seeking to exist within the light of spirit.

Thus, the need for a common language cannot be delegated to one or the other; it is a joint responsibility. Neither interest can take a position of arrogance, standing apart from the other and suggesting that what is known by them can never be understood by the other. It is the obligation of both to live, write, and speak in such a way as to build a bridge of understanding between the two. Physicist and philosopher Fritjof Capra said, "Science does not need mysticism and mysticism does not need science; but humanity needs both." It is essential that both come from positions of credible compassion, of a common humility focused on uniting the global societies. As the two communities are being merged by scientific and spiritual discovery, each community and each of us within our respective communities must build toward one another. Each of us individually, and all of us collectively, must recognize the importance of bowing our heads and our efforts to ensure that this marriage is a lasting one. Humanity can little afford another century of exile—the consequences of decisions made in a forced separation of science and spirit grow potentially more dire with each passing moment. We simply must understand this, and we must use our scientific tools and spiritual gifts to unite the legions of the status quo—for the good of all life on this planet.

As you read further, understand that nothing is an absolute in this life. Physics used to be taught in terms of absolutes, referencing what are called the *absolute laws of physics*. In new physics, the physics of this century being led by those young men and women who are willing to risk reputation in an effort to stand on the edge of knowledge and look beyond, there is a complete resignation from the absolutes of physics. Instead, there exists in new physics a surrender to the awareness that we exist in a universe of approximations. Every day in any number of fields of scientific endeavor, what we thought we knew yesterday gives way to some new theory, some new understanding or suspicion. The cycle of discovery is spinning faster than ever imagined possible.

Theoretical physicists from Imperial College in England, as well as from other highly regarded universities throughout the world, are pioneering research into the mathematical evidence supporting, among other revelations, the variable speed of light. If you do not come from a scientific background, the significance of this work may not register, but essentially, what is being called into question is the basis of Relativity and its implications for the last century of physics—that the speed of light remains constant regardless of the velocity of the observer. You must recognize that, early in the twentieth century, this seeming absolute of the speed of light was the subject of heated debate. The old guard of physics at the time would have nothing to do with it or with those proposing it. Einstein remarked, looking back on the opposition to the special and general theories of relativity, "Great spirits have always encountered violent opposition from mediocre minds." And now the old guard of present physics—those who have built a lifetime of understanding and teaching upon the supposed absolutes of science—are quivering angrily at the prospect that what they "know" to be an absolute is being questioned by a bunch of young upstarts. Bravo to the upstarts who, like Aldous Huxley, admit, "Science has 'explained' nothing; the more we know, the more fantastic the world becomes and the more profound the surrounding darkness."

Einstein, Bohr, Dirac, Feynman, and every other brilliant scientific mind of the twentieth century were once considered young upstarts. Where would we be without them and their courage to push the envelope of scientific understanding? Physicist Max Planck said of this relationship, "A new scientific truth does not triumph by convincing its opponents and making them see the light, but rather because its opponents eventually die, and a new generation grows up that is familiar with it." Addressing the stubbornness of the old guard, Planck reveals the unfortunate in human nature: so many of us are so conditioned as to what we "believe," that we would rather die "believing" in something than have the courage to explore and "know" that we really "know very little." Author Gerry Spence put it another way: "I would rather have a mind opened by wonder than one closed by belief." What is significant about these men and women, these new thinkers, is that not one of them ever questioned the existence of spirit or the need for the unexplained. Unlike those wishing the world could continue in a realm of absolutes, these men and women knew there were things that simply could not be explained through the current efforts of science. It did not mean a particular ability or event did not exist or happen; it only meant it could not be explained in the present condition, and this includes the human ability to see distantly in space-time.

PART ONE: THE UNIVERSE OF POSSIBILITIES

I would like to define a number of the terms we will be working with. These definitions constitute a basic scientific language you should become familiar with, as this will, in part, become your new lexicon, the language of the Coordinate Remote Viewer and beyond. Each new level of your training beyond this basic CRV course will add to this lexicon. There is no need for you to commit these definitions to memory; I assure you that you will hear them so frequently in Remote Viewing that they will soon become a part of your everyday vocabulary.

Metaphysics

Metaphysics is a division of philosophy that is concerned with the fundamental nature of reality and being. The study of metaphysics includes ontology (dealing with the nature of being, or of reality), cosmology (the scientific study of the form, content, and origin of the physical universe), and often epistemology (the study of the sources, origins, nature, and limits of knowledge).

The Mind

In the lexicon of the Remote Viewer, the language pertaining to the levels or categories of the mind is simplified drastically. For our purposes, the mind is divided into three levels: the conscious mind, the subconscious mind, and the unconscious mind. Remember that I have trained thousands of physicians, and several hundred of them have been psychiatrists. I have never had a psychiatrist question the use of these terms; all seem to recognize that language is just that—language—and language can be tailored to meet the needs of the endeavor.

The Conscious Mind

A pure textbook definition of the conscious mind might look something like this: "Perceiving, apprehending, or noticing with a degree of controlled thought or observation; recognizing as existent, factual, or true; recognizing as factual or existent something external; present especially to the senses; involving rational power, perception, and awareness." In the lexicon of Remote Viewing, a more suitable definition is used: The conscious mind is that aspect of self which guides one through the tasks of the physical, four-dimensional world. The conscious mind is responsible for assembling all the data derived by any combination of the unconscious mind and the subconscious mind into coherent thought form.

The conscious mind is responsible for assembling fragments of thought into larger chunks or concepts, often abstract concepts related to life in the physical. The conscious mind is that part of you that is in constant choice between the cycles of observer and evaluator. The conscious mind is in recurrent analysis of all that is perceived, categorizing data, assembling and piecing it together, providing some meaning, even if contrived out of fragments of distant experience. The conscious mind is in operation while the Remote Viewer is awake and aware in a beta brain-wave state, an alpha brain-wave state, and, in rare cases, a shallow theta brain-wave state. In a deep theta brain-wave state or in an ultradeep delta brain-wave state, the conscious mind is considered to be inactive, disengaged, and unaware.

The Subconscious Mind

Again, a textbook definition: "Existing in the mind but not immediately available to consciousness; affecting thought, feeling, and behavior without entering awareness; also considered to be the mental activities just below the threshold of consciousness." For your purposes as a Remote Viewer, think of the subconscious mind as a holding tank, a processing lab, a place where data derived by the unconscious mind is held until it can be assembled by the conscious mind for use in the physical. It is sometimes considered analogous to a garden hose with water running through it. When the flow of data (water) is terminated (turned off at the spigot), there is still a flow of data in the subconscious mind. Even after there is a termination or interruption of the Remote Viewing session, the Viewer can still produce residual data for a matter of minutes. This flow of data is considered to be coming from that portion of the flow which is backed up, or waiting in the subconscious mind.

The Unconscious Mind

In the lexicon of the Viewer, this is that aspect of the mind which is considered connected to the infinite, to the realm of the unmanifested, to the collective unconscious, to the global mind—to the mind of God. You are in constant contact with this aspect of self, and you always have been. It is believed that you were born with a perfect awareness of where you came from (the Source), and this constitutes a complete connection and opening to the vast resources of the unconscious mind. It is through the conditioning of the conscious mind that access to the all-knowing aspect of the unconscious mind is abandoned.

During a Remote Viewing session, the Viewer detects eight-dimensional waveform data using the unconscious mind and decodes this data with the conscious mind. The conscious mind assembles waveform fragments into four-dimensional thought forms of language and visual perspective and proportion. The altered state of consciousness sought by the Remote Viewer during the cooldown is designed to open the conduits into the unconscious, whereby the Remote Viewing process may begin.

Nonlocal Domain

Nonlocal domain is a field of quanta where there is no continuum of time. It is a realm where everything exists purely in waveform; thus, everything is in an omnipresent state, existing everywhere at once. My friend Deepak Chopra often describes this domain using the story of a nursing mother and her child. Though separated by a distance of thousands of miles, when the child cried from hunger, the mother instantly began lactating. The relativity of the space-time continuum would assume a time lag, since the energetic signal from the child to the mother would have to cover several thousand miles. However, in this example, such was not the case. The reception of the signal by the mother was instantaneous, indicating an omnipresent condition in the nonlocal domain. The connection between the mother and the child is without space or time limitations.

Space-Time

Space-time is a four-dimensional continuum with four Cartesian coordinates, the three dimensions of space and one of time, in which any event (or incident) can be located; it is called the space-time continuum in the lexicon of physics. This four-dimensional continuum can more accurately be expanded into a model of eight-dimensional hyperspace. Regardless of the model used, all Remote Viewing targets are conceptualized in relation to this continuum, whether in relation to time, past, present, or future, or in relation to space, near or distant. Actually, when the model is expanded into the eight-dimensional model, the concept of distance is nonexistent, as the model enters the nonlocal domain of the realm of the unmanifested. In this context, there is no element of time and distance, as all exists in the quantum-physics language of omnipresent waveform.

Wave or Waveform

A wave or waveform is a disturbance or variation that transfers itself and energy progressively from point to point in a medium or in space in such a way that each particle or element influences the adjacent ones. This may be in the form of an elastic deformation or of a variation of level or pressure, of electric or magnetic intensity, of electric potential, or of temperature. In classical physics, there are any number of wave types, but we are not interested in defining these types as they apply to various focuses of physics. We define the wave or waveform in generic terms, since the application of the term is broad in the world of Remote Viewing.

FIGURE 4.1 **Energy Is Everything and Everything Is Energy**
Therefore, everything can be expressed as waveform.

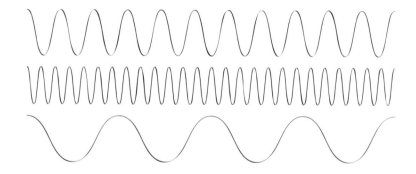

FIGURE 4.2 **Constructive Wave Interference**

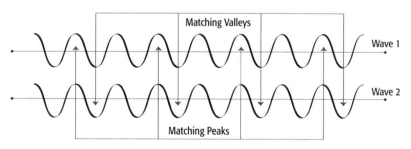

Waves combine into a wave exactly twice the strength of the original two waves—increased amplitude.

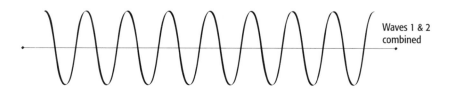

FIGURE 4.3 **Destructive Wave Interference**

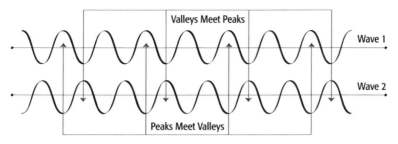

Valleys Meet Peaks

Wave 1

Wave 2

Peaks Meet Valleys

Waves cancel each other out—neutrality, balance.

Waves 1 & 2 combined

While energy can be modeled in many ways, for our purposes, we state that if everything is energy, then everything can be expressed in waveform at some level (see Figure 4.1). In quantum physics, nothing is solid; it only appears to be. In actuality, once all matter is distilled down to it smallest form, at the subatomic level it all exists as energy in the form of waves. These waves can affect other waves with positive and negative effect (see Figures 4.2 and 4.3). The notion of constructive and destructive interference can be linked to individual and collective human thought and action on a local or nonlocal scale. Hate can be reinforced by hate or neutralized by an opposite construct such as love. Like waveforms can reinforce one another and double the amplitude or frequency of the wave.

FIGURE 4.4 **Energy Is Everything (Frequency/Amplitude)**

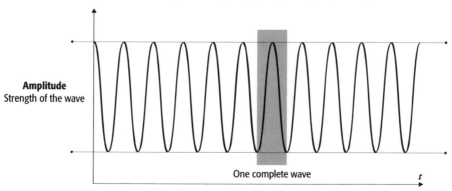

Amplitude
Strength of the wave

One complete wave

t

Frequency
Number of waves in a given interval of time

Waves are broken into two components: frequency and amplitude (see Figure 4.4). The frequency of a wave refers to the number of waves in any given interval of time, measured horizontally on the graph. The amplitude is a measurement of strength as indicated by the vertical height of the wave. In terms of sound, the amplitude, the vertical height of the wave, equals the volume of the sound. The higher the amplitude, the louder the sound. The frequency, faster or slower (more or fewer waves completed within a given segment of time), determines the pitch of a musical note. Remembering that everything is energy, both light and sound are only the portions of the spectrum that are detected by our physical eyes and ears. Beyond what we are capable of perceiving through our physical senses lies an infinitude of waveforms—for example, the sound of the dog whistle that a dog can hear but we can't.

When speaking of the frequency of a wave in terms of the human condition, we can think of any given act within the human condition. Let us use the example of prayer, considering the frequency as related to the number of times a prayer is offered to aid another human being. The amplitude in this example is related to the intention of the person offering the prayer. One can have a very high frequency of prayer with little or low amplitude—in other words, with low commitment or weak intention. Thus, when relating it to its energetic properties, the prayer must have both a high frequency and a high amplitude in order to maximize the prayer effort.

Everything is energy and energy is everything—thus, everything is in waveform on some level. This includes your thoughts, your words, and your deeds in relation to self and others. As you think it, so shall it be. Norman Vincent Peale said it appropriately: "Change your thoughts [they are waveform], and you change your world [your frequency and amplitude affects the thoughts of others]."

The Matrix Field

The word "matrix" comes from the Latin word for mother or womb, meaning an enclosure within which and from which something originates and develops or is stored and recorded. Often referred to as the *Source* when used in the lexicon of the Remote Viewer, it connotes a matrix convergence, a sea of all quantum waveform data in existence. It is considered a sea of photons with no charge or mass, but with momentum and energy. *Field* refers to a wide and unbroken expanse, a physical quantity specified at points throughout a region of space-time, a realm of knowledge.

The Matrix Field has been described as a huge, nonmaterial, highly structured, mentally accessible framework of information containing all data pertaining to everything in both the physical and nonphysical universe. In the same vein as Jung's collective unconscious, the Matrix Field is open to and comprises all conscious entities, as well as information relating to everything else, living or nonliving per accepted human definition.

This Matrix Field can be envisioned as a vast, three-dimensional, geometric arrangement of dots, with each dot representing a separate information bit. Each geographic location on Earth has a segment of the Matrix Field corresponding exactly to the nature of the physical location. In the Remote Viewing process, when the coordinate or other targeting methodology prompts the Viewer to access the signal line, data is then derived from the Matrix Field. By successfully acquiring or detecting this information from the signal line, and then coherently decoding it through the conscious mind and faculties, the Viewer makes it available for analysis and further exploitation (or use) by other analytic platforms.

TRAINED AND UNTRAINED OBSERVERS OF ALTERNATE REALITIES AND MATRIX FIELDS

The word "observer" is used in place of "Remote Viewer" in order to make clear that what we are talking about here is the ability to interpret eight-dimensional signal line data as it is perceived in waveform. You are always observing in the physical, four-dimensional world and beyond, and this section of the book is a minor treatise on understanding how time spent in an alternate reality will initially have no bearing on your ability to decode what is observed, but will eventually increase your awareness and accuracy of interpretive input. In other words, the harder you work to build a relationship between your conscious and unconscious mind, the more significant your observations will be—and the greater your Viewing experience will be.

Figure 4.5 illustrates the relationship between time spent in the physical world, the four-dimensional world of conscious thought, and time experiencing the Matrix Field. Clearly, all of us have conduits into the Matrix, but most of us spend very little objective time focusing on what we experience there. Our time spent looking into the Matrix can be expressed as spike activity—minor perturbations or brief glimpses into another reality. This experience can be by-chance exposure (instinct, intuitive perceptions) or can be by design and practice (such

FIGURE 4.5 **Matrix Realities 1**

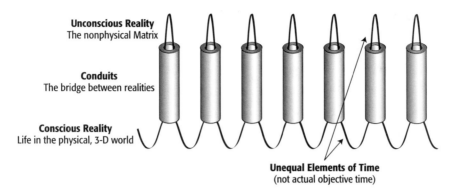

Unconscious Reality
The nonphysical Matrix

Conduits
The bridge between realities

Conscious Reality
Life in the physical, 3-D world

Unequal Elements of Time
(not actual objective time)

FIGURE 4.6 **Matrix Realities 2**

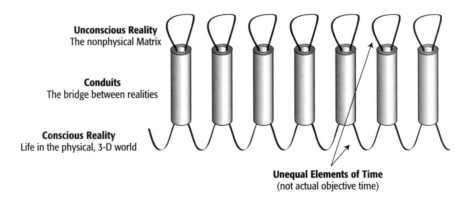

Unconscious Reality
The nonphysical Matrix

Conduits
The bridge between realities

Conscious Reality
Life in the physical, 3-D world

Unequal Elements of Time
(not actual objective time)

as with meditation, Remote Viewing, and so on). With training and practice, you will develop what is depicted in Figure 4.6.

To the untrained observer who experiences these brief spikes of activity, it is difficult to make any connection between the mind and brain and what is perceived outside the physical reality. You are there for a moment, but you communicate nothing back into the brain—nothing reaches the conscious-thinking level. It is analogous to subliminal messaging or to driving along a highway while conscious of the requirements of the physical world, yet also spiking into and out of another world of thought. The experience is too short to prompt a conscious coherent thought image, even though your subconscious mind will pick up the waveform and respond.

With time and practice in experiencing alternate realities, really focusing on task-driven journeys into alternate realities—into the Matrix to explore with purpose and focus—you will develop increased expertise in observing what is there. As a trained observer, you can observe and decode, imprinting information quickly and accurately. You will even be able to imprint your observations into thoughts. Thoughts will become action in the moment, and so you will create for yourself all that you desire.

You are here to experience the journey, to learn a new method of exploration, a new manner of perception outside the physical reality that you, due to your conditioning, are so completely familiar with. Through the individual collective experience of this program, you are learning to develop a coherent picture of the journey (the session) and of what is observed there.

Skill comes through dedicated devotion to the art combined with a voracious intake of information—you are on the correct path. Football coach Vince Lombardi said it best: "Practice does not make perfect. Only perfect practice makes perfect."

DEFINING THE MOMENT

Paul Dirac, Ph.D., won the Nobel Prize in physics for his work in theoretical mathematics and physics, specifically for his work that expanded Albert Einstein's general and special theories of relativity. In the mid-twentieth century, Dirac, among others, opened a branch of physics called quantum mechanics. What you see in Figure 4.7 is a synthesis of some of his work by me and one of my students, Kjetil Utne, an experimental mathematician from the Royal Norwegian Naval Academy.

The inherent difficulty in using and understanding this model is due to the fact that I am taking an eight-dimensional hyperspace concept and illustrating it using a simple two-dimensional diagram. To further complicate the issue, I am using a four-dimensional language (three dimensions of space and one dimension of time) to explain this eight-dimensional concept to an audience that speaks a four-dimensional language to reference a three-dimensional existence. Doesn't that hurt your head?

This naturally makes the model appear daunting, but it is not—not really. If I could use a three-dimensional model, which I obviously cannot in this book, then your understanding might accelerate a bit. Working from a two-dimensional illustration is a handicap we will just have to live with for now. The

FIGURE 4.7 **Dirac's Delta Function**

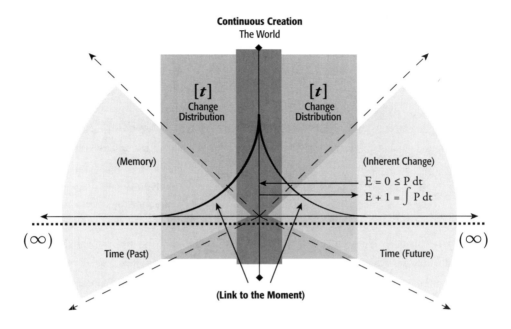

The Moment $= \displaystyle\sum_{\substack{0\to\infty \\ \infty\to0}} \left[\begin{array}{l} E=[(C\to0)+(T\to0)] \\ E=[(C\to\infty)+(T\to\infty)] \end{array} \right]$

Continuous Creation
The World

$[t]$
Change
Distribution

$[t]$
Change
Distribution

(Memory)

(Inherent Change)

$E = 0 \le \int P\,dt$
$E + 1 = \int P\,dt$

(∞)

(∞)

Time (Past)

Time (Future)

(Link to the Moment)

simplest definition of the model's concept is that it defines the moment as the point at which the past meets the future and the future meets the past; but that is not where I want to leave it. I would like you to have a more complete understanding of the concepts surrounding time past, time present (the moment), and time future, even if you cannot completely relate to the model.

In lay terms, the model illustrates the moment and defines it as the point at which all energy related to possibilities in time approaches zero, or the infinite, but never reaches either zero or the infinite. The moment—and this is a critical concept—is our only reality; it is truly all that we have that is real. All else is conceptual illusion. Conceptual illusion refers to our conscious mind's ability to juggle the energy related to some event or experience in the future or the past. It can never hold the illusion in one form; it is constantly morphing it, dropping it, fragmenting it, coloring it—you get the idea: it is illusion and not reality. If it is not in the moment, then it is illusion, an energetic representation of something outside of the moment.

The model is a Newtonian illustration, which means it is linear in construct. It represents time as something that moves from the future (on the right-hand side of the model), through the moment (in the center of the model), into the past (the left-hand side of the model). We all know that time is not linear. In fact, time is considered nonlinear *quantum foam*; it churns much like cream poured into hot coffee. While this is understandable in the world of physics, you cannot get yourself to work using this quantum foam model—you need the Newtonian model of linear time. While I am discussing the model of time, I want to be clear that linear time (the Western model) and cyclic time (the Eastern model) are no different in that they are both human constructs serving human purposes. Quantum time, on the other hand, relates to a model completely outside of our linear or cyclic human needs. Time is not linear, but the model, by necessity, is—and it is a limitation.

If you follow time through the model, you look to the right of the model and say, "I am now in the future. In the future, I exist in waveform as pure illusion, and I am surrounded by quanta, subatomic particles that exist in a delicate balance between energy and matter. I am in the realm of the unmanifested; all possibility exists here in energy form but cannot manifest until it enters the moment." For example, all possibility exists in the field of quanta as energy until I think of it, which in physics terms can be called *observation*. Once observed, this energy collapses into an incident in space-time, now manifesting itself as a particle, an idea, an object, an event, a person, a thought, and so on.

The further I am from the moment, the greater the field of energy surrounding me, and the vaster it is, thus the greater the number of possibilities that exist. This is defined as a cone of probabilities, $[(E + 1 \rightarrow \infty)] = \int P \, dt$, which, loosely interpreted, illustrates the mathematical understanding that the further we are from the moment, whether we are in the future or the past, the less the potential that we will experience any one particular possibility.

Now, do not get lost in this explanation. Here is another way of looking at it: If I am just on the other side of the moment (in the model), think of me as standing right there with my face pressed against the moment, getting ready to step into it in the next second. In this condition, the potential for me to experience a certain possibility, shall we say "abundance," will be greater than if I am looking eighty years into the future. Looking eighty years into the future, I may still see abundance for myself, but the sheer mathematical number of possibilities and the variables shifting those possibilities lowers the potential that the specific possibility of abundance will ever manifest. How I control this is to see myself in abundance while in the moment, to contemplate my existence surrounded by the things that I desire in my life, in the moment. As I contemplate this possibility and see it as a reality, I increase its potential. As I live my life in the moment, filling the moment with the kinds of things I desire, I will manifest from the future all that I desire.

Once my experience in the moment passes out of the moment into the past, it is no longer real. My recollection of the moment is just illusion; my version of the moment is constantly changing, morphing, being recolored by my memory—it is absolutely conceptual illusion. Mathematically, this conceptual illusion passing into history is increasing in potential, thus the equations related to the future are equally accurate when used as templates for the past. The further from the moment into the past I reach, the greater the number of possibilities for my memory. What was real in the moment is now expanding conceptual illusion. All that is real, all that you are in charge of, is the moment. To be effective in your choices, you must have an understanding of the moment. To the Remote Viewer, the moment is all you have. Even if you are looking a thousand years into the past, you are Viewing it in the moment, and you are describing what you are perceiving in the moment. The moment is all you have—never negate it or waste it.

To define the moment, you can use the equation at the top of Figure 4.7. The equation is read as follows: "the moment" is equal to the sum total (Σ) of all possibilities in change (C) and time (T), as change and time approach zero $[(C \to 0) + (T \to 0)]$, or the infinite $[(C \to \infty) + (T \to \infty)]$. Change and time can only *approach* zero or the infinite; they can never actually reach it. It is a mathematical impossibility.

The equation can be read as a collective whole or as individual and separate elements, and it remains equally correct. The understanding of the notion of continuous creation is outside the scope of this book; at this time, I would ask you to ignore that portion of the model and focus instead on a basic understanding of the moment as it is defined mathematically.

The future exists, expressed in the model as possibilities in time, P(t) or Pt. When one looks further into the future, one experiences increased possibilities in time. The further into the future you look, the more possibilities there are; conversely, the closer to the moment you approach, the fewer the possibilities. Time is not fixed; therefore, possibilities are boundless and infinite—for that reason, so are you.

Change (C) is expressed as a part of the equation, but it is not expressed in the model for the following reason: In our perspective, "change" is a word that asks us to look backward into the past to evaluate who we are now. In other words, if you refer to "change" in your life, it means you are comparing yourself with what was. To "change" yourself from a circle to a square requires you to maintain some conceptual reference to having been at one time a circle. To "know" you are a square, you must compare what you are, a square, with what you were, a circle. This is the only way to know that change has occurred. Transformation, on the other hand, implies movement forward and a condition within the moment that does not require looking backward for comparisons.

The past exists, but it is not fixed; it is illusion existing as waveform energy. The past, as it is expressed in the model, exists as increasing possibilities in time, constantly transforming as each recall of memory brings the illusion of a past event absorbed in waveform energy back into an event, or incident, in space-time. The only element of the past that remains fixed is your conceptual illusion of what it means, what it should mean, what you thought it meant, and what you were told it should mean.

What does this mean when expressed as manifesting from the realm of the unmanifested? How do you bring what you desire to you? Where does precognition fit into this concept? If you are having difficulty understanding this model and my explanation of it, you should embrace another definition of the moment that I shared with you earlier: The moment is the point at which the past meets the future, and the future meets the past. While this definition excludes the science of the moment, it does give a conceptual notion of the existence of science.

EXPLORING TIME FUTURE AND TIME PAST

I have already covered this concept indirectly. The bottom line is for you to know that anything past or future is illusion. It is illusion simply because it is energy, it is waveform energy, and it is not manifest as either event or matter within the moment. You cannot hold tomorrow in any tangible way, except to carry a visual illusion of what it might be, of what it could be, or of what you think it should be. This does not mean that you should not dream your dreams. What it means is that you should dream your dreams, and then live your life in the moment so as to create the space for those dreams to manifest—and they will.

FIGURE 4.8 **Your Life in the Physical World; Continuous Creation**

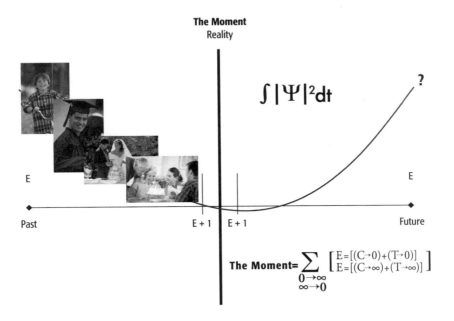

$$\int |\Psi|^2 dt$$

The Moment
Reality

E   E

Past   E + 1   E + 1   Future

$$\text{The Moment} = \sum_{\substack{0 \to \infty \\ \infty \to 0}} \left[\begin{array}{l} E = [(C \to 0) + (T \to 0)] \\ E = [(C \to \infty) + (T \to \infty)] \end{array} \right]$$

It also means that you should let go of the conceptual illusion of the past. Most of us spend the vast majority of our lives looking backward into the past, dwelling on the illusion of some event that we choose to keep giving energy. We assign emotion and belief to the past and accept some identity based on that emotion. We are living in the twilight of illusion, energy that is constantly in flux, never real, but tragically defining who we are. If you keep looking backward, you are going to miss this life. Let go of the illusion of the past as well as the illusion of the future. Choose your intended outcome, and let go of the illusion of it; do not spend time locking into something that has not happened, living in the future instead of living in the moment in such a way as to manifest what it is you seek.

ANYTHING IS POSSIBLE ON THE OTHER SIDE OF THE MOMENT

Physicist John von Neumann said, "The sciences do not try to explain; they hardly even try to interpret; they mainly make models. By a model is meant a mathematical construct which, with the addition of certain verbal interpretations, describes observed phenomena. The justification of such a mathematical construct is solely and precisely that it is expected to work." This is precisely what has been done with all the illustrations in this chapter, models built to describe an observation in the phenomenon of Remote Viewing and the life of the Remote Viewer. Figure 4.8 depicts a model of possibility. You can see by way of the photographs that I am indicating that your life is made up of innumerable events. These events create an energetic template, which, by your own acceptance of it, begins to filter from the future, thus limiting what is possible for you in the moment. What is important for you to know from the illustration is that the process is not fixed; it is in constant flux and is entirely dependent on your acceptance of the past.

The equation shown on the curve reaching out to a question mark is Schrödinger's probability density equation, the full explanation of which is, again, outside the scope of this book. However, a brief explanation is in order: Essentially, the equation is integral $\int$; absolute quantity (must be positive; you cannot have negative values); probability density 2; absolute quantity again, $\leq$; followed by distribution in time, dt. The equation means that along the future path of your life, there are patterns of potentialities. These patterns are dictated by the past as long as you give energy to the past and choose to live outside of the moment. Choose to define your possibility by living and Viewing in the moment, and the patterns of potentiality will shift accordingly.

The moment continues to be defined as the point at which $0 = \infty$ or when the past meets the future or the future meets the past. The moment can also be written as $\infty = T = 0$, where T is equal to time. Simply put, the equation illustrates that anything is possible on the other side of the moment, meaning that anything is possible for *you* on the other side of the moment.

When you understand and accept this fact, that your life is nothing but possibilities, then you exist in an empowered condition. The illustration reinforces the notion that your future is hinged upon the present and upon your ability to manage that. *As a Remote Viewer, the present is your most important ally.* Any time you step from the present, you enter the realm of conceptual illusion, and it is in the realm of conceptual illusion that the quality of your Remote Viewing data begins to decay. Know that the path of your life is not fixed, is not locked, then choose to live in the moment in such a way as to manifest all that you desire.

PART TWO: THE EXPRESSION OF THE UNIVERSE

The Ether

Ether is that medium in which the Remote Viewer travels—also called the Matrix Field. It is an unseen medium between the physical dimension (world) and the target site—the medium of space-time, in the lexicon of the quantum physicist. It can be expressed as Newtonian (that is, linear space and time) or Einsteinian (that is, the "frothy" fabric of space-time, sometimes referred to as *quantum foam*).

The Infinite

The infinite is considered endless, inexhaustible, subject to no limitation or external determination—extending beyond, lying beyond, or being greater than any preassigned finite value, however large.

Omnipotent

Omnipotent is defined as having virtually unlimited authority or influence. In terms of being a Remote Viewer, it means possessing this ability to control your own destiny, to choose your life's path, and to choose to exist as an observer in the moment.

Omnipresent

Omnipresent is a state of being present in all places at all times.

Omniscient

Omniscient is defined as having infinite awareness, understanding, and insight—possessed of universal or complete knowledge.

Atoms and Subatomic Particles

How small can we go? The British physicist J. J. Thompson said, "Could anything at first sight seem more impractical than a body which is so small that its mass is an insignificant fraction of the mass of an atom of hydrogen?" Atoms, the basic building blocks of the universe, are constructed of two types of elementary particles: electrons and quarks. The first **subatomic particle** discovered was the electron, identified in 1898. Ten years later, Ernest Rutherford discovered that atoms have a very dense nucleus, which contains protons. In 1932, James Chadwick discovered the neutron, another particle located within the nucleus.

The **electron** is a subatomic particle that occupies a space around the atom's nucleus. **Quarks** are subatomic particles that make up protons and neutrons, which in turn make up the atom's **nucleus.** A quark is a fast-moving point of energy, and there are several varieties of them. Protons have a positive electrical charge of +1. Neutrons are neutral and thus are considered to have a charge of 0.

In quantum physics, the subatomic world is one which cannot be described in diagrams. Subatomic particles are not dots in space, as usually seen in science diagrams; rather, they are "dancing points of energy," or waveforms. They are not considered particles unless they are observed.

Capacitor

A capacitor is much like a battery in that it stores electrical energy, although it cannot produce it as a battery can. I am defining this loosely for you because it is this notion of storing or reflecting energy that applies to Figure 4.9, which depicts the electrostatic field of planet Earth. If you were to run a wire from the negative pole of a battery to a sheet of aluminum foil, you would have one-half of the capacitor. If you were to run a wire from the positive pole of a battery to a separate sheet of aluminum foil, you would now have the two elements of a capacitor. If the sheets of foil were brought together but not allowed to touch, you would have a capacitor. The sheets of foil can be separated by what is called a *dialectic*, which can be air or anything that does not conduct electricity. When this model is complete, the air, or dialectic, between the sheets is filled with a reflective electrical charge. In Figure 4.9, the capacitor is formed by the positive and negative charges of the ionosphere.

Ionosphere

The ionosphere or thermosphere is a very thin layer of the Earth's atmosphere, and it carries a positive ionic charge. Farthest from the Earth's surface, it is responsible for absorbing most energetic photons from the sun. It also reflects radio waves, making long-distance radio communication possible. And it reflects, to a degree, all other electrical waves. In Figure 4.9, the ionosphere constitutes the positive element of the capacitor formation.

Monochromatic Light

Monochromatic light is a single color of light with a very narrow bandwidth, or frequency. The light spectrum consists of all available visible and invisible

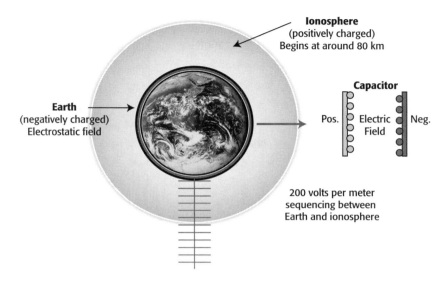

FIGURE 4.9 **The Electrostatic Field of the Terrestrial Plane**

Ionosphere
(positively charged)
Begins at around 80 km

Capacitor

Earth
(negatively charged)
Electrostatic field

Pos. Electric Neg.
Field

200 volts per meter
sequencing between
Earth and ionosphere

frequencies of light. Traditionally, in very simple terms, the major frequencies of light that are decoded by the human eye are red, orange, yellow, green, blue, indigo, and violet. If you were to select any one of these frequencies of light, you would have monochromatic light.

Coherent Light and Lasers

The trick in generating coherent light—of a single frequency or just a few frequencies going in one precise direction—is to find the right atoms with the right internal storage mechanisms, and create an environment in which they can all cooperate to give up their light at the right time and all in the same direction. In a laser, the atoms or molecules of a crystal—such as a ruby or a garnet—or of a gas, liquid, or other substance are excited in what is called the *laser cavity*. As monochromatic light in the form of a photon with a particular frequency (this determines the color of the light) is passed through the crystal, all the photons will be considered in phase and will be moving in the same direction. This process is called *stimulated emission,* and it produces a sudden burst of coherent radiation as all the atoms discharge in a rapid chain reaction, producing coherent light in the form of a laser. The word "laser" was originally an acronym for "light amplification by stimulated emission of radiation." The word is commonly used today as a noun to describe a device that creates and amplifies a narrow, intense beam of coherent light in the form of a laser.

Crystal

You may know crystal under many different conditions, from a wine glass to a quartz crystal sitting on a shelf in your home. By its pure definition, a crystal is considered a solid material in which the molecules or ions are arranged in regular patterns so that the bulk of the material forms a mass with flat surfaces. Crystals form when a material solidifies, either by a melt or by precipitation from a solution. The larger the crystal is, the slower the growth process of that crystal. For the purposes of addressing the Holographic Matrix Field, described next, I state that coherent light can be made by the use of a crystal. When monochromatic light is passed through the crystal, the molecular alignment of the crystal will align the photons of the light into a more radical, flat wave, or balanced frequency, which would now be called coherent light, or a laser.

Hologram and the Holographic Matrix Field

A hologram is often described as a three-dimensional image. While this is a good way to get a general idea of what you would experience looking at one, holography has very little in common with traditional photography.

While a photograph has an actual physical image, a hologram contains information about the size, shape, brightness, and contrast of the object being recorded. This information is stored in a microscopic and complex pattern of interference. The interference pattern is made possible by the properties of light generated by a laser.

The light reflected by a three-dimensional object forms a very complicated pattern that is also three-dimensional. In order to record the whole pattern, the light used must be highly directional and must be of one color, called *monochromatic light*. In addition, such light must be coherent, in the form of a laser. Because the light from a laser is one color and leaves the laser with one wave in phase with all others, it is ideal for making holograms.

When you shine a light on a hologram, the information that is stored as an interference pattern takes the incoming light and recreates the original optical wave front that was reflected off the object. Your eyes and brain now perceive the object as being in front of you once again. What is critical to know is that any piece of a hologram, even the slightest fraction of it, contains all the necessary coding to produce the entire image.

It is for this reason that the science of holograms can be modeled to facilitate an understanding of the nature of the universe, the three-dimensional world, and all other dimensions. I am using the model of the Holographic Matrix Field to put forth the notion that you are omnipresent, omniscient, and omnipotent, because no matter where you stand in this existence, in the conscious mind or the unconscious mind, in the physical or the nonphysical, you have all the coding.

THE HOLOGRAPHIC MATRIX FIELD

Figures 4.10 through 4.18 model the omnipresent, omniscient, and omnipotent nature of the human condition at both the individual and the collective levels. The series demonstrates the nature of a hologram and compares the waveform expressions of the stones in the water to the waveform expressions of all things within the electrostatic field of the planet and beyond—into the eternal and infinite of the Matrix Field.

Figure 4.10 shows a stone being thrown into a body of water, which will create ripples or waves, as seen in Figure 4.11. If you follow the waveforms in Figure 4.11, you will see that they billow outward until they meet the sides of the body of water, at which time they rebound back across the body of water. In order for this demonstration to work, two conditions must be present: first, the water can be frozen instantly, and second, there can be no effect of gravity. The gravity would pull the waves down until there were no more waves, which is a condition of using water for the demonstration—actual waveform energy, for example, from a human thought, would not be subject to these conditions.

In Figure 4.12, you can see that the waveform expression of the stone has now completely saturated the body of water with rebound waves. Each wave contains all the encoded information pertaining to the stone (that is, its mass and density, its dimension, the texture of its surface, and so on). All this information about the stone is transferred into the waveform and into the water via the waveform.

In Figure 4.13, you can see that no matter where you might stand in the water, you would have access to all the waveform data pertaining to the stone—because the entire body of water is filled with the waveform. This is what a holographic universe would be filled with: all the waveform data pertaining to absolutely everything. Since everything is energy and energy is everything, then everything can be expressed in waveform on some level.

FIGURE 4.10 **The Holographic Matrix Field 1**

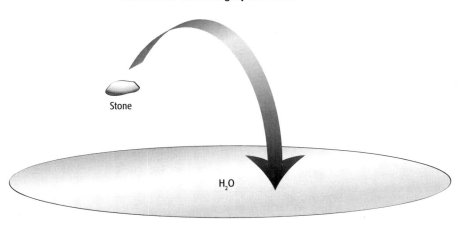

Stone

H_2O

FIGURE 4.11 **The Holographic Matrix Field 2**

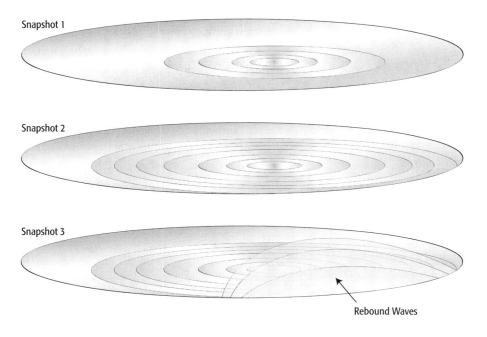

Snapshot 1

Snapshot 2

Snapshot 3

Rebound Waves

FIGURE 4.12 **The Holographic Matrix Field 3**

Rebound Waves

Each wave contains all the information regarding the mass,
density, dimension, and texture of the stone.

FIGURE 4.13 **The Holographic Matrix Field 4**

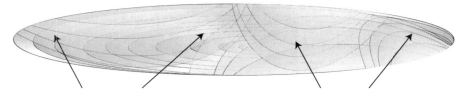

No matter where you stand in the Matrix, the information is always available in waveform.
Ask yourself, "How can I detect, decode, and record this information?"

In order to create the media from which to read or display our hologram, at this point, we will freeze the body of water solid, locking all the waveform data into place. If I had thrown three stones into the water, then the mass, density, dimension, and texture of each of the stones would be locked into the frozen hologram (see Figure 4.14). In order to carry the experiment further, we need to develop some coherent light.

In Figure 4.15, you can see the bent light waves of monochromatic light being passed through a crystal. The molecular properties of the crystal straighten the light waves, blend the frequencies, and form a concentrated stream of electrons guided by a self-generated electromagnetic field—in other words, coherent light is formed, making a laser. It is the laser that will be used to decode the waveform information that is contained in the frozen body of water.

However, what Figure 4.16 reinforces is the fact that what is present in the ice is the waveform information pertaining to all three stones, and that

FIGURE 4.14 **The Holographic Matrix Field 5**

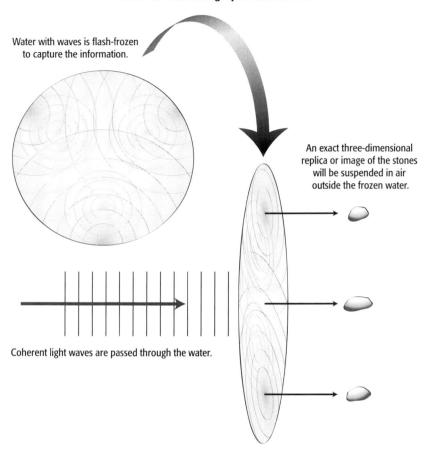

Water with waves is flash-frozen to capture the information.

An exact three-dimensional replica or image of the stones will be suspended in air outside the frozen water.

Coherent light waves are passed through the water.

FIGURE 4.15 **The Holographic Matrix Field 6**

The light is passed through a crystal in order to align the light waves, forming coherent light.

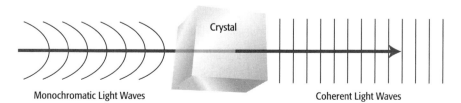

Monochromatic Light Waves

Crystal

Coherent Light Waves

FIGURE 4.16 **The Holographic Matrix Field 7**

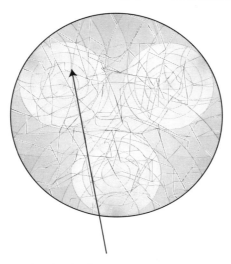

If we drop the sheet of ice on the floor, it will
break into a large number of pieces. We want
only one piece for our experiment.

no matter where you might look in the ice, the data will be present for all the
stones—an omnipotent, omniscient, and omnipresent condition. If you drop
the ice on the floor, it will shatter into many small pieces of ice. Each small
piece of ice on the floor will now have the holographic data pertaining to the
stones, even though there is not even one stone in that small piece of ice. The
arrow on the illustration indicates a shard of ice that you might select, which
has no stones within it.

In Figure 4.17, the model shows coherent light being passed through the
small shard of ice, and all three stones being projected outside the shard in perfect three-dimensional detail.

In Figure 4.18, the nature of the model reinforces the notion that we exist
in a Holographic Matrix Field, a universe—and beyond—of waveform energy.
There is no physical place in this existence that is not part of this field, which
is why you are omnipresent. There is no place or condition that can exist where
you would not have access to the infinite information contained in the Holographic Matrix Field, which is why you are omniscient. There is no time or place
in this existence or within the Matrix Field where you do not have the power of

FIGURE 4.17 **The Holographic Matrix Field 8**

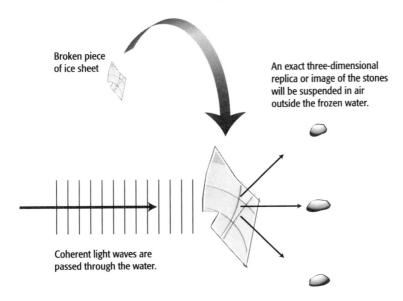

Broken piece
of ice sheet

An exact three-dimensional
replica or image of the stones
will be suspended in air
outside the frozen water.

Coherent light waves are
passed through the water.

Each segment of the ice, no matter how small or seemingly insignificant, will contain all the
necessary data to reproduce the image. The same is true of the MATRIX of ALL CREATION.

choice, do not have access to infinite information, or cannot influence with your
thoughts or actions, which is why you are omnipotent. In the Matrix Field, you
are eternal because you are energy—and energy is timeless.

YOU ARE 99.9 PERCENT SPACE

Your connection to the Matrix Field is made clear once you understand the nature of
your physical body at the subatomic level. Essentially nothing is solid, not you, not
the car you drive, the house you live in, or the chair you are sitting on—absolutely
nothing in this physical existence is solid. A piece of metal appears to be thick, solid,
and rigid. If you could expand the metal to take a closer look, you would begin to see
a very different texture to its surface. If you zeroed in on a particular section, continually enlarging the section, the metal surface would eventually appear porous. As you
continued your journey inward, your view of the metal would keep changing until
you were able to see the molecules of which it is made.

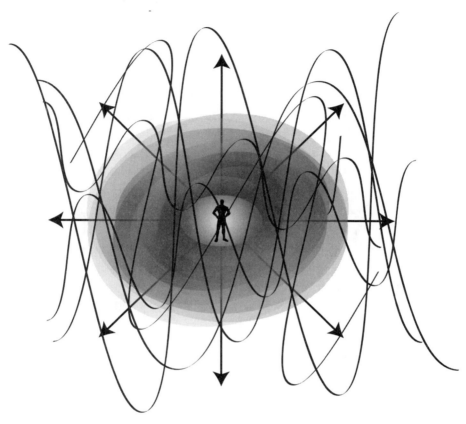

FIGURE 4.18 **The Matrix Field Concept**
Omnipresent, Omniscient & Omnidirectional Dimensions

It is at this, the molecular level, that the metal "agrees" to be solid. Beyond the molecular level, you see the atoms making up the molecules of the metal. If I asked you to find the nucleus of only one of the atoms, you would have to continue expanding the atom until it was the size of a professional football stadium—only then would you be able to find the nucleus. Once inside the atom, near the nucleus, you would now be aware of the subatomic particles making up the nucleus. Remember that if the atom is now the size of a sports arena, the nucleus would be the size of a small dried pea, and the subatomic particles, the electrons around the nucleus, would be roughly the size of small grains of sand.

To get some perspective, think about the grains of sand, the small dried pea nucleus, and the sports arena, which constitutes the exterior of the atom of the metal. What is there a great deal of in this model? Space! And this space is what you are made of. This space is filled with nothing more than waveform data, because there really are no particles at all. At the subatomic level, it all exists in waveform as dancing points of energy. Only when you observe these dancing points of energy do they hold briefly as particles. Once you stop observing them, expecting them to be particles, they revert to their natural state—pure waveform energy. This is why you are 99.9 percent space and why you exist in a Holographic Matrix Field filled with the waveform expression of all things, all thoughts, all actions, all life, everywhere in the infinite universe.

THE FOUR TURNINGS OF THE GLOBAL SOCIETY

Despite our cultural differences, whether we grow up in Australia or the United States or any other country, all of us are subject to a larger cycle of human energetic evolution that has been tracked by the scholars of history for nearly two thousand years. The world, the human condition, cycles through four turnings. The first turning is a high, an upbeat era of strengthening and rebuilding global perspectives oriented toward the collective whole. Focus on self is minimized, and work honors the possibility of a new global paradigm. The second turning is a sustainment phase, focused on awakening self. It is a passionate era of spiritual interest and upheaval. The third turning is a time of unraveling, a downcast era in which loss of interest in self causes values and order to stagnate. The fourth turning is a destructive phase of chaos and war.

The human condition, the global society, has been subject to a cycle whose duration is approximately one long human life. In this cycle, the global society experiences an alternation between a period of global growth and ideological conformity, and a period of global decay and ideological divisiveness. The cycle is driven by the changes in values and attitudes of each new generation, defined as categorical imperatives, which develop under the conditions inherited from, but distinct from, those within which its parental generation was raised.

The theory, developed by William Strauss and Neil Howe in *The Fourth Turning: What Cycles of History Tell Us About America's Next Rendezvous with Destiny,* addresses *saeculum,* or the cycle that divides the global evolution into four phases or turnings. Although I consider their work phenomenal, I find it limited in that the analysis of the turnings is applied only to the United States. Thus, the model takes an individual (national) perspective rather than a collective (global) perspective. As such, six years ago I adopted the model to the global societal perspective, using nine other sociological and economic models to develop the current, more far-reaching application.

In the model, within each turning, a new generation is born, exhibiting a distinct collective persona described, in part, by an archetype. Each global generation is shaped by the mood and orientation of the turning in which it is raised, and each has an important part to play in the whole cycle. As one turning gives way to the next, the global society's mood shifts, because the generations age from one phase of life to the next, bringing their unique perspectives and tendencies into their new global social roles.

In the First Turning of the cycle, the rebuilding phase, the global society expands and prospers, and its children are raised optimistically in a secure environment and encouraged to explore the frontiers of social values in an atmosphere of increasing freedom. These children develop into a Prophet generation, obsessed with meaning and distrustful of authority. When the Prophet generation enters young adulthood, it defies the power of the political regime, which at that point seems overly repressive and out of touch with reality.

Thus, the Second Turning, the sustainment phase, begins, in which the global society maintains a form of equilibrium. A spiritual fervor sweeps the land, and children are more or less left to themselves as adults become preoccupied with self-discovery and new movements, awakening themselves in preparation for the new millennium. The adults within the global society spend tremendous amounts of time focused on self rather than on the collective whole. The global youth develop into a Nomad generation, tough and wild, which earns a bad reputation and withstands the worst of the blame for the ensuing social chaos.

With the global society's institutions discredited, a civic decay sets in and the Third Turning, or the unraveling phase, begins. The Nomad generation has a rough-and-tumble coming of age as traditional bonds and associations are broken and scattered. Meanwhile, children are raised pessimistically in a dangerous environment, restricted by ever-tightening codes and harsh judgments from their elders. The global society finds cause to go to war and generates a moral and ethical unraveling to justify a masked agenda; and the Hero generation finds itself. Compare and contrast this turning with what you see happening in the world today, as warfare on an ever-increasing scale of lethality and precision escalates. Young men and women of this global society are called to war in more than forty-nine declared armed conflicts around the world.

The young men and women of the global society will be forged by the epic trials of the coming Fourth Turning, the destructive phase of the global evolution, in which the world goes to war on an incomprehensible scale. In this grotesque condition, the Hero generation comes of age and the political order is transformed according to the new values, which arose in the earlier, Second Turning phase. The global heroes understand that if a shift does not occur, the protraction of the destructive phase at this time in human history carries the potential to end the species. This is a dangerous and difficult time, during which children are heavily protected, developing into a sensitive and caring Artist generation. This Artist generation prepares for the subsequent First Turning of the new cycle, as the inheritors of the new regime.

These four turnings—the rebuilding, the sustainment, the unraveling, and the destructive—are all motivated by categorical imperatives driving the human condition. What I would like you to know about this model is that nothing is fixed. Remember, anything is possible on the other side of the moment as long as you keep your focus on the moment.

Each of the turnings will come; there is no escaping the cycle. However, through the awareness of how our actions affect the Matrix Field, you can make a difference in the length and intensity of each of these turnings. The duration of each turning, whether it is protracted or contracted by positive or negative human thought and action, is entirely up to us. We individually and collectively have a choice, in the moment, to give nothing to the global past, understanding that anything is possible on the other side of the moment—even a collective shift in human destiny. If we all exist in the electrostatic field of this planet, then it is our thoughts and actions in the moment that generate the positive, optimistic energy of transformation. Do your part each day to make a difference. Bring love and joy into the equation at your level, and the contagions of your promise and possibility will initiate a shift.

Figure 4.19 depicts the four turnings of the global society, showing their repetitive or cyclic nature. These turnings are protracted or contracted by categorical imperatives affecting the human condition, such as rage, hatred, fear, and greed, which can be contrasted by love, compassion, joy, and sacrifice. The turnings are considered fuzzy measurements of time, meaning the imperatives affecting them can extend or shorten their respective durations. The two waveforms indicated in the model illustrate the positive and negative energies within the human condition. If you reference the destructive or constructive wave interference theories

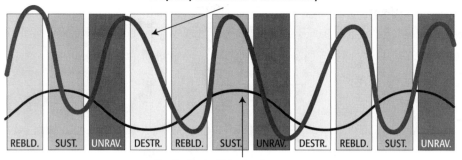

FIGURE 4.19 **Global Societal Evolution**

**The "Collective" Dominant Human
Frequency Measured as a Global Society**

| REBLD. | SUST. | UNRAV. | DESTR. | REBLD. | SUST. | UNRAV. | DESTR. | REBLD. | SUST. | UNRAV. |

**The "Collective" Nondominant Human
Frequency Measured as a Global Society**
Increase consciousness and focus on the "positive" categorical
imperatives to create a shift in the collective global society.

previously discussed, you will see that if our individual efforts rise powerfully to a collective effort, we can bring about a positive shift in human consciousness. In so doing, we can shorten the unraveling and destructive phases of the global societal evolution and lengthen the rebuilding and sustainment phases.

5

Terms of Reference

Only I can change my life. No one can do it for me.

Carol Burnett

Much of the vocabulary used in this book is technical terminology coming from a variety of disciplines, such as quantum physics, human physiology, and psychology. Sometimes more common words are used to convey less familiar meanings that are specific to the art and science of Remote Viewing. Still other terms are new and completely unique to Remote Viewing. It is important that you become familiar with these, so you can be fully engaged in the discussions that follow. These terms of reference will bring you closer to actually performing the progressive stages of the Coordinate Remote Viewing protocol; you should be comfortable with these terms and have an overall sense of where they apply. This chapter also serves as a reference anytime you need further clarification or to refresh your memory. While there are relevant definitions with full explanations within each chapter, this chapter includes brief, "snapshot" definitions that will provide answers to your questions, no matter which chapter you are reading.

"A" Component: The "motion" component of the ideogram. The motion is essentially the impression of the rise and fall, shift, angle, curve, across or down response to the ideogram.

Advanced Visuals (AV): Any visual data that appears during the cooldown period at the beginning of a Remote Viewing session.

Aesthetic Data (AD): The Viewer's sensitivity of response to a given site. More completely, an appreciation of, a response to, or a zealous reaction to the aesthetics of a target. Relating to or dealing with aesthetics, or the beautiful, for example, aesthetic theories, aesthetic values, aesthetic features, aesthetic architecture. One of the signal line categories in the Stage IV matrix and the Stage VI verbal sensory matrix.

Aesthetic Impact (AI): A sudden awareness of the presence of aesthetic data significant enough to affect the Viewer. A Viewer objectifies this experience by declaring AI when it appears, especially in the early stages (Stage I through Stage III) of the CRV session, where the focus is on verbal and visual data, and aesthetic data is not yet being sought out.

Analytical Overlay (AOL): Subjective interpretation of signal line data, which may or may not be relevant to the site. The analytic response of the Viewer's mind to signal line input. An AOL is usually wrong, especially in the early stages, but often does possess valid elements of the site that are contained in the signal line. When perceived, an AOL is declared throughout the stages of a CRV session. AOL is one of the signal line categories of the Stage IV matrix.

AOL Drive (AOL=D): This occurs when the Viewer's system is caught up in an AOL to the extent that the Viewer at least temporarily believes he is on the signal line, even though he is not. When two or more similar AOLs are observed in close proximity, AOL drive should be suspected. One or more of the following indicates AOL drive: repeating signals, signal line ending in blackness, peculiar (for that particular Viewer) participation in the signal line, or peacocking.

AOL Signal (AOL/S): (Stage IV) Occurs when an AOL produced by the Viewer's analytical mental machinery almost exactly matches the site and the Viewer can, to some extent, look through the AOL image to perceive the actual site.

Aperture: An opening or open space, hole, gap, cleft, chasm, or slit. In radar, the electronic gate that controls the width and dispersion pattern of the radiating signal or wave.

Attributes: A characteristic or quality of a person or thing. Attributes apply to those characteristics of the site that contributed to cognitron formation and the Viewer's original response. A category of data elicited in Stage V.

Auditory: Of or pertaining to hearing, to the sense of hearing, or to the organs of hearing. Perceived through or resulting from the sense of hearing.

Automatic vs. Autonomic: By pure definition, there is little or no difference. Automatic refers to a reflexive response or completion of some thing, some task, some process. Autonomic is usually applicable to a mental, physical, or physiological response, which is involuntary to actual conscious thought. In Remote Viewing terms, autonomic refers to the reception and movement of the signal line information through the Viewer's system. Further, this information is objectified via an autonomic process as opposed to an automatic one, which itself implies an action arising and subsiding entirely within the system rather than from without.

Autonomic Nervous System (ANS): A part of the vertebrate nervous system that innervates smooth and cardiac muscle and glandular tissues, governs actions that are more or less automatic, and consists of the sympathetic nervous system and the parasympathetic nervous system.

"B" Component: The first (spontaneous) analytic response to the ideogram and "A" component. In CRV the only allowable responses are "natural" or "manmade."

Bi-location (Bi-lo): The phenomenon whereby the Viewer's body begins to manifest the physiological indicators of what is taking place in the target gestalt. For example, body temperature may rise in response to high temperatures present in the target site, or a Viewer may experience nausea because of something moving rapidly in all directions, such as a roller coaster or a fast-moving vehicle.

Break: The mechanism developed to allow the system to be put on "hold," providing the opportunity to flush out AOLs, deal with temporary inclemencies, or make system adjustments. This allows the Viewer to achieve a fresh start with new momentum. In CRV there are ten types of breaks: analytic overlay (AOL break), confusion (confusion break), too-much (TM break), aesthetic impact (AI break), AOL drive (AOL=D break), bi-location (bi-lo break), emotional impact (EI break), break, missed break, and personal inclemency (PI break).

"C" Component: The step where Viewers determine the principal element of the target gestalt and record their perceptions using one of the following allowable descriptors: "mountain," "land," "water," "land-water interface," "structure," or "life form."

Coding—Encoding and Decoding: The information conveyed through the signal line is encoded, that is, translated into an informational system (a code) allowing data to be transmitted by the signal line. Upon receiving the signal, the Viewer must decode this information through the proper CRV structure to make it accessible and reliable. This concept is very similar to radio propagation theory, in which the main carrier signal is modulated to convey the desired information.

Cognitron: This word was invented by the Remote Viewing community circa 1984, a combination of "cognition" and the acronym TRON, to connote a combination of neural patterns. A cognitron is an assemblage of neurons, linked together by interconnecting synapses, which, when stimulated by the mind's recall system, produce a composite concept of their various subparts. Each neuron is charged with an element of the overall concept, which, when combined with the elements of its fellow neurons, produces the final concept, represented by the cognitron. As a human learns new facts, skills, or behaviors, neurons are connecting to form new cognitrons, the connecting synapses of which are more and more reinforced with use.

Conscious: Perceiving, apprehending, or noticing with a degree of controlled thought or observation. Recognizing as existent, factual, or true. Recognizing as factual or existent something external. Present especially to the senses. Involving rational power, perception, and awareness. Also, the state or quality of being aware, especially of something within oneself. The state characterized by sensation, emotion, volition, and thought: mind.

Cooldown: The cooldown process is the preparation for the Remote Viewing session. At the beginning of every session, the Viewer will enter an altered brain-wave state, much like a deep meditative state. For CRV sessions, the Viewer will go from the conscious, waking beta brain-wave state to the relaxed, focused alpha brain-wave state. For Extended Remote Viewing sessions, the Viewer will go deeper, accessing theta and delta brain-wave states.

Coordinate: *Webster's Dictionary* defines a coordinate as "any of a set of numbers used in specifying the location of a point on a line, on a surface, or in space." In Coordinate Remote Viewing, the coordinates consist of two sets of four single-digit numbers, randomly assigned, thereby giving them an encrypted quality. The numbers (or coordinates) represent the concept of the target in the Matrix of the collective unconscious. Theoretically, it can be said that the numbers give Remote Viewers an address, linking them to the focal point in the fabric of the infinite for the specific concept of the target. The coordinates are *not* Grid Mercator (a military form of land navigation), Cartesian (the classical mathematical, statistical, or scientific *x-y* axis), nor latitude and longitude (another form of surface navigation traditionally used by pilots and naval navigators).

Cosmology: A branch of metaphysics that deals with the nature of the universe, or a branch of astronomy that deals with the origin, structure, and space-time relationships of the universe.

Data Bleed-Through: Occurs when aesthetic, emotional, or intangible data expected to be detected and decoded much later in the session has appeared in the session out of sequence. The structure of the CRV protocol is designed to regulate and give order to the flow of data perceived; however, when a target gestalt contains strong aesthetic, emotional, or intangible aspects (normally detected in Stage IV), impressions may seep into the Viewer's awareness in earlier stages. When these impressions are noticed, they are objectified, or declared, so that the Viewer may continue with unobstructed clarity of mind in the stage he is currently working in.

Data Clusters: The repeating of various forms of Stage II categories of data. For example, any series of colors that repeat over a number of pages in Stage II indicates the clustering of color data. Clusters may indicate that the Viewer is perceiving a significant element of the target gestalt. Recognizing and identifying data clusters is part of preparing the session summary.

Data Strings: The smooth flow of verbal sensory data in the Stage II process. Theoretically, the verbal sensory data is backed up and waiting for an opportunity to be objectified into the two-dimensional media of the session. Given the opportunity to purge the data from the biological brain, the flow, or strings, of data are significant. A long, uninterrupted list of descriptive words on the page can indicate a strong signal line or an abundance of data in the target site. Shorter data strings can be an indication that the flow of data has dried up, and it is time to move to Stage III.

Decoding: The second of two kinesthetic activities, detecting and decoding, in which the mind consciously, at the speed of thought, assembles waveform expressions of target data into four-dimensional thought form (height, width, depth, time). Decoding follows detecting. It is the distinct act of codifying detected waveform data into expressions of four-dimensional thought-form. Additionally, it is considered the process of forming, distinguishing, or recognizing—to make out or identify waveform data via the biological brain and the neural patterns associated with it. Decoding further includes formation of words (verbal sensory data), or images (visual sensory data) in the biological brain all filtered by the Viewer's previous human experience (the experience rolodex) and the Viewer's principal modality of perception—tactile, digital, auditory, kinesthetic—as well as non-principal modalities—olfactory and gustatory. For example, if you are primarily a visual perceiver, you will decode more of what you detect into visual data; if you are a tactile perceiver you will decode more textures or touch sensory data. In CRV, decoding is immediately followed by objectification on paper in a near seamless process; the decoded thought-forms (concepts) are recorded two-dimensionally, on paper, as verbal and visual descriptors.

Detecting: The first of the two kinesthetic activities, detecting and decoding, in which the mind unconsciously distinguishes and then separates eight-dimensional waveform expressions of target data into four-dimensional thought form (height, width, depth, time). Detecting precedes decoding. It is the conceptual act of perceiving eight-dimensional waveform data from a target distant in space-time: to observe, to take in, to sense, to feel, to become aware of or realize. It includes reaching into the Matrix field without overt physical means; to perceive holographically, and it is loosely linked to proprioception, exteroception, and interoception. For CRV, the process requires a "softened" or alpha brain-wave state, focused attention, target coordinates, CRV structure, paper, and black pen. The Viewer attempts to close out external environmental noise in order to "detect" waveform data directly linked to the target, to detect waveform from a specific target, and to unconsciously limit perception to a precise spectrum of target data.

Diagonal: Something that extends as a line between two or more other things or points; a line connecting two points of intersection from one angle to another; not adjacent; within a polygon; oblique; slanting. In CRV or ERV, this is a dimensional perception perceivable to the Viewer.

Dimension: Extension in a single line or direction as length, breadth, and thickness or depth. A line has one dimension: length. A plane has two dimensions: length and breadth. A solid or cube has three dimensions: length, breadth, and thickness. The ether world of the Remote Viewer can have four dimensions: the three spatial dimensions listed plus time.

Dimensional Data (D): Information from the target site that can be detected and decoded into mass and density, contour, verticals, diagonals, horizontals, curves, and arches. This type of information is sought out in Stage II and is also one of the signal line categories in the Stage IV matrix and the Stage VI verbal sensory matrix.

Emotional Data (ED): The perceived emotions or feelings of the people at the target site; emotional impressions accumulated in the site. Sometimes the site itself possesses an element of intense emotion, which is imprinted with long or powerful associations with human emotional response (such as a WWII Nazi death camp). Emotional data can also include the perceived emotions of the Remote Viewer relating to the target. One of the signal line categories of the Stage IV matrix and the Stage VI verbal sensory matrix.

Emotional Impact (EI): As with aesthetic impact (AI), when a Viewer is affected by a sudden perception of emotional data in the early stages of a session, it is declared so the Viewer can continue working in that stage. CRV structure allows for emotional data to be detected and decoded fully in Stages IV and VI.

Ether: That medium in which the Remote Viewer travels. It is an unseen medium between the physical dimension (world) and the target site—the medium of time and space. It can be Newtonian (linear space and time) or Einsteinian (the "frothy" fabric of space and time, sometimes referred to as "quantum foam").

Evoke: To call forth or up; to summon; to call forth a response; to elicit. Iteration of the coordinate or an alternate prompting method is the mechanism that evokes the signal line, calling it up, causing it to impinge on the autonomic nervous system and unconsciousness for transmittal through the Viewer and on to objectification.

Extended Remote Viewing (ERV): A hybrid form of Remote Viewing learned only after a demonstrated proficiency in Coordinate Remote Viewing. ERV escapes the normal structure-driven format of CRV. In ERV, the Viewers enter an altered state, often referred to as ultradeep, and venture into the target site, where they will remain for extended periods of time, up to two or three hours. The book *Psychic Warrior* mainly portrays the use of ERV rather than CRV.

Feedback (also Session Feedback or Target Feedback): The evidence identifying a particular Remote Viewing target, presented at the end of a Remote Viewing session after summaries have been completed. In resident classes, feedback is presented as a video or printed narrative (with or without photos, depending upon the target) sealed in an envelope. Feedback provided to Viewers in the early stages of training, and to more experienced Viewers in conjunction with "calibration target" sessions, indicates if they have detected and properly decoded site-relevant information. Feedback provides Viewers with closure regarding the target site in relation to their experience and session summary data. It also allows them to assess the quality of their performance more accurately.

Front Loading: A technique normally reserved for advanced Remote Viewers—pertains to the advanced briefing of specific elements of a target site. This information is usually given to a Viewer prior to the beginning of a session. In other cases, the information would be given only after the Viewer has demonstrated he is on target—for example, when the results of the Viewer's first session clearly indicate that the Viewer is where the monitor or program manager wants him to be. The Viewer may then be front-loaded with specific target information or specific intelligence requirements. This is not a recommended procedure for anyone but the most experienced Remote Viewers. In the military's Remote Viewing unit, only Viewers with twelve to eighteen months of experience and a well-documented accuracy rate were given front-loading information. Trainees—and many experienced Remote Viewers—will usually spin rapidly into AOL drive when given advanced information about the target.

Gestalt: A structure or configuration of physical, biological, or psychological phenomena so integrated as to constitute a functional unit with properties not derivable from its parts in summation. Any given target site has an overall nature or gestalt. The gestalt of a target site is what makes the target uniquely what it is. The target gestalt consists of any of the integrated structures or patterns that define the total experience of the target site, such as emotions, temperatures, aesthetics, tastes, dimension, color, texture, energetics, and so on. Essentially, it is best for you to understand or think of the target gestalt as the total package of all waveform data relating to a target.

I/A/B/C Sequence: The core of all CRV structure, the I/A/B/C sequence is the fundamental element of Stage I. It is composed of the ideogram; the "A" component, or "motion"; the "B" component, which is the analytic response to the origin of the target, "natural" or "manmade"; and the "C" component, or first analytic response to the signal line.

Ideogram: A picture, a conventionalized picture, or a symbol for a thing or an idea, but not a particular word or phrase for it. In Coordinate Remote Viewing, the reflexive mark made on the paper as a result of the impingement of the signal on the autonomic nervous system and its subsequent transmittal through this system to the arm and hand muscles, which transfers it through the pen onto the paper. There are four types of ideograms: single, double, multiple, and composite.

Inclemency: A personal consideration, such as illness, physical discomfort, or emotional stress, that might degrade or even preclude psychic functioning. In general, these are discussed and declared as physical, emotional, or spiritual inclemencies.

Intangible Data (I): Qualities of the target site that are perhaps abstract or not specifically defined by tangible aspects of the site, such as purposes, nonphysical qualities, and categorizations—for example, "governmental," "foreign," "medical," "church," "administrative," "business," "data processing," "museum," "library," and so on. One of the signal line categories of the Stage IV matrix, used further in Stage V. Also, one of the signal line categories of the Stage VI verbal sensory matrix.

Intention: A concept formed when the mind is directed toward an objective or outcome. Also considered the act or fact of intending, determination to do a specified thing or act in a specified manner. Intention is the general word implying having something in mind as a plan or design, or referring to the plan in mind. An intention in Remote Viewing carries the same definition as in a metaphysical discipline. Intention governs every act in the protocols of Remote Viewing. Intention is linked to the assignment of the coordinates to the target. Intention governs the selection of the target. Intention is specifically important in Stage V for eliciting emanations from the objects, attributes, subjects, and topics relevant to the target. Intention focuses the Viewer in every aspect not only of the session, but also of life. Intention precedes all other acts, if these acts are to be purposeful and transformational.

Limen: The threshold of consciousness—the interface between the unconscious mind, the subconscious, and conscious mind.

Liminal: At the limen; verging on consciousness.

Mass: Extent of whatever forms a body—usually matter—usually associated with density as well. An element or aspect of target sites to be detected, decoded, and objectified by Remote Viewers.

Matrix: Something within which something else originates or takes form or develops—a place or point of origin or growth. The lexicon of CRV or ERV often refers to the "matrix of the collective unconscious" or the "matrix of the universe" or the "matrix of creation."

Mental Noise: The effect of the various types of overlay, inclemency, and so on, which serves to obscure or confuse the Viewer's reception and accurate decoding of the signal line. Noise must be dealt with properly and in-structure to allow the Viewer to accurately recognize the difference between a valid signal and his own incorrect internal processes.

Metaphysics: A division of philosophy that is concerned with the fundamental nature of reality and being, and includes ontology, cosmology, and often epistemology.

Modalities of Perception: The sensory systems associated with the Viewer's perception of target data. Broken down into four principal and two non-principle modalities. The principle modalities are: Tactile (related to the sense of touch), Digital (wherein the viewer can "see" in the mind's eye the word for what is being perceived), Auditory (related to the sense of hearing), Kinesthetic (related to the ability to feel sensations and movements of the body). The non-principle modalities are: Olfactory (related to the sense of smell), and Gustatory (related to the sense of taste). Example: I see the word for the color red (digital); I hear the word for the color red (auditory); I feel the color red (tactile); I see the color red (visual).

Monitor: The individual who assists the viewer in a Coordinate Remote Viewing or Extended Remote Viewing session. Most often used in CRV. The monitor provides the encrypted coordinates and observes to help ensure the viewer stays in the proper structure. The monitor records relevant session information, provides appropriate feedback when required, and provides objective analytic support to the viewer as necessary. The monitor plays an especially important role in training beginning Viewers. In the RVT development process, monitors must attend a training course before they are permitted to conduct sessions with other Remote Viewers.

Motion: The act or process of moving. For the Remote Viewer, this corresponds to the target or elements of the target being in motion relative to the Viewer's stationary form. For example, the motion of a machine part, the motion of a train or a vehicle, or the flow of some fluid. It can also represent the movement, flow, or motion of energetic data within the target.

Movement and Mobility: The state or quality of Remote Viewers being mobile in the target area; the ability of the Viewers to reposition themselves within the target site. This ability can take on at least two different modalities: "involuntary movement" and "voluntary movement." Involuntary movement describes the Viewer's ability to move within the target without having to think about it, whereas voluntary movement involves consciously directing one's movements, changing one's perspective within the target site. The control mechanism for this voluntary movement process is the use of movement brackets; during the session, the Viewer writes down movement commands, enclosed in brackets. This is differentiated from "motion," which is the Viewer's perception regarding elements of the target site.

Movement Brackets: Written brackets framing your movement instructions, such as "[move up 500' and look down]."

Moving Forward: When Viewers become aware of an accumulation of data pertaining to a previous stage in the CRV session, they declare that they are "moving forward" into the previous stage and then work in that stage to purge the backlog of data. The option to move forward into the previous stage is always available in CRV.

Neuron: A nerve cell with all its processes—the apparent fundamental physical building block of mental and nervous processes. Neurons are the basic element in the formation of cognitrons and may be linked into varying configurations by the formation or rearrangement of synapse chains.

Noise: The effect of the various types of overlay, inclemency, and so on, which serves to obscure or confuse the Viewer's reception and accurate decoding of the signal line.

Objectification: The act of physically saying out loud and writing down information. In Coordinate Remote Viewing methodology, objectification serves several important functions: recording of information derived from the signal line; re-input of information into the system as necessary for further prompting; and expelling of non-signal-line-derived material (inclemencies, AOLs, and so on) that might otherwise clutter the system and mask valid signal line data.

Objectify: To cause to become or to assume the character of an object—to externalize visually.

Objects: A thing that can be seen or touched. Objects can be understood as those physical items present at the target site that helped cause the cognitrons to form in the Viewer's mind and hence prompt the appropriate response. A category of data elicited in Stage V.

Omnipotent: Having virtually unlimited authority or influence.

Omnipresent: Being present in all places at all times.

Omniscient: Having infinite awareness, understanding, and insight; possessed of universal or complete knowledge.

Ontology: A branch of metaphysics concerned with the nature and relations of being. Also known as a particular theory about the nature of being or the kinds of existents—an abstract philosophical study; a study of what is outside objective experience.

Peacocking: The rapid unfolding, one right after another, of a series of "brilliant" AOLs, each building from the one before, analogous to the unfolding of a peacock's tail.

Physiology: A branch of biology that deals with the functions and activities of life or of living matter (as organs, tissues, or cells) and of the physical and chemical phenomena involved. As pertains to Remote Viewing, this science is predominantly used in various descriptions of the Remote Viewer's bi-location to the target site, whereby the Viewer's physical body will begin manifesting the physiological signs relating to conditions present at the target.

Probing: The symbolic act of placing a pen onto the surface of the ideogram, into the signal line on a page, into a sketch, and so forth. Probing requires the Viewer to actually place the tip of his pen onto the page, to connect energetically to the signal line in the detect mode, engaging the unconscious mind. The act of probing serves as a mechanism of focus, training the Viewer's figurative antennae in one direction.

Ratcheting: The recurrence of the same AOL over and over again, as if trapped in a feedback loop.

Remote Viewing (RV): The term codified by scientists at SRI International in the early 1970's as "the acquisition and description, by mental means, of information blocked from ordinary perception by distance, shielding, or time." A more recent definition, applied by the Defense Intelligence Agency and the Central Intelligence Agency, is "the learned ability to transcend time and space, for the purpose of viewing persons, places, or things remote in time or space, and to acquire and report intelligence information on the same." For the purposes of this book, the author's definition is "the learned ability to use two inherent kinesthetic human abilities to detect and decode eight-dimensional waveform data into coherent four-dimensional thought form, and to further objectify this data into two-dimensional media." Encompasses the protocols of both Coordinate Remote Viewing (CRV) and Extended Remote Viewing (ERV).

Rendering: Version; translation; drawing (often highly detailed). In CRV, visual data is objectified in Stage VI in the form of detailed drawings or renderings.

S2: Stage II of the CRV protocol. As one of the signal line categories of the Stage IV matrix, it signifies Stage II verbal sensory data. Note that in the structure of CRV, the stages are written on the page as follows: Stage II is S2, Stage III is S3, Stage IV is S4, and so forth.

Sense: Any of the faculties, such as sight, hearing, smell, taste, or touch, by which a person perceives stimuli originating from outside or inside the body.

Signal: A sign or means of communication used to convey information. In radio propagation theory, the modulated carrier wave that is received by the radio or radar-receiving set.

Signal Line: The hypothesized train of signals emanating from the Matrix and perceived by the Remote Viewer, that transports the information obtained through the Coordinate Remote Viewing process.

Sketches, Drawings, and Renderings: There are two methods for objectifying visual sensory data in the Remote Viewing session: sketching, and the more detailed drawing or rendering. In Stages II, III, and IV, the method used is the sketch, meaning to draw the general outline without much detail, to quickly describe the principal points of the target. A sketch is considered a simple objectification of visual data, a rough design, capturing dimension, texture, and form, without spending exorbitant amounts of time in the process. It is in Stage VI that the aperture will be opened to it widest point and you can begin objectifying the visual data through the development of detailed drawings or renderings.

Space: Distance interval or area between or within things; "empty distance."

Stage IV Matrix: The word "matrix" in this context refers only to the signal line categories used in the Stage IV process of CRV. A Remote Viewer completes the matrix format by listing each of the abbreviations for the signal line categories from left to right across the top of the page. This format—S2, D, AD, ED, T, I, AOL, and AOL/S—must be written across the top of every page in Stage IV. It provides the structure for detecting, decoding, and objectifying the data.

Stage VI Verbal Sensory Matrix: In Stage VI, the Remote Viewer works with two pages simultaneously, one of which is the Verbal Sensory matrix. This is the same list of signal line categories as used in the Stage IV matrix, written at the top of the page and used together with a second page, the Stage VI Visual Sensory matrix.

Stage VI Visual Sensory Matrix: This is the page used for objectifying and developing visual data in Stage VI, used together with the Stage VI Verbal Sensory matrix.

Structure: The single most important element in Remote Viewing theory— signifies the orderly process of proceeding from general to specific in accessing the signal line, and of objectifying in proper sequence all data bits and RV-related subjective phenomena, such as aesthetic impact, emotional impact, and bi-location effect. The structure of CRV is executed in a format and sequence using pen and paper. When used correctly, the structure will keep the Viewer on track in a target session even when mistakes are made; hence, it is considered to have a self-correcting aspect.

Subconscious: Existing in the mind but not immediately available to consciousness; affecting thought, feeling, and behavior without entering awareness. Also considered to be the mental activities just below the threshold of consciousness.

Sub-gestalt: Each major gestalt is usually composed of a number of smaller or lesser elements, some of which may, in and of themselves, be gestalts. A sub-gestalt, then, is one of two or more gestalts that serve to build a greater "major" gestalt.

Subjects: A subject is defined as "something dealt with in a discussion, study." A category of data elicited in Stage V. In Stage V, subjects are emanations that might serve a nominative function in describing the target site, or they are abstract intangibles, or they could be more specific terms dealing with function, purpose, nature, activities, and inhabitants of the site.

Subliminal: Existing or functioning outside the area of conscious awareness. Influencing thought, feeling, or behavior in a manner unperceived by personal or subjective consciousness; designed to influence the mind on levels other than that of conscious awareness and especially by presentation too brief and/or too indistinct to be consciously perceived.

Tactile: Of, pertaining to, endowed with, or affecting the sense of touch. Perceptible to the touch; capable of being touched; tangible.

Tangible Data (T): One of the signal line categories of the Stage IV matrix and the Stage VI verbal sensory matrix. Objects in or characteristics of the site that have solid, "touchable" impact on the perceptions of the Viewer—tables, chairs, tanks, liquids, trees, buildings, intense smells, noises, colors, temperatures, machinery, and so on.

Tracing: The act of using your pen to follow the contour of a sketch, of a texture, or, specifically in Stage I, of the ideogram as you decode the "A" component of the ideogram.

Unconscious: Not marked by conscious thought, sensation, or feeling. In Remote Viewing, we often refer to the unconscious as that part of us that is connected to the collective unconscious, the global mind, nirvana, the Matrix of all creation, God.

Vision: One of the faculties of the sensorium, connected to the visual senses out of which the brain constructs an image. Remote Viewers learn to use nonphysical sight or vision through the construct of the Coordinate Remote Viewing structure.

Volume: A quantity, bulk, mass, or amount, detected in relation to elements at a target site.

Wave: A disturbance or variation that transfers itself and energy progressively from point to point in a medium or in space. This occurs in such a way that each particle or element influences the adjacent ones, and it may be in the form of an elastic deformation or of a variation of level or pressure, of electric or magnetic intensity, of electric potential, or of temperature.

6

The Journey Inward Begins:
Coordinate Remote Viewing—Stage I

The illiterate of the twenty-first century will not be those who cannot read and write, but those who cannot learn, unlearn, and relearn.

Alvin Toffler

Before you begin this chapter, you should have an understanding of the information contained in the previous chapters, particularly the general terms of reference as they pertain to Coordinate Remote Viewing. As I begin covering the structure of each stage of the protocol, you will need this understanding, because I will spend little time explaining the lexicon again. There will be some review; however, each new chapter will focus on comprehension of the theory and method, and will not necessarily address definitions from previous chapters. To prepare for this chapter, you should know the theory of waveform as I have explained it. You should understand the theoretical notion of the holographic brain, universe, and beyond. You should also have an understanding of other theoretical notions governing the human ability to detect and decode waveform data pertaining to a target distant in space-time. As you begin this chapter, your focus must be on method and structure, not on understanding how or from where the information about a target is made available.

You are about to enter the environment of the Coordinate Remote Viewing structure. You have what it takes to learn this structure. Taking it all one step at a time is important; consider that you are building a foundation for your practice. You must know the fundamental elements completely before you move forward.

In the CRV protocol, each stage feeds the following stage. Omit something in an early stage, and you will be missing a critical block in the foundation of the entire structure. This does not mean you have an irrecoverable error; it means you will have to recognize the problem and take corrective action. It is far better to stay on track throughout the session than to try to retrace your steps to determine the source of a problem. You should use the Reference Sheets on pages 140 and 141 for Stages I through VI; make notes on the Reference Sheets as you read this text, and use them in your practice sessions. Having all your notes in one place will be far better than trying to look something up in this book while you are working in the session. Throughout the instruction that follows, you will be asked to refer to the Sample Session (Chapter 12), which is an example of the work produced by an experienced Remote Viewer adhering to the CRV structure you are about to learn. Remember that you can e-mail my office at homestudy@davidmorehouse.com if you have questions or need clarity on something contained in this book.

THE TARGET

Stage I involves the use of the coordinates that were previously assigned to the concept of the target—a specific concept of the target, implying a coherent four-dimensional concept of an eight-dimensional waveform expression of the target, within the event arc of the target. I know this is a mouthful, so here it is in simpler terms. Let us use the 1,815-foot Canadian National Railway (CN) Tower in Toronto, Canada—the target in the Sample Session. Everything has an event arc, which is a history of its beginning, its inception, its birth, if you will. This event arc moves from the point of origin, through the past and present, into the future until, conceptually, there is an end point in time. Therefore, whoever assigns the coordinates to the target must have locked into their mind a concept of exactly what it is that they expect you to be able to see in this target—we call this the point of origin. For this example, let us say the concept of the CN Tower target is the exact moment that the helicopter lowered into place the last of forty individual, seven-ton metal elements of the tower's 335-foot communications mast. Let us further define the exact moment of the event as the point when the helicopter cut loose the cables attaching itself to the mast element. This is the concept of the target that the person assigning the coordinates must hold in his conscious mind as he assigns the coordinates.

This process involves taking a waveform expression of an event distant in space-time and holding it in conscious thought as a coherent four-dimensional concept. This four-dimensional concept, held in the mind, is then further objectified as a set of random numbers. The idea of the exact moment in the target is captured by writing the coordinates on a piece of paper (or on the outside of a target packet envelope). Thus, you have a two-dimensional theoretical address to a four-dimensional concept of the tower mast being lowered into place in 1975, which is no longer real, as it only exists in memory as waveform.

Put another way, you have taken the macro, the waveform construct of the target, and distilled it into the micro, the two-dimensional expression of the waveform in numbers. During a Remote Viewing session, you begin working from the micro, the coordinates, and it is the coordinates that propel you at the speed of thought back into the macro, the waveform, where you begin the process of detecting and decoding. You detect in the macro, you decode in the micro, and so forth.

To initiate the process of detecting and decoding, you "take the coordinates," which means to write the coordinates down on a piece of paper.

TIME YOUR SESSION

Before you begin a session, you should set an alarm, especially when you are first learning this protocol. Eventually your internal clock will set itself, and you will move through all six stages of the protocol within the ninety-minute time limit. However, while learning, an alarm will tell you when to end the session and begin preparing your session summary. A word of caution: place the alarm in another room where you will hear it, but where it will not shock you out of your socks when it goes off—unless you can adjust the volume on the alarm of your desk clock.

COOLDOWN

To begin a Remote Viewing session, you will have to enter an altered brain-wave state, much like a deep meditative state. The cooldown process is your preparation for the session. To cool down, you should find a place that is quiet, where you will not be disturbed for at least thirty minutes. It does not need to be in the same room where you will be doing your session. The concept is to spend some time drifting from the conscious and awakened state of beta brain-waves to the relaxed and focused brain-wave state of alpha.

The CD provided with this book will make that happen, but you must select the right place for it to happen. The session itself is done while sitting at a table. Some people prefer to listen to the cooldown at the same table. In the resident training seminars I teach, students cool down in the same place they work in, but they can sit on the floor or lie down next to their desks. Your posture during the cooldown is not critical. You should do whatever is most comfortable to you; after all, the object is to relax and let go of the outcome. I like to lie down on a bed or sofa and, after I cool down, move to my desk for the session. I occasionally fall asleep during the cooldown, which is okay by me; I like to work when I feel refreshed yet still a little heavy-eyed. You should not cool down too far from where you will be doing the session. If you have to walk through the entire house to get to your desk, you will likely lose the desired altered state while you are negotiating a path through the furniture—a few feet away or in the next room is fine, but no farther.

THE PURPOSE OF STAGE I (S1)

The purpose of Stage I (S1) is nothing more or less than to establish target contact and to gauge or control the opening of the target aperture—your "peephole" to the target. Years ago, an inordinate amount of time was spent developing information in Stage I, but I have found this to be of little value. Consider, then, that Stage I is like looking through a tiny peephole to see and experience a vast and eternal universe. You will look through the peephole, the smallest opening of the aperture, to begin perceiving the target in a vast realm of possibility. As such, you will not base your entire experience on what you can see as a voyeur on the other side of the peephole. Instead, you want to use the Stage I opening to establish your presence in a controlled way, to open the door and begin your journey, using each step of the stage's widening aperture to experience more and more of the target.

Before we go any further, let us look at a finished S1 product. The first two pages of the Sample Session (see pages 248 and 249) contain an example of a complete heading and a completed S1. Notice that S1 consists of five elements:

the coordinates, correctly recorded, which are followed by an ideogram. The ideogram is decoded into the "A" component, which includes a brief description of the contour, motion, and movement of the ideogram; the "B" component, which includes a decoding of the principal element of the gestalt as either "natural" or "manmade"; and the "C" component, which includes a decoding of the principal element of the gestalt as "mountain," "land," "water," "land-water interface," "structure," or "life form." This is what you will be doing in S1; this is S1 in its simplest and optimum form.

Stage I of the CRV protocol should take a skilled Viewer approximately three to five minutes to complete before moving to Stage II. With this caveat, it is understood that you, as a new Viewer, will not move this quickly through the structure. It takes time and practice to become comfortable with the structure, to remember what you are supposed to be doing at any given time, to flow through the structure instead of referring to notes and the Reference Sheets while you stumble from one stage to the next. Consequently, it may take you as long as ten to fifteen minutes to get through Stage I at first, but rest assured you will shorten this time exponentially as your skill and experience levels increase.

THE SESSION HEADING

As soon as you are finished with the cooldown, the session formally begins with the session heading. This heading is important, not only from the standpoint of its being critical information, but also that it is a part of the ritual of CRV. Ritual is significant to us for many reasons; put simply, it connects us with the efforts of all who have gone before us. Ritual is an energetic engagement with the past, present, and future, and should not be ignored. A shaman does not just make it up as he moves through life; he adheres to a strict regimen, a protocol, a ritual, that connects his efforts, his prayers, and his thoughts to this energetic library we call the Matrix Field. In so doing, he figuratively drinks from the pool of wisdom collected through the millennia, a pool known by many names: the Akashic Record, the global mind, the collective unconscious, and so on. Keep vigil during your session by adhering to the protocols as they are taught and by not varying from or violating any principle you are given, and the quality of your Remote Viewing sessions will be optimized.

To begin filling in the heading, you will take a clean sheet of 8½-x-11-inch unlined paper and, at the top right corner of the paper, write your

FIGURE 6.1 **The Heading of the Stage I Format**

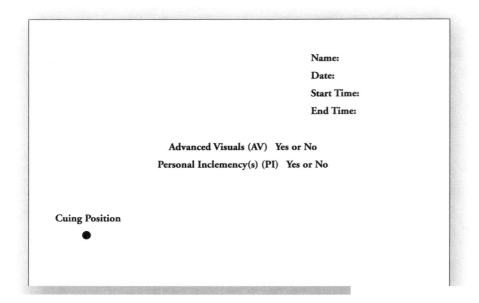

name, the date, and the time, which indicates the start time for the session. You will leave the end time blank and move to the top center of the page, where you will declare advanced visuals (AV) and personal inclemency (PI). See Figures 6.1 and 6.2 .

ADVANCED VISUALS

In the center of the page, near the top and just below the "end time" entry (see figures 6.1 and 6.2 and the first page of the Sample Session on page 248), you declare any advanced visuals. Advanced visuals consist of any visual data that came to you during the cooldown period and *only* during the cooldown period. If something came to you in a dream or while you were drinking tea in the morning, do not record it here. The only imagery that pertains is that which developed during the preparation period. This "objectification" of the information is an opportunity to declare, or write down, any mental noise or images before taking the coordinates. You may abbreviate the declaration as "AV" instead of writing the entire phrase out as "Advanced Visuals." In declaring the advanced visuals, you are responsible for indicating whether or not visuals were present by writing "yes" or "no." You write "AV yes," or, if no visuals were perceived, you write the declaration as "AV no." If you indicate "yes" for advanced visuals, then you must briefly describe how the visuals appeared to you.

Because the visual modality of perception differs for each of us, the protocol establishes some simple guidelines to follow. The visual data is categorized as either a fixed and repeating series of related images or a montage of scattered and unrelated images. Let us say that for our example of the CN Tower, during the cooldown, you had a series of images that came to you as a tall piece of concrete, a person walking through a glass door, the rippled surface of water, a blackbird flying overhead, and so forth. These would be considered unrelated images, a montage, with no direct link to anything; thus, you would write your declaration like this: "AV yes, a scattered montage of images."

As another example, let us say that during the cooldown, you experienced the following: a tall piece of metal, two pieces of metal bolted together, a man turning a wrench to tighten a bolt in two pieces of metal. In this example, the imagery seems to show a relationship, and as such, you would indicate that you recognized this relationship. You would objectify your perceptions as "AV yes, a fixed and repeating series of images involving pieces of metal and the bolting of this metal together," or words to that affect. The exact wording is not critical; you are trying to purge the information from the conceptual mind, where it exists as illusion, by placing it into two-dimensional media, where it can be interpreted later.

PERSONAL INCLEMENCY

Once the advanced visuals are declared, you move your pen to the place directly below the advanced visual declaration, still in the center of the page, and indicate if you are experiencing any kind of personal inclemency, whether physical, emotional, or spiritual. The declaration of personal inclemency works the same as with visuals. As the Viewer, you are responsible for completing the declaration by stating "yes" or "no" to the existence of inclemency. As with the advanced visuals, if no inclemency is present, you record the declaration like this: "PI no." If you declare "yes," then the inclemency must be stated, "PI yes, tired and hungry."

The latter is a declaration of a physical inclemency, and such inclemency may adversely impact your session. Because you are tired, you may make structure mistakes, and this declaration alerts the monitor or the analyst looking at your session to this possibility. Because you are hungry, food smells, tastes, and other categories of data may be heavily emphasized in your session. Your target may be the CN Tower, but all you are describing is the menu from the restaurant on top. Thus, the declaration of what is happening to you physically, emotionally, or spiritually before you begin the session will lend critical evidence as to why certain pieces of data may be repeated or absent from the session.

An inclemency is defined in the lexicon of Remote Viewing as a personal consideration, such as illness, physical discomfort, or emotional stress, that might degrade or even preclude psychic functioning. These are usually declared as physical, emotional, or spiritual. What is important for you to understand is that any inclemency strong enough to affect the session will possibly limit your ability to perceive certain elements of data, which is why it is declared. For example, if you are congested, your olfactory modality of perception will undoubtedly be impaired, and your olfactory data will be limited. If you are sad about something, which is an emotional inclemency, it is likely that during the session, any emotional data relating to the target that is sad or upsetting will exacerbate your present emotional condition. Does a declaration preclude any impact on the session? No, it does not; however, it lets anyone looking at your session analytically know that you had a reason for being overly emotional about the session. Therefore, the declarations are made so that anyone reviewing your session will know what was going on with you physically, emotionally, and spiritually before you began the session.

A physical inclemency is the most common inclemency, and may include such conditions as a severe cold, congestion, or a headache. What to declare is your call; you are in charge of the session once you begin. You should not become a hypochondriac and list everything you think is infirm about you, from the top of your head to the bottom of your feet; just stick to what you feel will adversely affect the session. Think of these inclemencies as a set of filters that process certain types of information, leaving other categories of information behind; thus, you need to know what filters are in place from session to session and day to day.

Emotional inclemency is the next most common category and includes such indications as sadness, anxiety, and anger (perhaps anger about your drive to class or work, or anxiety about how you think you might do on your first practical Remote Viewing exercise—things of this ilk). Any time a significant emotion is present, regardless of its source, you should declare it before you take the coordinates and move forward in the session.

A spiritual inclemency is very rare but does occasionally manifest. An example of a spiritual inclemency might be an epiphany you have as a result of suddenly realizing you *are* more than the physical. It has happened repeatedly that students have suddenly recognized their calling in this physical existence, bringing on an overwhelming abundance of emotional data that must be declared before they can progress in the session.

As a suggestion, not a rule, if you ever find that any inclemency is extremely pronounced, feel free to terminate the session before it begins, and pick it up on another day, when the inclemency has subsided. Do not be afraid to wait—it is far better to wait than to fight your way through a session, dragging some heavy physical, emotional, or spiritual inclemency with you.

While we are on the subject of terminating a session before you get too deeply into it, there are other conditions and criteria to consider. An external or environmental inclemency, such as lightning or sunspots, can affect the Remote Viewing session. While inclemency of this type rarely occurs, there is evidence that it does adversely affect the Viewer and thus the session; therefore, we identify it as *environmental inclemency*. Extremely low frequency (ELF) electromagnetic radiation may have a major role in this. Experience and certain research suggests that changes in the Earth's geomagnetic field—normally brought about by solar storms or sunspots—may degrade the Remote Viewer's system, causing him to be unable to function effectively. Ongoing research projects are attempting to discover the true relationship, if any, between solar storms, ELF, and human psychic functioning, but there is an effect. Therefore, if you know there is increased solar activity, and radio and television broadcasts are stating that computer and communications systems may be interfered with, it is probably not the best day to try a Remote Viewing session. The same is true for electromagnetic storms in your immediate area. If there is lightning and thunder, you probably should not be doing a Remote Viewing session; if you do, do not expect to do your best work.

TAKING THE COORDINATES

Once the inclemency declaration is complete, the Viewer moves to the cuing position (see Figure 6.2). At this point, the heading for the session is complete, and you are now waiting in the cuing position to receive the coordinates. This position exists for several reasons. First, it is where you will record the coordinates; second,

FIGURE 6.2 **Cuing Position for Receipt of Coordinates**

Name:

Date:

ST: 1300

ET:

AV/Yes dog on a porch

PI/Yes tired

Cuing Position

●

FIGURE 6.3 **The Receipt-of-Coordinates Position**

Waiting in the cuing position

Waiting in the receipt-of-coordinates position

FIGURE 6.4 **Improper Position for the Receipt of Coordinates**

Improper hand position   Improper elbow position

it is a place to rest and wait until you feel you are ready to take the coordinates. In Figure 6.3, you can see that the hand is relaxed; the tip of the pen is resting lightly on the paper. The Viewer is relaxed, eyes closed.

If you were working with a monitor, the monitor would now say the co-ordinates aloud, slowly, and you would silently record the coordinates, digit by digit, until you had two sets of four consecutive digits stacked as shown on the first page of the Sample Session (see page 248). Because you are working solo through this book, you will give yourself the coordinates from the target packet envelope. You will look at the coordinates and then record them on the page in the area designated "cuing position."

As you finish writing the coordinates, you will flow out of the last digit into the reflexive generation of a line. This line constitutes the ideogram, the first graphic representation of the principal element of the gestalt, which is then decoded into its three components. This mark, or ideogram, is the result of the impingement of the signal line on the autonomic nervous system of the Viewer and its subsequent transmittal through this system to the arm and hand muscles, which transfer it through the pen onto the paper.

SIGNAL LINE

Taking the coordinates and completing the ideogram initiates and anchors the Viewer's contact with the signal line. The signal line is the hypothesized train of signals emanating from the focused concept of the target in the Matrix Field and running to the Viewer in the physical, four-dimensional world. The signal line is the Viewer's vital link to the target. If the signal line runs dark, or weakens, the strong flow of waveform data will diminish. This indication notifies the Viewer that it is time to move on to the next stage, thereby opening the aperture to the target to a new level or lens. It may also mean that the Viewer has lost the signal line by some other means, such as becoming emotionally involved in the target, bi-locating, or perhaps becoming engrossed in analytic overlay to the point of obsession. I encourage new Viewers to think of the signal line as a fiber-optic cable (this is only a figurative illustration). Each filament of this massive cable carries various channels or categories of verbal and visual data.

DEVELOPING THE IDEOGRAM

In Stage I, everything is performed from top to bottom and from left to right, as it will be in all the stages and all the protocols of CRV. In this stage, each piece of data is derived from the theoretical center of mass of the principal element of the gestalt. This means, as you finish recording the last digit of the coordinates and produce the ideogram, your ideogram is formed from the center of mass of the target. Figure 6.5 illustrates this. Your tracing and probing of the ideogram is always from left to right.

FIGURE 6.5 **Theoretical Center of Mass of the Principal Element of the Gestalt**

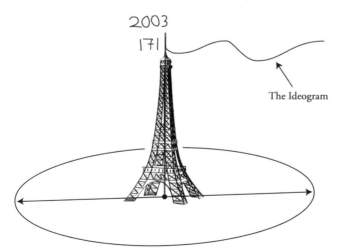

The Ideogram

This is your point of contact with the target site: Note that the ideogram begins at the exact point where the last digit of the coordinates terminates. You are theoretically landing in a location in the target site oriented on the theoretical center of mass of the principle element of the gestalt.

The last digit of the coordinates will always be the number 1 because the digit 1 facilitates the development of the ideogram. That is, moving smoothly into an ideogram from a number 1 is far easier than doing it from a number 4 or 8. As you record the last digit, you must begin pulling your hand from left to right across the page for several inches. This point is critical: *you* must begin pulling your hand; nothing is going to do that for you. There is no unseen force that grabs your hand—the initiation of the process is up to you. Thus, as you finish recording the last digit, you will respond reflexively from left to right across the page with an ideogram.

There are several methods of developing the ideogram. The most important thing to remember is to relax. Tens of thousands have come before you, and everyone, to some degree, struggles with this part of S1. You will see that it is not difficult, and with a few sessions behind you, this will be nothing at all; you will produce an ideogram in seconds and decode it in minutes. For now, you just need to relax. Record the coordinates slowly, with very little pressure from your hand. Pay no attention to your penmanship; it does not matter at all. You will see that the deeper you go into the altered state, the more sloppy your handwriting becomes. Now, as you record the last digit, try to think about what it would feel like if you suddenly had a surge of electricity pass through your body. Your pen never leaves the paper to execute the ideogram. It should be a smooth flow out of the last digit of the coordinates into the ideogram. This presents itself as a spontaneous or reflexive mark produced on the paper by the motion of hand and pen from left to right.

As I trained myself to respond with an ideogram in the military unit, I often imagined I was plugging into the signal line, and that the signal line contained so much information in waveform, so much voltage, that it shocked my hand into a reflexive response across the page. It sounds odd, but it worked for me. Again, I kept my eyes closed, recorded the coordinates, and imagined I was receiving a bolt of information in the form of energy, and that energy reflexively produced contour in the ideogram. I began pulling it across, from left to right, without thinking, and the energy produced some degree of contour.

On the first two pages of the Sample Session, you can see the contour in the ideograms. If you slow down the process, deliberately moving the pen from here to there on the page, then you are not producing an ideogram; you are sketching, and this is not what you are after.

Look at the coordinates, close your eyes, and write them, two sets of four. As you finish the last digit, eyes still closed, quickly move your hand to the right, feeling as if a bolt of electricity shot through you.

If you want to practice this, make up some coordinates of your own. Remember, these coordinates do not relate to any target concept; therefore, you are free to use any numbers you wish, as long as the last digit is a 1. As you will soon see, producing the ideogram is only half the process; it still has to be decoded, which is what we will discuss next.

DETECTING AND DECODING

Remote Viewing theory relies on a rather Freudian model of human consciousness levels. The lowest level of consciousness is paradoxically named the unconscious. This label really means that the part of our mental processes we know as physical awareness or consciousness does not have access to what goes on there; it is this part of the individual's psyche that first detects the signal line. As discussed in previous chapters, the unconscious mind is that aspect of us that exists within the framework of the Matrix Field; it is the unconscious mind that exists in an omnipotent, omniscient, and omnipresent state.

Detecting is the act of receiving, of looking or searching for, information in waveform. This is done using your pen to either trace or probe a sketch, an ideogram (as you are doing in Stage I), or the theoretical signal line on the page. Every time your pen goes to the paper, you are entering the unconscious Matrix of the mind, asking for information. The information received is then decoded by the conscious mind into coherent four-dimensional thought, and it is then objectified, or written down, as verbal data in the form of words or as visual data in the form of sketches.

As soon as you produce an ideogram, you can begin decoding it into the three components; this is called the *A/B/C component process*. This is what completes S1.

"A" COMPONENT

To begin, immediately after you produce the ideogram, move your pen all the way to the right and slightly below the ideogram, and write the letter "A" (see Sample Session beginning on pages 248 and 249). Next, place the tip of your pen on the ideogram at the point where the last digit flows into the ideogram. Remember, this position is considered the theoretical center of mass of the principal element of the gestalt. Therefore, as you move to the right along the ideogram, you are theoretically moving farther away from the center of mass of the target, which is why you always decode based on your first perception (more on this in a minute). In order to decode the "A" component, you must trace the ideogram from left to right. Trace slowly and softly, with a very light touch. With your eyes open, follow the contour of the ideogram with your pen; you are sensing the motion, the movement, the feeling of the ideogram. After tracing the ideogram with your eyes open for a few passes, close your eyes and trace smaller sections, working from left to right. Do this several times to get a feel for the contour, the motion, the movement of the ideogram. What do you perceive here? You are looking for feeling and contour. This feeling is the first (spontaneous) analytic response to the ideogram and the "A" component, and contour can precede or follow the feeling. See Figure 6.6.

There are at least five types of feelings possible: solidity, liquidity, energetic, airiness (that is, there is more air space than anything else, such as some suspension bridges might manifest), and temperature. Other feeling descriptors are possible, but are encountered only in rare circumstances and are generally connected with unusual sites. Use your own words to describe this feeling and contour. As you trace, does it feel as if the ideogram is airy and rising, solid and falling, liquid and spinning left, turning right, curving, arching over or under, peaking, dropping, cupping? Do not worry if your pen drifts slightly to the right or left of, or above or below, the ideogram; you are still tracing the contour, which is what is important. In your own words, describe what you sense here by writing it down after the "A" on your page.

FIGURE 6.6 **Decoding the "A" Component**

"A" component: Describe in your own words the motion, the contour, the feeling of the ideogram. Always decode the ideogram based on how it feels, never on how it looks.

2003
1721

Begin here, at the theoretical center of mass of the principal element of the gestalt, and retrace the ideogram. Retrace it again, even with your eyes closed, until you get a feeling of the ideogram. Describe in your own words what you feel it is doing.

Sometimes, closing your eyes will help you "feel" the ideogram, letting go of the desire to decode it based on how it looks. Always remember this: decode the ideogram based on how it feels, never on how it looks. The reason for this has to do with the unconscious mind.

Ideograms may be encountered (objectified) either parallel with the plane of the horizon (horizontal) or perpendicular to it (vertical). For example, the Gobi Desert, being predominantly flat, wavy sand, would likely produce, in the motion portion of the Stage I "A" component, the response "across . . . flat . . . and wavy," or similar terminology, to indicate a horizontal ideogram. The Empire State Building, however, might produce some sort of vertical response, such as "up . . . angle across and down," in the motion portion of "A," to indicate a vertical ideogram.

However, the crucial point to remember is that the objectification of the ideogram is completely independent of either its appearance or direction on paper. What determines the vertical or horizontal ideogram orientation is the target site's inherent manifestation in the physical world, not how or in what direction the ideogram is executed on the paper.

Simply observing how the ideogram looks on paper will not give reliable clues to what the orientation of the ideogram might be (not that you are looking for clues—because you are not). As you record the coordinates and respond with the ideogram, the unconscious mind, that aspect of mind which exists within an eight-dimensional construct, is presenting information to you from a perspective that greatly exceeds the conscious mind's perspective. Your unconscious mind does not care about up, down, left or right, front or back; these are tools of the conscious mind. Your conscious mind will want to decode the ideogram based on its appearance on the page, that is, unless you remind yourself that it is what you feel that counts. Tracing the ideogram gives you a mechanism for detecting the information presented by the unconscious mind as the feeling or abstract sense you perceive.

The ideogram objectified as "across . . . flat . . . and wavy" for the Gobi Desert might, on the paper, be an up-and-down mark. The ideogram for the Empire State Building could possibly be executed horizontally across the paper. You may one day trace an ideogram that looks as if it is dropping straight down, yet you will feel as if you are climbing straight up as you trace it. This is why the ideogram is always decoded based on how it feels, never on how it looks. Looks may, in fact, deceive; however, your feeling perceptions will seldom deceive, and with practice and skill, they will consistently be more accurate than the illusion of the physical world.

"B" COMPONENT

When you have finished decoding the "A" component of the ideogram, you will move directly below it and write the letter "B" (see Figure 6.7).

To decode the "B" component, you probe, not trace, the ideogram. You are looking for a simple piece of data: Is the principal element of the gestalt natural or manmade? That is it, nothing more. For your training purposes, you are permitted only the following words: either "natural" or "manmade." You may write either one in the "B" decoding, but never both, and never some composite descriptor such as "manmade hole in the ground."

You begin by probing the ideogram from the same point you began tracing from—the theoretical center of mass of the principal element of the gestalt. You probe in small increments, say a quarter of an inch, lifting the tip of your pen and

FIGURE 6.7 **Decoding the "B" Component**

"B" component: Is this target natural or manmade?

Put the tip of your pen here, at the theoretical center of mass of the principal element of the gestalt, and ask: natural or manmade? Be prepared to go with the first answer that comes. If nothing comes, move along the ideogram in quarter-inch intervals until you get an answer.

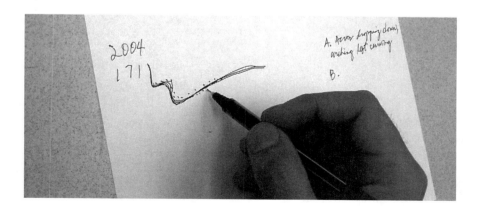

moving from left to right, touching down and pausing briefly, for eight to ten seconds, at each probe point to wait for information. If nothing comes to you, if no modality of perception is present, if you draw a blank, then pick up the pen and move right along the ideogram to the next probe point and wait again, eyes closed, descending into the detect mode, perceiving, detecting, and decoding the subtle nuances of waveform data that come to you.

This was a very odd thing for me to engage in when I was in the military unit. I mean, after all, it is an ink line on a page, and you are probing and tracing it to extract information from it. Yes, you are, and it works, because everything is energy and energy is everything, and everything exists in waveform on some level. It is not just an ink line; it is a two-dimensional representation of eight-dimensional waveform data. All you are doing is exercising a protocol that facilitates a focused perception, the opening of the conduits into the unconscious mind that allows you to detect, decode, and objectify this waveform data. So, stop feeling silly, and get on with it. Keep probing all along the ideogram until you come to the end of it. Do not make a second pass for the "B" component; if you perceived nothing in the first pass, you will have to follow another procedure that I will discuss later in the chapter.

FIGURE 6.8 **Possible Visual Percepions of the "B" Component**

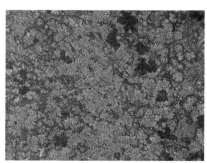 

Natural   **Manmade**

For now, let us assume that you did perceive something in the first pass. Your perceptions for the "B" component of the ideogram may be natural or manmade. What is important for you to remember is that you may select only one of these descriptors—never both. Again, both may be present in a complex gestalt, but you are after the principal element of the gestalt, not just any element present. You will develop your own technique for decoding this information.

This new language between the unconscious mind and the conscious mind is different for each Viewer. You will have to practice "perceiving" many times to learn exactly what that language is for you, in other words, what modality of perception will be most pronounced in your RV sessions. Draw no conclusions at this point; it is way too early in the process.

"C" COMPONENT

The final step in S1 is decoding the "C" component of the ideogram. As soon as the "B" component is decoded, you move your pen to a position on the paper below the "B" responses. Here you write "C," and immediately begin to probe the ideogram again to determine the principal element of the gestalt and record your perceptions (see Figure 6.9). The only allowable descriptors in decoding the "C" component are "mountain," "land," "water," "land-water interface" (for example, an island, a beach, or a river delta), "structure," or "life form." No combinations are permitted; you can have only one.

As you did with the "B" component, probe from left to right all along the ideogram, in quarter-inch increments, stopping at each probe point for approximately eight to ten seconds. If nothing is perceived, move along the ideogram to the next point, keeping in mind that the farther along the ideogram you go, the more distance you are placing between yourself and the theoretical center of mass of the principal element of the gestalt.

As I indicated earlier, you have to discover exactly how you will decode this information—what your principal modality of perception is. Each Viewer will

FIGURE 6.9 **Decoding the "C" Component**

"C" component: Is this target mountain, land, water, land-water interface, structure, or life form?
You have to determine which one of these six categories the target falls under.

2003
1721

Put the tip of your pen here, at the theoretical center of mass of the principal element of
the gestalt, and ask: mountain, land, water, land-water interface, structure, or life form?
Be prepared to go with the first answer that comes. If nothing comes, move along the
ideogram in quarter-inch increments until you get an answer.

develop as an aural, a tactile, a digital, or a visual perceiver, learning to decode data perceived in the mind using available sensory analysis. You will ask yourself what this new language between the unconscious and the conscious mind is and how it will manifest itself for you.

You must be careful in the "C"-component decoding to not let the aperture open too quickly, allowing too much data to rush in unchecked, uncontrolled, and without structure. If this happens, you will be overrun by data, and you will lose control of the session within a few minutes of entering it. The trick is to perceive data without really hearing or seeing anything that carries both form and function, which would be analytical overlay (AOL) and would necessitate declaring a break and taking the coordinates again after resuming the session (more on this later).

In other words, you do not want to see a mountain in order to decode a mountain for the "C" component. This may sound ridiculous, but it is the structure, and it works. If you see a mountain in your mind's eye, then you have form and function together, which means you have an AOL. What you want is something to indicate a mountain to you without actually developing a verbal or visual AOL that would drive the session from this point forward. For me, that means visual textures because, as I mentioned, I am a visual perceiver. Photographs 1 through 6 in Figure 6.10 illustrate the visual textures that I use to decode the "C" component. Of course, your perceptions may vary from mine, especially if you are an aural, tactile, or digital perceiver.

The methods of perception are unique to each of us, and I provide you these photographs, not so you will try to make your perception match mine, but to give you some idea of how the imagery develops for me. Allow your perceptions to develop for you over time and through experience—do not try to force it, or you will slow the developmental process.

At this point, you'll notice you're beginning to identify your language and make an agreement between the conscious and the unconscious mind. This is part of honoring the structure of CRV, which establishes an orderly, manageable flow of data from the Matrix Field to the conscious mind. If you set limits early on, they will be honored by the unconscious mind. If you establish as your intention that you desire to see a texture without it becoming a full-blown image, then that is what you will see. Therefore, what you want to do at this point is simply to state your intention about what language you will use to decode these elementary aspects of the target site.

FIGURE 6.10 **Possible Visual Perceptions of "C" Component Categories**

1. Mountain: The texture may appear as this: slanted and sloped, a diagonal.

2. Land: The texture may appear as this: a soft contrast between dark and light.

3. Water: The texture may appear as this: reflective and wavy.

4. Land-Water Interface (LWI): The texture may appear as this: a reflective fluid over solid.

5. Structure: The texture may appear as this: a smooth and polished surface, cold and slick.

6. Life Form: The texture may appear as this: flaky and organic-looking.

Even though there will be several elements present in any given target gestalt (you will be working in complex gestalts, so there will always be an abundance of data present), you are always after the principal element of the gestalt, which means you must select the one that is most pronounced. Remember, the only allowable descriptors are "mountain," "land," "water," "land-water interface," "structure," and "life form."

The first two pages of the Sample Session, pages 248 and 249 make up Stage I. Upon completion of Stage I, you will have all five elements present: the co-ordinates, the ideogram, the "A" component, the "B" component, and the "C" component. You will be ready to proceed to Stage II of the CRV protocol.

RELY UPON THE STRUCTURE

Stage I will be the most difficult for you to master, simply because your analytical conscious mind will make it so. I will admit that when I was training in the unit at Fort Meade, I considered this the most peculiar thing anyone had ever asked me to do up to that point in my life. I understood the concept, but I doubted that it could be done, and therein lay the obstacle. I had to overcome this obstacle, and you will, as well. My strategy was no strategy at all. I put my trust in the structure, recognizing that I had no other way of proving to myself whether the ability existed or not. I knew this protocol was a part of the military, and I had learned, through being a soldier, that you trust your equipment and you rely on your training; from my perspective, this was nothing more or less than training. If I doubted that my parachute would open on a mass tactical combat jump, then I would be ineffective as a soldier, a leader, and so on. I had no reason to doubt that what I was being trained to do was any less effective than any other training I had received in the prior thirteen years. You may not have the benefit of this mind-set; if you don't, then resonate with mine. This is a scientifically developed protocol, born in a bed of science, by scientists; it was used as an intelligence collection methodology and continues to be used even today. Regardless of how far outside your conditioned comfort zone these protocols take you, keep reminding yourself of where this came from and why it was developed. If you can relate to this, you will have no trouble accomplishing your goals in Remote Viewing.

It is all about the power of your intention; it is about being the observer in this process, not the evaluator; it is about trusting the process that has been proven to work for decades. Therefore, if you want to do this, if you really want to know what is beyond the physical world, you have to get out of your own way by understanding the theory and engaging the process as the observer.

Structure is the key to usable Remote Viewing technology. It is through proper structure and discipline that mental noise is suppressed and signal line information is allowed to emerge cleanly. "Content be damned, structure is everything!" As long as proper structure is maintained, the information obtained may be relied on.

POTENTIAL CHALLENGES

Before we move on to Stage II, I want to discuss some potential snags that may pop up. Stage I can present you with a number of challenges, and you will need to know how to use the structure to your advantage. These problems are considered critical in Stage I, since this element of the structure is so vital to the rest of the process. Since you are only trying to establish target contact and to control the opening of the aperture, strict adherence to the protocols must be observed. Be aware that some of what I am showing you here in Stage I may also appear in future stages, and you will have to know how to address each situation independently. All of this will become second nature after you have a few Remote Viewing sessions under your belt.

During your actual session, you will use your Reference Sheets (see pages 140–141) as an outline document to help you remember the structure. You will want to have the Reference Sheets handy to make notes while you read this next portion of the book. During RV sessions, you need to quiet the mental noise and stay in an altered state, so you will rely on the Reference Sheets as a checklist. Flipping through a notebook or this book for instructions would draw you out of the relaxed alpha brain-wave state.

ANALYTICAL OVERLAY (AOL)

Analytical overlay is a result of the linear, analytical thought processes of the normal, waking conscious mind—enhanced and ingrained from our earliest stages of cognitive development. While extremely useful in a society that relies heavily on quantitative data and technological development, such analytical thinking hampers Remote Viewing by the manufacture of analytical overlay, or AOL. Put simply, AOL is the tendency of the mind to jump to conclusions, to process details and bits of information into a recognizable form. It is a process of the conscious mind, the imagination; it is an analytic response of the Viewer's mind to signal line input.

As the signal line surges up into the threshold areas of consciousness, the mind's conscious analytical processes feel duty-bound to assign coherence to what at first seems to be virtually incomprehensible data coming from an unaccustomed source. The mind must make a logical assessment based on the impressions being received. Essentially, it jumps to one of a number of instantaneous conclusions about the incoming information without waiting for sufficient information to make an accurate judgment. This process is reflexive and happens even when it is not desired by the individual. Instead of allowing a holistic right-brain process, through which the signal line apparently manifests itself, to assemble a complete and accurate concept, the untrained left-brain analytic processes seize upon whatever bit of information seems most familiar and forms an AOL construct based upon it.

For example, given the coordinates to the CN Tower construction, a flash of a complex, manmade metal structure may impinge on the liminal regions of your mind, but so briefly that no coherent response can be made to it. The conscious mind, working at a much greater speed than you expect, perceives bits and pieces, such as massive angles, thick concrete, and tall, riveted girders. This may create a sense of feeling "roofed over" and "boxed in," whereupon it suggests to your conscious awareness that the site is the outside of a large oil tank or a metal wall. The "image" is, of course, wrong, but it is at least composed of factual elements, though these have been combined by your overeager analytic processes, your conscious mind, to form an erroneous conclusion.

AOL is anything you perceive, through any modality of perception, that has both form and function. For example, a simple circle image as perceived by the Viewer is not AOL; it is only form. However, when suddenly the Viewer perceives the circle as having spokes and a hub, then the form takes on function as well, and is now analytical overlay, "a wheel." AOL is usually wrong, especially in early RV stages, but often possesses valid elements of the site that are contained in the signal line. Hence, a lighthouse may produce an AOL of "factory chimney" because of its tall cylindrical shape.

To give you a better sense of how AOLs take shape, read the following description which you might find in the Session Summary written by an experienced Remote Viewer:

As I look around, I see a large hard and flat base of some sort. It looks as though it is very large and round, thick, and perhaps made of concrete or metal. There is a large object sitting in the center of this base. I can see what look like vehicles driving up to and away from the object. The object itself is very large, maybe 150 feet tall or more. The object is hollow. It appears to have a thin outer skin or covering that is wrapped around a heavy metal frame. I see wires and tubing running all throughout the object and all kinds of electronic devices, inside and outside. I perceive monitoring equipment and sense that someone is watching me. This object is pointed at the top and wider at the base. There are four distinct corners, or perhaps sharp fin-like elements, at the bottom. I can see people inside the object at the top, who appear to be looking out very small windows or portholes, and they have a tremendous view around the area.

The Viewer has described, for the most part, what is called pure data—information from the unconscious mind that is devoid of analysis—but even here, you can see that life forms have been named "people" and small openings have become "windows or portholes." By now, your mind has probably stitched together these details into a single image, perhaps a rocket ship or missile. Indeed, all the aspects of such a target are present; however, you can see in Figure 6.11 that the target being described is actually the Washington Monument.

FIGURE 6.11 **An Example of How AOL Can Distort Pure Data**

This image is AOL.   **This image is the described target.**

You will recognize AOL in several ways. First, if there is a comparator present, such as "It looks like . . . ," or "It's sort of like . . . ," then the information present will almost inevitably be an AOL, and should always be treated as such. Second, a mental image that is sharp, clear, and static—there is no motion present in it, and it appears to be a mental photograph of the target site—is also considered AOL.

AOL is not a bad thing in Remote Viewing; I would like you to think of it as a category of data. You should not be afraid of it; you should not try to eliminate it from your session, nor could you even if you wanted to. Rather, you should understand that it will always be present, and you should not buy into it at any time—it cannot be trusted. In one moment, it may prove to be highly accurate target data, and then in the next, it swings at the speed of thought into highly inaccurate data.

As such, the way you handle it is to objectify it and move forward in the session. AOL will be present in every session, and in every stage of the session, you work with it.

In Stage I, however, AOL is not permitted, and when it manifests itself, you will have to take a break and take the coordinates again before you can continue with the session.

BREAKS AND RETAKING THE COORDINATES

There are instances in Stage I when you are required to retake the coordinates, some of which involve intentionally taking a short break and then resuming your session. There are thirteen types of breaks in Coordinate Remote Viewing, six of which can occur in Stage I. What is important to know is that each time you see or hear the word "break," a certain CRV protocol is used.

Essentially, a break, also described as a temporary termination of the signal line, is the mechanism in CRV that was developed to allow you to put the system on hold, providing you the opportunity to flush out AOL, deal with temporary inclemency, or make system adjustments. Declaring a break permits you to begin again, making a fresh start with new momentum.

In brief, here is the protocol you will use for all types of breaks. The protocol itself involves recognizing that there is a requirement to take a break when, for example, AOL is present, you missed the coordinates, the ideogram split, and so forth. Once you recognize that a break is needed, you declare the break, which means writing down the type of break on the right-hand side of the page you are working on. Next, you place your pen on the table and sit back in your chair to relax for a moment. When you are ready, after a minute or so has passed, you pick up the pen, write "resume," and begin work in the session again. The word "resume" is the symbolic gesture that you are ready to reestablish signal line contact and continue the session. In Stage I, upon resuming the session, you would take the coordinates again. This protocol, as with much of CRV, is a ritual, and it does work when followed.

As you can see in the sample session beginning on pages 244 and 245, the Remote Viewer took the coordinates a total of three times. The following discussion explains the situations you may encounter and instructs you on how to address each one.

Missed Break

This is a break declared when the Viewer takes the coordinates and does not produce an ideogram. In session, this condition will manifest immediately after you take the coordinates. As you finish recording the last digit, you know that you are supposed to respond with an ideogram, but nothing happens; you freeze. This is analogous to jumping off a platform, attempting to grab hold of a rope, and missing it. You have missed the signal line and fallen into darkness. That is a rather ominous-sounding way of saying something went wrong. We have no idea why this happens. It could be because you were nervous or because something distracted you, if even for an unwitting instant. We just do not know. The bottom line is that the structure does present us with a tool when this happens. You simply move to the right-hand side of the page and declare a "missed break," putting your pen down and relaxing for a moment. When ready, write "resume," the symbolic gesture that you are reengaging the signal line, and take the coordinates again. See Figure 6.12.

FIGURE 6.12 **Missed Break**

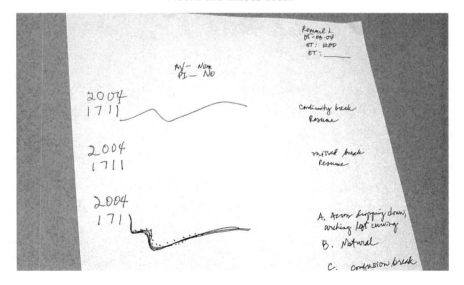

Continuity Break

This occurs when there is a break in the line of the ideogram, whereby the ideogram produced is not a single continuous line. Here again, we do not understand beyond theory why this happens. Years ago, this condition would have been considered a "split ideogram," and you would have been asked to decode the A/B/C sequence for both lines, treating them as separate elements of the gestalt. However, I do not want you to waste time decoding separate ideograms; remember that your mission in Stage I is to establish target contact and to control the opening to the aperture. Therefore, all that is necessary is for you to temporarily disengage the signal line, allowing the unconscious mind to repackage the data stream into a more user-friendly delivery. And it will do just that as long as you follow the structure and declare a break when the system delivers something less desirable. If you have a continuity problem in Stage I, move to the right-hand side of the page and declare "continuity break," placing your pen on the desk and relaxing for a moment. When ready, write "resume," and take the coordinates again. See Figure 6.12.

When no interruption occurs and your ideogram is a single continuous line, you must decode the ideogram that develops; you cannot ignore it and take the coordinates again. I mention this only because some new Remote Viewers will take the coordinates, respond with an ideogram, and then decide they do not "feel good about this one," prompting them to take the coordinates again. This is called "not feeding back to the system" and can cause the signal line to abruptly shut down. Essentially, when you ignore an ideogram and take the coordinates again, the language between the unconscious mind and the conscious mind terminates. The unconscious mind, which originally delivered the information, is now confused by the conscious mind ignoring the data flow. If you decide to move on to the next engagement, taking the coordinates again, the unconscious mind is likely to shut down the flow, and you will flatline, or receive no data. By the way, this is true in any stage of CRV. You must acknowledge and objectify everything that presents itself to the conscious mind without censoring, or you risk losing the clear flow of signal line data. Acknowledging and objectifying is accomplished by declaring a break, which is a symbolic gesture to acknowledge the error and reinforce the corrective action. You would then take the coordinates again, and decode the new ideogram that is presented.

"B" and "C" Component Decoding Challenges

Two other problem areas that can occasionally manifest in Stage I occur during the "B" and "C" component decoding processes. These challenges do not require you to take a break; however, they do require you to follow protocol in order to effectively reengage the signal line and continue the session. These conditions are usually present with newer Viewers. They seem to be indicative of the struggle to find one's particular modality of perception. Once the principal modality of perception is recognized and developed through experience and skill, these conditions dissipate rapidly and seldom appear in session again. That said, when they do appear, here is how you handle them.

No "B" Component

This condition may manifest during the probing of the ideogram in Stage I. You begin probing, but in eight to ten seconds, nothing is perceived, so you move along the ideogram a quarter of an inch to the right and pause to probe again for eight to ten seconds, but nothing happens. Sometimes you may move all the way down the ideogram and still have no discernible "B" data; that is, you are unable to determine if the "B" component is natural or manmade.

When this happens, do not repeat the decoding sequence, and do not start again on the ideogram. Move to the right-hand side of the page and write "no B." Figure 6.13 illustrates this. You do not have to put down your pen, because you are not declaring a break. You are not using the word "break." Thus, all that you do after declaring "no B" is to take the coordinates again and move on in the session. The reason you objectify "no B" is so that the system will know that

FIGURE 6.13 **No "B" Component**

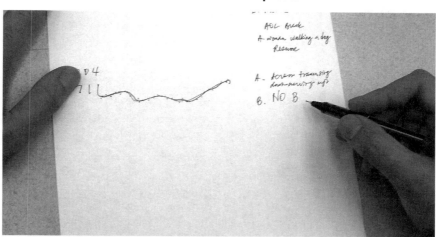

something went wrong. The process is called "feeding back to the system"; you are telling the unconscious mind that you were unable to decode the information in the ideogram, and that it must be repackaged and produced in a more pronounced way.

No "C" Component

This condition may manifest in relation to the "C" component during the probing of the ideogram in Stage I. You begin probing, but in eight to ten seconds nothing is perceived, so you move along the ideogram a quarter of an inch to the right and pause to probe again for eight to ten seconds, but again nothing happens. Sometimes you may move all the way down the ideogram and still have no discernible "C" data; that is, you are unable to determine if the "C" component is mountain, land, water, land-water interface, structure, or life form. When this happens, you move to the right-hand side of the page and write "no C." You do not have to put down your pen, because you are not declaring a break. After declaring "no C," take the coordinates again and move on. As with "no B," you objectify "no C" so that the system will know that something went wrong and that the information in the ideogram must be produced in a more pronounced way. You can see that the Viewer did this on the first page of the Sample Session (see page 248).

AOL Break

Taking an AOL break allows the signal line to be put on hold while AOL is expelled from the system. The AOL is present, and you recognize it as anything with form and function together. You declare the break, describe the AOL, put down the pen, write "resume" when ready, and take the coordinates again. In the Sample Session, at the bottom of page 248 and the top of page 249, you can see the entire break process. The Viewer experienced an AOL while decoding the "C" component: a sudden visual of a marina with small boats. You already know this is not permitted, because in decoding the "C" component of Stage I, you are looking only for mountain, land, water, land-water interface, structure, or life form. Therefore, the instant that form and function appeared, the Viewer recognized that this was an AOL, went to the right-hand side of the page and wrote "AOL break, a marina w/sail boats," and set the pen down. The Viewer resumed the session by writing "resume" and taking the coordinates again.

FIGURE 6.14 **Confusion Break and Too-Much Break**

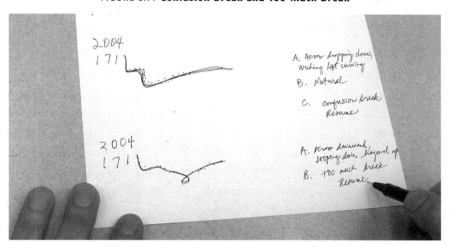

Confusion Break

If you become confused by events in the decoding environment—that is, information in the signal line as you are decoding the A/B/C sequence is hopelessly entangled—a confusion break is called. For example, as you are probing the ideogram decoding the "B" component, you are unable to determine if the presentation of the data is confirming "natural" or "manmade." The decoding process is flipping back and forth so rapidly that you cannot determine if it is the one or the other. Therefore, the environment confuses you, and you must declare a "confusion break." You move to the right-hand side of the page, write "confusion break," put down your pen, and take as much time as necessary for the confusion to dissipate. When you feel ready, pick up the pen, write "resume," and take the coordinates again to resume the A/B/C-sequence decoding. It is important to note that this condition may occur in the "C" component as well as in the "B" component.

Too-Much Break

When, all at once, too much information for you to handle is provided by the signal line, a "too-much break" is called and written down (objectified) on the right-hand side of the page. This type of break occurs when you suddenly find that the signal line is overloading your ability to sort the data. For example, during Stage I, in which you are asking for simple elements of data, you want to know, via some modality of perception, if the principal element of the target gestalt is a structure or a life form—when suddenly the aperture springs open, and a rush of data flows to you. This closely resembles the conditions present in a confusion break, yet there are distinct differences. "Too-much" indicates that you are unable to handle the flow of data; it relates to the volume of information, not necessarily the speed with which it is delivered by the unconscious mind. You are focusing on a texture (if you are visual) in decoding the "B" or "C" component, and now you have textures, colors, sounds, tastes, perhaps some emotional data, and so on. Thus, the flow is overwhelming and cannot be accommodated in Stage I; you must declare the break. To declare a too-much break, move to the right-hand side of the page, write "too-much break," and set down your pen, which tells the system to slow down and supply information in order of importance. When ready, after the overload is dissipated, write "resume," and take the coordinates again. An overly elaborate ideogram often indicates that a too-much break could follow shortly.

Break

Breaks can be declared at any stage during the session. If, at any point in the process, the Viewer must take a break that does not fit into any of the other categories, a simple break is declared. If the break is extensive, say twenty minutes or longer, it is appropriate to objectify the length of the break by including the time of the break and the time you resume the session. You use this break if you are feeling overwhelmed, if too many things are going wrong, or if some other difficulty is present such that it would be better if the session is just put on hold for a while. You declare the break on the right-hand side of the page, put your pen down, and when ready, write "resume" to symbolically reengage the signal line, and take the coordinates again. Any time the word "break" is used in CRV, the same protocol is used. However, it is only in Stage I that you must retake the coordinates after resuming. Also be aware that in Stage V, you are not directly engaged with the signal line, so no breaks are permitted.

TRANSITION FROM STAGE I TO STAGE II

There are two important things to point out here as you transition into Stage II. First, recognize that the Viewer never looks back to an earlier ideogram for any reason. When you retake the coordinates, you work only with the data from the new ideogram, always moving forward. While detecting and decoding the second ideogram, the Viewer decodes everything in the A/B/C components related to the second ideogram; this is exactly what must take place. You cannot decode A/B/C components that relate to an earlier ideogram—all decoding must be directly linked to the most recent ideogram produced.

I often say, "Never look back during the session." This means you must stay in the moment, detecting and decoding only in the moment, without censoring, without comparing what you perceive with what you've previously written down. Think of the words of the author Jim Bishop: "Nothing is as far away as one minute ago." That is exactly the attitude you need to be an effective Remote Viewer. Understand that every time you take the coordinates, you are setting down and opening the aperture in a different place within the target gestalt. When you retake the coordinates repeatedly, you can think of it as "tea-bagging," plopping yourself down into the target site as one might dunk a teabag several times into a cup of water. There is no one place in the target area that is designated as the best vantage point for Remote Viewers, and the target data you perceive may appear to you differently depending upon your vantage point. This is nothing to worry about; just know that this happens and is a reason you always follow the structure, stay in the moment, and never look back during a session.

The second important point is that you must successfully complete each part of Stage I before you move to Stage II. This means that if you have seven ideograms, each with its own problem area, you keep taking the coordinates and producing ideograms until you can decode the A/B/C components for that ideogram. Then, and only then, are you able to move to Stage II.

This concludes the chapter on Stage I of the Coordinate Remote Viewing protocol. You should be completely familiar with every aspect of this chapter before moving on to Stage II. If you are having difficulty at this point, be sure to e-mail us and ask whatever questions are necessary to gain clarity.

REFERENCE SHEET I

Name:

Date:

Start Time:

End Time: *(leave blank until session ends)*

Advanced Visuals or Perceptions (AV)
(Yes or No) if Yes, describe them

Physical or Personal Inclemency (PI)
(Yes or No) if Yes, list them

STAGE I

• This is the **Cuing Position** – tip of pen to paper
Coordinates: followed by the **Ideogram**

"A" Component: Describe the *feeling/motion* of the Ideogram

"B" Component: Describe the *feeling* as:
  • Natural
  • Manmade
  (can only be one or the other—never both)

"C" Component: Describe your *perceptions* of the major component of the gestalt as only *one* of these:
  • Mountain
  • Water
  • Land
  • Land-Water Interface
  • Structure
  • Life Form

STAGE II

Begin Stage II here, in the center of this page only after you complete an A/B/C-component decoding in sequence.

Remember to sketch on the left and write on the right.

Colors
Textures
Smells
Tastes
Temperatures
Sounds
Dimensionals *(can include verticals, horizontals, mass & density, diagonals, arches)*
Energetics

Break *(AOL, AI, EI, PI, BI-LO, confusion. too-much)*
Resume

AOL: here
[Movement Brackets here]

Sketches here

STAGE III

new stage, new page

Drawings in the form of simple dimensional or contour sketches
Remember to probe and label them.

Remember to sketch in the middle of the page now.

REFERENCE SHEET II

PHASE II – REFERENCE SHEET (STAGE IV, V, VI)

STAGE IV

Stage II, Dimensional, Aesthetic Data, Emotional Data, Tangibles, Intangibles, AOL, AOL/Signal

You are still sketching on the left and writing on the right within the Stage IV matrix.

STAGE V

Work from one cue word selected from Intangibles, AOL/S, or AOL in sequence.

a. (Cue Word)
   OBJECTS
   physical items present in the site
   Data?

          b. (Cue Word)
            ATTRIBUTES
            characteristics or qualities of a person or thing
            Data?

                    c. (Cue Word)
                      SUBJECTS
                      function, purpose, nature, activities
                      of site or inhabitants
                      Data?

STAGE VI

You are now working off of two pieces of paper simultaneously.

STAGE VI MATRIX

S2 D AD ED T I AOL AOL/S

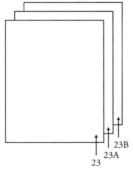

23
23A
23B

STAGE VI RENDERINGS

More fully developed sketches

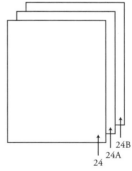

24
24A
24B

End of Session
(record end time at top of first sheet)

At the end of your session only, write a session summary. This should be a brief summary of all your sensory perceptions. You should include references to your verbal data as well as your sketches. Begin your paragraph with the words "My perceptions of the target site are…"

7

The Journey Inward Continues:
Coordinate Remote Viewing—Stage II

I do not want the peace that passeth understanding.
I want the understanding which bringeth peace.

Helen Keller

In this chapter, you will continue working with the Sample Session on the CN Tower (Chapter 12). Before you read further, I would like you to look at pages 249 through 260, which illustrate Stage II (S2). Look carefully at the flow of the data and the verbal descriptors used by the Viewer in the session. Become familiar with these pages, as you will refer to them to reinforce this chapter.

The Remote Viewer who did this session is obviously very skilled; his structure is impeccable. I know that the Sample Session looks intimidating; however, in time, and with effort, practice, and experience, your skill at Remote Viewing will be much the same as his.

THE METHOD

Stage II is a verbally driven stage. You will remember that the purpose of Stage I is to establish target gestalt contact and to control the opening of the aperture and the flow of data. In Stage II, the aperture is opened wider to allow the Viewer's perception of the following categories of data: colors, textures, smells, tastes, temperatures, sounds, dimensional data, and energetic data. Stage II presents you with cognitive signal line data that is relevant to physical sensory input. The classic explanation of this is that such data is exactly equivalent to sensations you would experience if you were physically present at the site. In effect, this allows you to come into closer contact with the signal line through recognition and objectification of sensory facts relevant to the site. This information revolves around the five physical senses—touch, smell, sight, hearing, and taste—and can include temperature both as a "hot" or "cold to the touch" tactile sensation and as a general environmental ambience. It also includes dimensional data, that is, diagonals, curves, and so on, and energetic data, such as magnetism, strong radio broadcasts or waveform, nuclear radiation in blast or thermal energy, high-vibration energy, shaking, and so forth. Stage II data is generally simple, described using fundamental words dealing directly with a sensory experience, such as "rough," "red," "cold," "stinging smell," "sandy taste," "soft," "moist," "green," or "gritty." Although Stage II includes simple sketching as images present themselves, your primary focus will be detecting and decoding signal line data in a verbal mode.

STAGE II FORMAT

Looking at the Reference Sheets (pages 140 and 141) and pages 249 through 260 of the Sample Session, you can see how the Stage II format flows. You work from top to bottom in the center of the page because the signal line is theoretically in the center of the page at this point in the structure. You work down the center of the page probing, detecting, and decoding verbal data. You can also see that you sketch any visual data on the left-hand side of the page, and you declare breaks, objectify AOL, and move your position, etc., verbally on the right-hand side of the page.

Look for AOLs and how the Viewer tracked them. Look for breaks, for movements, and for other difficulties, making note of how the Viewer handled them. You can see that no matter what happens, there is a structural procedure to deal with it. As long as you know what to do and when to do it, you will always complete the session, you will always be in control of the session from start to finish, and you will always produce usable and accurate information pertaining to the target distant in space-time.

THE S2 HEADING

On page 249 of the Sample Session, immediately after completing the A/B/C-sequence decoding, that is, when all five elements of Stage I are present and complete, the Viewer drops down a level, places his pen in the center of the same page (from left to right), and indicates he is transitioning into Stage II by writing "S2" and drawing a line underneath. Stage II is the only stage that can follow this procedure; all other stages must adhere to the adage "new stage, new page," meaning that you must take a clean sheet of paper to begin a new stage. Every page in Stage II is labeled by writing "S2" at the top center of the page.

DETECTING AND DECODING

The signal line inherent in Stage II is said to theoretically run through the center of the page. Of course, there is nothing literally "running through the center of the page"; this is an adopted term addressing the ritual of CRV. I mentioned ritual in a previous chapter, but I want to reinforce it here: ritual is significant because it facilitates coherent communication with the subconscious levels of the mind and strengthens our practice by linking us to the collective experience of all who have come before us in the same practice. CRV is a structured dogma, a protocol that is easily considered a ritual. In the same way your pen returns to the same point when you probe the ideogram in Stage I, your pen must always return to the center of the page as you enter the detect mode in Stage II, standing in the unconscious mind of the Matrix Field, then shifting to the conscious mind as you decode the perceived data and objectify it onto the page.

You move at a metronomic cadence through the structure of Stage II, a detect and decode pace that will likely average eight to ten seconds for new Viewers and gradually speed up to two to four seconds with increased skill and experience. Each time you place your pen on the page, you close your eyes and wait for perceptions in the form of colors, textures, tastes, smells, temperatures, sounds, dimensional data, and energetic data. As these perceptions manifest, you record them vertically down the middle of the page.

VERBAL DATA AND LANGUAGE

What makes Stage II a challenge is not the structure or even the ability to begin perceiving data. What challenges most new Viewers is a lack of vocabulary, an inability to assign language to what they perceive during the session. Journalist and novelist Joan Didion said, "You will only become free in this life when you develop a command of the language." Further exploring the argument, she described herself in her work *Why I Write* as:

> *a person whose most absorbed and passionate hours are spent arranging words on pieces of paper. Had I been blessed with even limited access to my own mind, there would have been no reason to write. I write entirely to find out what I am thinking, what I am looking at, what I see, and what it means. What I want and what I fear. Why did the oil refineries around Carquinez Straits seem sinister to me in the summer of 1956? Why have the night-lights in the bevatron burned in my mind for twenty years? What is going on in these pictures in my mind?*

This example illustrates Didion's discovery that the images of the mind, the questions of the mind, are conceptual illusion detected and decoded into thought form, but are fleeting, moving, morphing, and uncontrolled as long as they are left to the mind.

To know what you are thinking, to understand your perceptions, you must objectify them; you must write them down. Write with a passion, for this is the tool for manifesting, for creating; this is the tool for objectification—without writing, all that remains is a transitory illusion. Stage II is a tool for manifestation. You stand there in the darkness of the Matrix Field, awash in a sea of waveform data, detecting and decoding. If your command of the language is limited, it will dampen your ability to apply language to what you see. This ability to describe the energetic world around you through a new set of eyes, to use words strung together like jewels on a string, requires effort, practice, and commitment. You should never be anywhere, from this moment forward, that you do not look at the world around you and ask yourself, "How would I describe this if I were to see it, to perceive it, in a Remote Viewing session?"

Work hard to become a person who describes the world in such a way that others fall in love with your version of it, with your descriptions, your interpretations. Someone once asked Oscar Wilde to comment on a sunset, and Wilde replied, "It is a second-rate Turner." The simplistic beauty of his words aside, he implied that the natural beauty of the sunset paled in comparison with the interpretive use of color and texture to depict a similar image of the setting sun by the painter J. M. W. Turner, probably the most acclaimed and prolific painter of landscapes. Turner was among the first impressionist painters, who in turn were the forerunners of the French Impressionists. During his lifetime, he produced over twenty thousand paintings and drawings, and his command of the brush earned him the title "the painter of light." Turner's command of the canvas, of the medium, so inspires us that we love his version of the world, how he speaks to us, how he shows it to us.

Words and our use of them are tools akin to the artist's brush. Words allow readers to see the world through a new set of eyes, nonphysical eyes, and this is your task as a Remote Viewer—to create an image of something distant in space-time. Who knows, you may become the next great poet of our time. We all have a savant aspect within us, and this aspect is shadowed and masked by our conscious minds. The author Zadok Rabinowitz said, "Your dreams are an index to your greatness." Know your dreams, and more important, know how to objectify them. If you can think it or dream it, you can write it down, and when you write it down, it will manifest itself in your life. Another author, Marilyn vos Savant, said, "To acquire knowledge, one must study; but to acquire wisdom, one must observe." As a Remote Viewer, you are in the business of observing, and objectifying what you observe.

You are a brilliant person. Your view of the world is unique in perspective and interpretation. What is lacking, often, is a command of language. This is not a measure of intellect, nor of creativity; it is a reflection of our conditioning. Due to the ever-increasing pace of our lives, most of us have learned to think and express in chunks, to express ourselves in one or two words, in sound bites.

I remember taking my son into the pavilion of the Capitol Building in Washington, D.C., when he was thirteen. He looked up at the enormity, the complexity, the delicate beauty of the ceiling. The artistry, color, and aesthetic property of the rotunda was distilled into a flatly stated "Cool." "Cool?" I asked. "Yeah, cool." "Is there anything else you can use to describe it?" I persisted. He looked more carefully this time, his eyes following the lines through the curvature of the dome and down the other side. "Really cool," he said.

This is a demonstration of conditioning, not of intellect, and most all of us fall into the same behavior. I have trained thousands of students worldwide, and it is the same in every part of the world. The youth of this planet, that is, the youth from the industrialized nations of this planet, are pressed through a compact disc, radio, television, film, and video-game version of the world. Little training goes into the work of self-expression, using language to communicate in beautifully expressive ways. Instead, a type of code is spoken, a limited verbal code, designed to distill one's expression, one's version of the world, into an accepted, widely understood, regional phrase.

Sometimes the limitation of language during a Remote Viewing session is brought on, not by a limited lexicon, but by an overwhelming abundance of data and an inability in the moment to forget the name of what you are looking at. If this happens to you, your reversal of the phenomenon is to dissect the image, all the sensory data, into its various components. My conditioning may trigger the limited response; my training as a Viewer, as an observer, graces me with the ability to forget the name of what I am looking at, to fragment and study what I am seeing in a different way. For example, think of a strawberry. What does a strawberry taste like? What does it smell like? What does it look like? Describe it in your own words, without using the word "strawberry."

In another example, I recently returned from a journey to Peru with an advanced RV class of Extended Remote Viewers. The class focused on the Remote Viewing of various sacred sites, followed by the feedback, which was to be on the ground (at the site) with shaman Jorge Ruiz Delgado and me. On the final leg of the class, we were leading the Viewers into Machu Picchu. To honor the event, Jorge conferred with me, and together we developed a plan to lead the Viewers up a particular trail with their eyes closed and holding hands. This would prevent them from seeing Machu Picchu until we asked them to open their eyes. This served two purposes. First, the Viewers would experience Machu Picchu with their nonphysical eyes, as well as their hearts. Second, they would exercise their ability to express their perceptions verbally while experiencing the target. The exercise was a success. You should have seen it: thirty-eight people in two groups, holding hands, walking up a trail, stepping cautiously onto a flat terrace to feel Machu Picchu, and then opening their eyes on command. There were great gasps, with a few "Magnificent!" and "Beautiful!" exclamations sprinkled in here and there. What was most notable to me was that even in experienced Remote Viewers, there was a distinct inability to find the words for the experience either before or after opening their eyes.

The older we get, the more we should be able to communicate, to express our perceptions of the world, our emotions, our feelings, our concepts and notions—yet the opposite is true. Most of us read less and watch more television, videos, DVDs, and films. We ride alone in cars for hours on the way to work and back again. We listen mindlessly to talk-radio shows or music, essentially being fed a version of the world second by second, never once working to create our own version of what we are hearing. At work, we may sit in a cubicle entering data into a machine, and our only interface may be with the machine. We may answer e-mail, but likely in a limited manner; because we have so many to answer, we have to be brief and succinct. If we sit in a boardroom and are asked to comment, we are reminded to keep it brief, no longer than two minutes, as the meeting must keep moving. You get the picture. We are conditioned to think, see, feel, and express our relationship with the world in simple, noncomplex language. Is it any wonder that the mental muscle necessary to describe the world is atrophying?

On average, North Americans use approximately 85 to 135 different words per day to communicate with their fellow human beings. Think about that: a maximum of 135 different words from a language that contains approximately a million words. If you include language from technical and regional vocabulary, Latin words used in law, French words used in cooking, German words used in academic writing, Japanese words used in martial arts, slang terms, computer jargon, and so on, in excess of one million words are available to us on a daily basis to describe the world around us. And we use what, 85 to 135? What is the matter with us? It is all about conditioning, training.

The good news is that no matter how atrophied this ability becomes, it is reversible. What you can train to in the negative, you can train to in the positive—it is a choice. At any given moment, you can begin training yourself to develop a better command of the language. All you have to do is to start. For instance, when you hear a wonderful descriptor for something, write it down, and use it in conversation. As I have said, you should never be in any place or situation again that you do not ask yourself the question "How would I describe this if I were in a session right now?" I am including here two exercises that will help you develop the language skills you will use as a Remote Viewer.

LANGUAGE EXERCISES

Sensory Journaling

You can train with a friend by taking the Stage II categories of data (listed on page 150) and going for a walk. Stop along the way at various things—trees, buildings, animals, water, structures, events—and ask each other how the other would describe the color of the tree, the texture, the smell, the taste (use caution here—don't go licking trees; some of them are toxic), the temperature, the sound, the dimensions, and the energy. You will be surprised how differently others see the world. The combination of information, the exchange of descriptors, is fascinating and educational. What you write down, you are far less likely to forget, and what you hear others use to describe the world, you are less likely to forget, as well. You will find this sensory journal exercise pays big dividends as you develop your skills in Stage II. Carry a journal, a small notebook, or a simple recording device, and capture every descriptor used to describe the world around you.

Descriptors for Stage II

The categories of data you will be detecting and decoding during Stage II are colors, textures, smells, tastes, temperatures, sounds, dimensional data, and energetic data. Even though I just spent pages encouraging you to improve your use of language, you have to use caution when assigning language to the Stage II categories of data. You want to be descriptive, yet you want to find language that does not carry both form and function—if you describe these elements of data in a form-and-function manner, then you have developed an AOL, and you must declare it. Again, an AOL is not a bad thing. It is inherent to any session, a category of data, but it must be constantly held in check, or it will drive the session.

Take a moment to look at the room you are in, and describe each of these categories in your own words, with as many descriptors as you can. I have provided some examples to illustrate some of the kinds of language that will work in each category. Understand that the lexicon should not be limited to the brief examples below. For example, you can perceive far more tastes than sweet, salty, sour, bitter, and natural.

Colors—any colors within the spectrum that you are able to assign language to

Textures—convoluted, soft, wavy, spiky

Smells—rotten, fresh, fragrant, chemical

Tastes—sweet, salty, sour, bitter, natural

Temperatures—hot, frosty, frigid, humid, steamy, icy

Sounds—rushing, clanging, banging, repetitive

Dimensional data—tall, heavy, porous, diagonal, vertical

Energetic data—vibration, heat, piercing wave, rolling force, stillness; a presence of energy pulsating, shaking, or exploding; nuclear, hydroelectric, electric, magnetic, microwave, combustion

Completing these exercises will help heighten your sensory awareness, activate your ability to choose descriptively precise words for what you perceive, and allow you to appreciate the abundance of words you have to draw from in your Remote Viewing sessions. As mentioned earlier in this chapter, anywhere you are, from this moment forward, whether you are sitting in a train station or lounging in a hotel lobby, you should be looking at your environment and asking yourself, "If I were looking at this in a session, how I would describe it?" Ask yourself, "What are the tastes in the air here? What are the smells? How would I describe that texture or this element of dimension?" You get the picture. You will build a lexicon of descriptors that you can call upon whenever you need to in the Remote Viewing session.

DIMENSIONAL AND ENERGETIC DATA

As you proceed through Stage II and approach Stage III, the aperture widens, allowing you to shift from a blind global (gestalt) perspective, which is paramount through Stage I and most of Stage II, to a perspective in which certain limited dimensional characteristics are discernible. Generally received only in the latter portion of Stage II, dimensional data is usually very basic: tall, wide, long, or big. More complex elements of dimensional data, such as "panoramic," are usually received at later stages characterized by wider aperture openings; in other words, the notion of "panoramic" might better describe an aesthetic element of data in Stage IV, or it might fall into a Stage IV intangible concept, depending on how you perceived it. If these more complex elements of dimensional data are reported during Stage II, they are considered "out of structure," and therefore unreliable. I will discuss the protocol for acknowledging data bleed-through later in this chapter.

The words you will use to describe dimensional data demonstrate eight dimensional concepts: vertical, horizontal, diagonal, mass, arch, curve, column, and space (or density). Notice what happens in your conscious mind when you read these descriptors. In most cases, as we think of these descriptors, our conscious mind conjures images to go with them. This is why we try to limit dimensional data until the end of the Stage II process. You cannot stop the flow of dimensional data, nor would you want to. However, you should establish your intention to push this data to the end of Stage II as much as it is practicable. The reason is that Stage II is a verbally driven stage, asking for an abundance of verbal descriptors, often as many as eight to ten pages. If your conscious mind begins developing dimensional images on your third page of Stage II, you may end up being prompted to move to Stage III prematurely, before you have purged all available Stage II data from the target as perceived through the Stage II aperture. You want to remain in Stage II and develop as much Stage II data as is reasonably possible, which is why the eight-to-ten-page guideline is suggested. Eight to ten pages of Stage II data is not a mandate and, in some targets, might actually be an impossibility. Rather, it is provided as a guide, a motivator to hearten your efforts in a difficult verbal stage.

The eight principal elements of dimensional data that can be decoded in Stage II are as follows:

Vertical—perpendicular to the plane of the horizon; the highest point or the lowest point (height or depth)

Horizontal—parallel to the plane of the horizon

Diagonal—something that extends between two or more things that are not adjacent; a line connecting two points of intersection or two lines of a figure

Mass—extent of whatever forms a body in space, usually matter

Arch—similar to curve: an arch can be considered a vertical curve

Curve—a curving element usually found on the horizontal

Column—vertical and cylindrical

Space (or density)—distance, interval, or area between or within things; an empty area, distance, or volume of particles; mass in a given area or quantities of matter

VISUAL DATA IN STAGE II

As we have discussed, verbal descriptors are listed down the center of the page. As Stage II progresses, visuals will develop. When you perceive something that appears via a visual modality of perception, you sketch this image data on the left-hand side of the page and then follow it with a probing and labeling procedure (which will be explained shortly).

Page 251 of the Sample Session begins with a string of verbal data that develops into a basic Stage II contour sketch on the left-hand side of the page. The sketch was probed and labeled with no development of form and function, thus no requirement to declare any AOL. As soon as the sketch was finished and labeled, the Viewer rejoined the signal line in the center of the page to begin decoding verbal data again. Note the spacing on the page and the flow of the data. The sketch interrupts the string of data, and the string begins again under the sketch. It is easy to see the flow of the decoded verbal data (down the center of the page) followed by the visual data sketch (on the left) and the verbal data continuing again in the center of the page.

In Stage II, you will capture simple textures and contrasts. Your sketches will develop further in later stages. Sketch everything that visually comes to you. It may begin as a series of white dots on a black background, but as you probe and label the sketch, it may prove to be highly valuable data in the overall target session. Remember, if you do not write it down, it does not count. Leave nothing behind; leave nothing to the conceptual illusion of the conscious mind. Objectify, objectify, objectify.

Unique to the sketch on page 258 of the Sample Session is the presence of the Viewer, depicting himself and labeling himself "me" at the bottom of the sketch. You should be aware of this ability during your session. Always look to see if you can see yourself in the target looking at the target. Do not give this too much analysis—it will only hurt your head. For some, the mere idea that they can be in one place physically, in an altered state, and looking at an energetic representation of themselves looking at something in a target site distant in space-time is, well, just plain freaky. Nonetheless, it does occur, and when it does, you must capture it.

Probe and Label

Every sketch you produce during your session should be probed and labeled. This procedure involves placing the tip of your pen into the sketch as well as on to certain aspects of the sketch. With your pen on the sketch, you close your eyes to detect and decode data relevant to the sketch.

In the various sketches produced in the Stage II portion of the Sample Session, you can clearly see the probe marks made by the Viewer. Every sketch, no matter how complete or simple, is probed and labeled. You must bear in mind that what you initially perceive as visual data may not sustain itself once you begin probing it. You may begin with a simple series of black dots on the page that, once probed, increase in data to become swirling points of energy, that further expand, through probing, into a controlled or harnessed flow of energy, that further expands into another, and still another, description. Simple textural sketches produced in Stage II, and even in Stage III and Stage IV, must always be probed to unveil other elements of data pertaining to the sketch.

Look at the sketch on page 252 of the Sample Session. If this sketch had not been probed and labeled, it would mean little to an analyst reviewing this session. However, since the Viewer had indicated there is movement, provided a direction for this movement, and probed the image to conclude that it is a fluid that is moving, the sketch has analytic meaning and is more usable data than if no labeling had been done. Likewise, in the sketch on page 253 of the Sample Session, you can see that the probing and labeling for data indicators like "soft and green," along with "rigid," lend more interest and usability to the sketch. If you look through the session, you will see that almost every sketch has been extensively probed and labeled in an effort to produce more data than was initially decoded from the perceived visual.

THE RIGHT-HAND SIDE OF THE PAGE

Any necessary declarations or descriptions are written on the right-hand side of the page; this includes AOLs, AI, EI, breaks, and movements. The structure of Stage II can be described as follows: "Detect and decode verbal sensory data down the center of the page, sketch visual data on the left, and write or declare verbal information on the right." You can see in the Sample Session that this simple structure was followed through the entire Stage II process.

Analytical Overlay (AOL) in Stage II

Remember that AOL is defined as anything, any visual or verbal data, that carries form and function combined. A circle is not an AOL. A circle (form) that is spinning under a vehicle (function) is likely to trigger your analytic conscious mind to assign a concept to the image: "AOL, a wheel."

Analytical overlay is considerably rarer in Stage I than it is in Stage II, and it is considered rarer in Stage II than it is in Stage III. You will remember that AOL is not permitted in Stage I and, if present, requires you to declare it, take a break, resume, and take the coordinates again. Once out of Stage I, AOL is handled as simply another category of data, which you objectify (declare) on the right-hand side of the page by writing "AOL" with a brief description.

Often long strings of verbal data will prompt AOLs. There are times when the process reverses itself; that is, visual data, simple Stage II sketches—as they are probed and labeled or as the Viewer follows the sketch with a string of verbal data used to describe the image—spring into sudden elements of "form and function" for the sketch, making it AOL.

Refer to page 251 of the Sample Session. The Viewer decoded a string of six pieces of verbal data before a verbal AOL of "a greasy spinning piece of metal" was declared. In other words, it appears that the string of verbal data prompted the AOL, which was declared and then was followed by the declaration of an image. If you pay attention to the stacking on the page, you can see how the verbal string prompted the verbal AOL declared (written) on the right and how, at the completion of this declaration, the Viewer moved to the left and sketched the image, probing and labeling it. The stacking is an indicator of how the data flowed into the session for the Viewer. Impeccable structure makes this information available to the analyst or trainer reviewing the session; you should strive to keep the same unimpeachable structure.

On page 252 of the Sample Session, the Viewer produced a long string of verbal data before declaring an AOL of "a sea smell," an olfactory AOL. Look at the list of verbal data, and you can see what prompted this: "wet smell," "water smell." The olfactory AOL "a sea smell" was declared on the right, and then the signal line was reengaged in the center of the page.

The Viewer decoded another string of olfactory data followed by a color and a texture before a visual developed. The visual data, this simple texture sketch, was declared on the left, and it was probed and labeled. The probing and labeling of the sketch prompted a visual of moving fluid—form and function together; thus, the Viewer moved to the right and declared (wrote) the AOL as "some sort of fluid moving."

AOL can develop via auditory and other modes of perception; it is not limited to visual perception. For example, on page 253 of the Sample Session, a string of data was produced with several sounds, and this produced another brief AOL of "people laughing & talking," which was declared on the right.

Analytical overlay occurs in every stage except Stage V, which is a stage separate from all others. There is something extremely basic about the sensory nature of the data perceived in Stage II, which strongly tends to avoid AOL. Some suppositions suggest that the sensory data received comes across either at a low enough energy level or through a channel which does not stimulate the analytical portion of the mind to action. In effect, the mind is fooled into thinking that Stage II information is being obtained from normal physical sensory sources.

However, I tend to strongly believe, and teach, that the reason Stage II can control the flow of AOL is due to the metronomic cadence of the structure, moving to a regular rhythm in the same way that a musician's metronome functions. I assure you that if you slow down the cadence, you will give the conscious mind sufficient time to generate AOL. You must keep moving forward; if you stall for too long—if you wait there, your pen on the paper, your eyes closed in the detect mode—you will generate AOL. If you do, then simply declare it and move on. Do not worry about the AOL, for it is just a category of data—and there will ultimately be plenty of it.

The combination of true sensory data received in Stage II may produce a valid signal line image consisting of colors, forms, and textures. Stage II visuals or other true signal line visuals of the site may be distinguished from AOL. In fact, they are perceived as fuzzy and indistinct, tending to fade in and out as you attempt to focus on the constituent elements, rather than as the sharp, clear, static images present with AOL. (This is what you will find in Stage IV, where I will define the difference between AOL and AOL signal, along with training on Stages IV, V, and VI of the Coordinate Remote Viewing protocol.)

AOL Drive

Years ago, the structure of Stage II required Viewers to recognize certain categories and conditions where AOL would appear. For instance, I was taught to recognize AOL, AOL drive, AOL ratcheting, and AOL peacocking. AOL drive indicated the presence of a repeating AOL, while AOL ratcheting indicated the repeat presence of the AOL despite the Viewer's best efforts to declare and diminish it. AOL ratcheting was described as analogous to a ratchet wrench. You would declare the AOL, and it would appear again somewhere in the session, cranking back down on you. You would declare it, perhaps even take a break because of it, and then it would reappear later, only to crank down on you again. AOL peacocking referred to the development of the AOL in more elaborate, repeating patterns; that is, you would declare the AOL only to have it reappear in more deliberate form, with more visual data attached than before. For example, you declare the AOL of "a ship at sea." Several pages later, the ship reappears, only this time it is a "four-masted schooner sailing in a gale." You declare this, even take a break, when several pages later, the AOL reappears as a "four-masted schooner, sailing in a gale, with all hands in the rigging." In this example, each occurrence of the AOL produces additional visual data, hence the analogy of the unfolding of the elaborate tail of the peacock—AOL peacocking.

What I would like you to do is simply to consider AOL as a single occurrence, in which case you will declare it as AOL and include a brief description. For example, "AOL, a ship at sea." If, however, the AOL appears a second time, no matter how many pages later, then you are in "AOL drive," and any occurrence of "drive" requires you to take an AOL break.

The first AOL break in the Sample Session occurs on page 257. The small sketch on the left was probed to indicate the perception of concrete in color "grey" and likely an element of mass and density similar to concrete, which is what prompted the Viewer to simply label the sketch as "concrete." This kind of sketching is typical in Stage II—simple, no-nonsense, not a lot of imagination or interpretation going on, just a two-dimensional representation of the perceived visual data. The probing breathed life into the sketch, but it also prompted the manifestation of AOL, which was declared on the right as "AOL, stacked or formed concrete blocks." The Viewer rejoined the signal line in the center of the page, placed the tip of his pen on the page, closed his eyes, and descended into the detect mode, where he immediately decoded two pieces of verbal data: "grey" and "flat."

These two elements of data likely prompted the reemergence of the visual of concrete, thus the Viewer moved to the right and declared "AOL break, concrete sidewalks." Notice it is a recurrence of data represented by the sketch on page 253—"AOL, a concrete sidewalk." Remember that because the AOL had developed twice, the Viewer knew that he was in AOL drive. The procedure for handling AOL drive is to take a break from the AOL each time it reappears. No analysis, no conclusions, no judgment—just take the break.

When taking a break because of AOL drive, you will go to the right side of the page and write "AOL break," followed by a brief description, put your pen down, and when ready, symbolically reestablish the signal line contact by writing "resume." In most cases, when you resume, you will execute a movement to voluntarily move out of the area and away from the source of the problem, which is what this Viewer does; he resumes and moves "right 100'."

Note that you will handle other types of breaks in the same way. For instance, on page 256, the Viewer moved to the right of the page and declared a confusion break, indicating that he felt he was out of focus, floating in his perceptions, and unable to stabilize the flow of target data. (The Viewer's Session Summary, Chapter 13, will likely tell a great deal more about what the Viewer felt was happening than this cursory analysis of the structure.) When the Viewer resumed, he made two distinct voluntary movements, indicated on the right: "[down 500']" and "[right 500']" Clearly, the Viewer was trying to move boldly out of the area, away from the source of the difficulty. Also, note that in Stage II and the stages that follow, such breaks do *not* require retaking the coordinates as they did in Stage I.

Movement within the target site is your choice; remember, you are in control of the session. On page 256 of the Sample Session, notice the AOL of "a brick and glass structure w/life forms moving in & around." Because this image of a manmade structure is carried over from pages 258 and 259, the Viewer determined that the image constituted AOL drive. Thus, the Viewer declared an AOL break, resumed when ready, and then chose not to move. Again, the written summary may shed light on why the Viewer chose not to move after the recognized presence of AOL drive. In this case, the Session Summary shows that the Viewer decided not to move because he felt the perspective in the target was fine, that he was safe, and that the AOL was under control.

Mobility/Movement and Using Movement Brackets

These terms refer to your ability to move within the target site, to change your position, to alter your perspective during the session. This ability can take on at least two different modalities: voluntary movement and involuntary movement. Involuntary movement describes your ability to move within the target without having to think about it. Many new Viewers do not have this ability; they actually find themselves fixed or static in the target area, as if they were stuck in mud. Involuntary movers have the ability to perceive various aspects of the target gestalt and move to them freely, without having to direct their movements consciously in any way. Think about your day-to-day movements in the physical world: you walk outside to the mailbox without having to pay too much attention; you do not have to actively think about doing it, you just decide to do it, or you do it as a matter of routine, and automatically move to the location and back. However, if you were recovering from an injury to your legs, you would have to plan your movement to the mailbox. You would be deliberate and focused—such is the voluntary mover in a Remote Viewing session. The control mechanism for this voluntary movement process is the use of movement brackets. The voluntary mover must, in effect, "volunteer" to move from location to location within the target gestalt, controlling the movement through the use of the movement brackets.

Movement brackets are training wheels, if you will—a tool to enhance stability and control in new Viewers. While they prove useful in early sessions and occasionally after you increase in skill and experience, they are something you will eventually want to use sparingly or not at all.

Specifically, movement brackets are written brackets framing your movement instructions, for example "[move up 500 feet & look down]." The brackets are used on the right-hand side of the page you are working on, and they must always include a direction and a distance. Look at pages 255, 256, 257, 259, and 260 of the Sample Session. On each of these pages you can see the application of movement brackets by the Viewer. In this example, the Viewer used movement brackets to illustrate his control and movement process during the session. If the Viewer had been an involuntary mover, the session would have been covered with notes indicating changes in position and perspective, which would be more difficult for you to follow in this instruction. Therefore, even though you are encouraged to go beyond the use of the brackets, that is, to become an involuntary mover, for instruction purposes, they help you in following the movements of the Viewer in any given stage. I told you that you will grow out of them, only because it is always better to be a flyer as a Remote Viewer than it is to be a deliberate plodder in the session—that said, you will have to find your own comfort level and work within that.

You should also understand that movement brackets do not have a mind of their own; they do not understand abstract concepts related to the target, such as "Show me what I am supposed to see here," or "Take me to the target." These are simple command tools used to start, stop, turn, climb, and drop. Do not make the mistake of thinking the brackets, as a tool, can think for themselves, that they know where something is—because they do not.

You will notice in the Sample Session pages for Stage II (pages 249–260) that the brackets were used after incidents requiring a break in the session work. The Viewer wisely used the movement brackets to move out of the area, the source of the stimuli in the target that triggered the AI break, the confusion break, and the AOL break.

You can also use movement brackets to change perspective if you feel that the signal line data is beginning to repeat itself. For instance, you keep detecting and decoding the same clusters of color or texture, over and over again, so you use a movement command to change your perspective five hundred feet to the right. Care must be taken when directing movements, simply because it does not take too many movements to completely remove yourself from the target gestalt. The gestalt is defined as having a one-kilometer diameter, or a five-hundred-meter radius, the latter being the invisible straight line drawn from the theoretical center of mass of the principal element of the gestalt to the perimeter of the gestalt. Understanding this, it would take only four or five large moves for you to walk yourself completely out of the target gestalt. Therefore, you must keep track of your movements; move only when you have a reason to move, for example, when the data begins repeating itself, when the signal line runs dark, or when there is a problematic incident such as an AI, EI, or AOL drive. When you move, bear in mind the fact that the curvature of the Earth will affect your ability to perceive; thus, the farther you move from the center of mass of the gestalt, the less usable target data you will likely decode.

Your movements must be deliberate enough, bold enough, to make a difference, yet they must be controlled enough not to remove you from the target altogether. You should be asking yourself right now, "What do I do if I walk myself out of the target?" That's easy. You take the coordinates again, and begin the session from a new position relative to the theoretical center of mass of the principal element of the gestalt. You see, the structure of Coordinate Remote Viewing provides for every eventuality. Every situation has a control mechanism that allows the self-correcting aspect of the structure to bring you back online, on signal line, to do the work of detecting and decoding target data.

Data Bleed-Through

Figure 7.1 depicts the "bleed-through" phenomenon. The structure of Coordinate Remote Viewing generally protects you during the session from any overwhelming abundance of data—it is the beauty of the structure that it keeps you in the flow of data you are asking for, and controls the rate at which it is delivered to you during the session. This flow rate and inherent control is what distinguishes Remote Viewing from any other mechanism for the perception of remote targets. On occasion, an incident in the Remote Viewing structure can manifest that produces certain elements of data that are out of stage, or out of sequence. When this occurs, it is called *bleed-through* or *data bleed-through,* and it means that data expected to be detected and decoded much later in the session has appeared in the session now.

The structure allows for this by directing you to declare the early arrival of the data, in its category, on the right-hand side of the page, or by parenthetically indicating the presence of such data next to the verbal data. For example, in the Sample Session, page 254, on the bottom right, you can see the declaration of the aesthetic impact (AI) "I feel very put upon—agitated." This is a declaration by the Viewer that he recognized a negative response to some aesthetic element in the target, in this case, most likely an energetic that was provoking the response in him. The sense of feeling agitated could be interpreted as an emotional, but the Viewer indicated a physical and emotional mix of feeling agitated, not simply an emotion of anger. If the problem had persisted and caught the Viewer off guard, the condition could have developed into an emo-

FIGURE 7.1 **Data Bleed-Through**

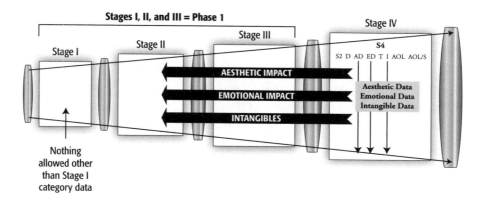

tional impact (EI), but the Viewer felt this had not yet occurred. However, on page 255 of the Sample Session, you can see that the Viewer experienced several more incidents of data bleed-through. In the verbal sensory data decoded in the center of the page, he recorded "monumental" and "pride," both of which are intangible concepts not expected to be present until Stage IV. Because they were present in the current stage, the Viewer noted his awareness of their presence by writing "(S4)," indicating intangible data that, according to the structure, would normally be detected in Stage IV. All the Viewer was doing was letting an analyst or anyone else looking at the session (including himself, for when he began preparing the session summary) know that he recognized that this data was bleeding through from Stage IV. Therefore, the data was not excluded, nor was it ignored; rather, it was recorded with comment.

Farther down the page, the Viewer experienced another incident of bleed-through, a bleed-through of energy that prompted another aesthetic response of "feeling overwhelmed by some energy" and feeling "small, even engulfed by something big." It appears the Viewer was linking this to the declaration made on page 254, because he declared a break in this instance, meaning he felt this was the second time the sensation had appeared, or he felt it was significant enough to warrant the break. Regardless, the presence of such data is significant and must be declared in the manner indicated. The analysis of such bleed-through indicates the data was so abundant in the target that it flowed through the preceding stage lenses and affected the Viewer. Other incidences of this are indicated on pages 256, 258, and 267 of the Stage II process.

Aesthetic Impact (AI)

In normal session structure, aesthetic data relevant to the target occurs only in Stage IV, where a signal line category for aesthetic data exists. As I've indicated, however, AI may occur more or less spontaneously in Stage II, especially when a site, such as the CN Tower in the Sample Session, is involved with very pronounced Stage IV elements. Again, I refer you to page 254 of the Sample Session, where you can see on the right-hand side of the page that the Viewer declared an AI, or aesthetic impact, indicating the presence of aesthetic data significant enough to affect him. Essentially, what happens is that the aesthetic data which should be available when the aperture is open to the Stage IV level bleeds through into the Stage II portion of the session and is noticed by the Viewer. When this bleed-through happens, it is declared as an impact because it is not expected to be present until Stage IV. Thus, the Viewer declared the AI and moved back into the session. In addition, notice that the Viewer objectified what was perceived: "I feel very put upon—agitated." This was his subjective response to the aesthetic data that will be asked for in Stage IV. It was showing up in Stage II because it was pronounced in the target gestalt, and as such, it had to be declared. Think of it as if you were blindfolded and led carefully to the edge of a precipice, where your blindfold was suddenly removed. The rush of awareness, or opening of the aperture, is the aesthetic impact, and it must be declared. It is important to remember that if this same aesthetic impact shows up again, it must be treated as an aesthetic impact break, requiring you to declare a break on the right-hand side of the page.

Some sites seem to consistently invoke similar AI responses in any person Remote Viewing them. For example, the scene of a nuclear blast or a catastrophe will always carry a certain powerful aesthetic value. Still, you must remember that your response to an AI is keyed directly to your own personality and emotional or physical makeup. Therefore, AI responses can differ, sometimes dramatically so, from target to target and Viewer to Viewer.

In the residential classes, I show several movies to reinforce this notion. The short film clips cause you to focus on certain elements of the film, only to surprise you with a sudden opening of the aperture, a sudden awareness of what is happening in the film, the environment of the characters, and so on. When this happens, students in the class always react, some excitedly, some with fear, some with laughter, and some with nothing more than a raised eyebrow. It is truly a subjective response. It is your call—nobody can tell you how you feel or how the target is impacting you—but it must be declared before you can move forward, or the aesthetic will develop into an emotional, a much more difficult impact to contend with. You will have to see what your subjective responses will be over time.

Emotional Impact (EI)

The general flow of impact data in the Remote Viewing session is said to unfold in a predictable manner; that is, dimensional data generally prompts aesthetic data, and aesthetic data generally prompts emotional data. While emotional data (expected to be found in Stage IV) is linked to some emotion present in the target site or in the inhabitants of the target site, an emotional impact indicates a significant presence of emotional data. As with aesthetic impact, when this emotional data is significant to the degree it is bleeding through the preceding stage lenses and "impacting" the Viewer in Stage II or Stage III (long before the Viewer would normally begin the process of detecting and decoding such data), then it must be declared as such on the right-hand side of the page.

Emotional data means data present in the target site, emotional data that may be attached to buildings, grounds, monuments, and the like. Emotional data can also be detected in the inhabitants of the site—the people, the animals, and so on; however, when this data is significant, for example, at ground zero of the World Trade Center site in New York, it can, and often will, bleed through into your session during Stage II and Stage III. When emotional impact occurs, you must declare it before you can move on in the session, or it will increase in severity.

Again, I call your attention to Figure 7.1, which depicts this bleed-through phenomenon. This illustration shows the Stage IV signal line categories for aesthetic, emotional, and intangible data bleeding through into Stage II and Stage III. This bleed-through is indicative of significant elements of these categories of data in the target gestalt. If emotional data is appearing in Stage II, you can bet it is significant in the target, as with aesthetic data or intangibles. In the Sample Session, no emotional impact came about in either Stage II or Stage III; however, multiple occurrences of aesthetic impact did manifest in the session.

Bi-location (Bi-lo)

Bi-location is the phenomenon whereby the Viewer's body begins to manifest the physiological indicators of what is taking place in the target gestalt. For example, your body temperature may rise in response to high temperatures present in the target site, or you may experience nausea because of something moving rapidly, such as a roller coaster or a fast-moving vehicle. This physiological condition can only occur if you have some incident from your past, from your "experience Rolodex," that your conscious mind can reference, producing the physiological effect. When this happens, you must move to the right-hand side of the page you are working on, declare the bi-location, and take a break.

This state normally follows Stage II dimensional data or appears in Stage III. This is a subjective condition and will affect each Viewer differently, or sometimes not at all. As a new Viewer, you should be aware of the potential for this to happen and know what to do if it occurs.

Years ago, I had a student who began experiencing a very unpleasant pain in her head and face during a session. The pain forced her to declare several bi-location breaks during the relatively short, forty-five-minute Stage III session. She did not understand what was happening or why she was experiencing pain; however, she followed the instruction and took a break. Every time she resumed the session, she failed to execute a movement exercise, which kept her in the exact spot within the target where the stimuli were inducing the pain. Thus, she would experience the pain again and again, each time forcing her to break from the target.

During the feedback process, when the feedback video of the target was shown, it became clear to the student why she had been experiencing pain. The target was the "sun catcher" in Daggett, California. The sun catcher is a tall metal structure in the desert, surrounded by computer-controlled mirrors used to focus the energy of the sun onto a boiler. The sun's energy superheats water, creating steam, which powers a turbine, thereby creating electricity for the surrounding community. Why was this student having so much difficulty with this target? The woman approached me at the front of the class immediately after the feedback video was shown. She was grinning from ear to ear, thrilled that she now understood what had happened. "Look at my face!" She said softly, "Can you see the surgery?" I looked but I did not notice anything. "I have had extensive surgery to remove several melanomas; it was a painful process and recovery, leaving me with emotional and physical scars. I have to stay out of the sun as much as possible, and I am very afraid of it, afraid that I will have to go through the surgeries again. That is why I was experiencing pain in this session. It was just as you said. Because I had experienced this before, I began experiencing it again; my body was protecting me from the source of my previous pain, which was the sun."

Let me explain this phenomenon another way. In the Army, if you have soldiers who have been heat casualties, who have suffered from heat stroke or exhaustion, then these soldiers are recorded and watched by the unit leadership. They are watched because they are now the weakest link in the unit when it comes to certain physical and environmental conditions. When you are stricken by extreme temperatures to such a degree that damage occurs to the brain and other body organs, the brain remembers the conditions that preceded these injuries. As an example, let us say that my old Ranger unit is marching in the hot sun of Honduras for fifty kilometers. Tactical road marches of this length were not unusual, and each Ranger would be carrying fifty to ninety pounds of equipment on his back. Each man had his own limits, and this was always a test of those limits. Once in a while, we would find young Rangers who had suffered heat stroke or exhaustion in basic training, or in high school football practice, or as children playing outside, or at some other time. People who have experienced heat exhaustion have a built-in buffer in their brain. Their biological brain developed neural patterns of memory that would trigger a physiological response in their body and begin shutting them down an average of 10 to 15 degrees before the temperature got hot enough to affect their colleagues who had not had a previous experience of heat stroke or heat exhaustion. For the Rangers, this was a good thing, a natural protective measure, a fuse if you will, that prevented them from hurting themselves again. Whenever the temperatures climbed, the gradual physical shutdown of those previously affected would develop like clockwork.

To better understand the bi-location mechanism, let us say that one of these young men is to take a Remote Viewing class. Now, in an altered state of consciousness, this young man begins detecting and decoding waveform information relevant to the target, and the target is the sun catcher in Daggett, California. If, during the session, the young man's biological brain with all its neural diversity begins detecting the waveform similarities of the heat associated with the sun catcher, his brain's pyramidal neurons will begin responding to the stimuli, triggering the neural code via the release of hormones, neurotransmitters, endorphins, and neuropeptides. This rapid unfolding of action potentials, mirroring the blinding speed of the brain to perform at least one quadrillion operations per second (a thousand times more than the best supercomputers), stimulates other physiological functions within the body that begin shutting the body down, protecting the body from injury. The young man becomes aware of this, as an actual physical experience during the session, even though he has no idea why it is happening. As his physiology changes, his hands begin to cramp, his vision blurs, he develops a slight headache—all conditions that existed when he succumbed to heat stroke days, months, or even years before. The condition can be potentially dangerous as the symptoms increase; thus, the recognition of the symptoms necessitates the declaration of a bi-location break.

Once the condition is recognized and the break is taken, it is important to remind yourself that you are merely detecting and decoding waveform data—you are not drowning; you are not overheating; you are not going to burn your skin again in the sun. Once you understand what is happening, you can resume the session and move forward without mishap. However, if you ignore the physiological indicators as they appear, you can draw the experience into a full-blown bi-location, which can be very unpleasant and, in extreme situations, dangerous. For example, if your doctor has advised you to avoid doing anything that would place stress on your heart, and you begin bi-locating in a Remote Viewing session into an element of the target site that triggers the release of adrenaline and speeds the heart, you could drive yourself into a heart attack.

Bi-location is nothing to fear, now that you know that it is possible and you know how to address it. Remember that you will not experience anything that is not in your "experience Rolodex" from the past. If you begin feeling something physical in your body, something that is changing during the session—such as your pulse increasing, your temperature falling or rising, your body sweating—do not let the condition progress further: declare a bi-lo, or bi-location break, and step away from the session for a few minutes. There is no established time limit for a break of this nature. You be the judge, and resume the session when you feel you are ready. When you resume, it is logical that you will want to move away from the source of the stimuli; therefore, you would direct a movement in the target gestalt. Finally, you will get back to the task and have fun.

TRANSITION FROM STAGE II TO STAGE III

You will continue the process of detecting and decoding verbal data in Stage II until the data begins to repeat significantly, even after you have executed several voluntary or involuntary movements, or until the strings of verbal data diminish and the potential or desire to sketch (to capture visual data) increases. Reviewing the Sample Session gives you a good picture of the flow of Stage II data. Initially, there are long strings of verbal data, then a mix of verbal and visual data on pages 251-257 of the Sample Session, until the visual data begins increasing noticeably on page 258 and finally overtakes the verbal data on page 261.

Deciding that the visual data was developing in prime, and that the verbal data was weak or was only supporting the visuals, the Viewer in the Sample Session decided to move to Stage III. A Viewer must always have a reason for moving to the next stage, not because of time or having filled eight to ten pages. Instead, the move is always made based on the following factors: significantly repeating verbal or visual data in the present stage, or the signal line shutting down, offering no perceivable data for the Viewer to decode.

Looking at the Sample Session, you should recognize that the visual data begins to increase significantly, while the verbal data slowly dwindles into dimensional or textural indicators leading to the next visual. Pay particular attention to how the verbal data is slowly replaced by visual data; this is an indicator that it may be time to consider moving to Stage III.

In this example, the Viewer made the decision to move for a combination of reasons. Clearly, there was no shortage of verbal or visual data in the session. However, the Viewer felt the visual data was getting ready to take off, while the verbal data was repeating as well as just offering supporting verbal descriptors of the next visual perception. For this reason, the Viewer decided to move to the next stage. Page 261 of the Sample Session begins Stage III, which we will explore in the next chapter.

8

The Journey Inward Continues: Coordinate Remote Viewing—Stage III

Among scientists are collectors, classifiers, and compulsive tidiers-up; many are detectives by temperament and many are explorers; some are artists and others artisans. There are poet-scientists and philosopher-scientists and even a few mystics.

Peter Brian Medawar, *The Art of the Soluble*

What should you expect in Stage III? Stage III is a visual stage, in which you will detect and decode visual information related to the target. Stage III requires you to objectify this decoded information by developing simple contour, textural, and dimensional sketches of data perceived about the target. Every sketch must be probed and labeled just as you saw in the Sample Session for Stage II. In Stage III, you may encounter everything that potentially manifested itself in Stage II, that is, aesthetic impact, emotional impact, and intangible elements of data that bleed through from Stage IV. You will still be tracking any AOLs that you may have encountered in Stage II.

As Stage III progresses, the aperture opens dramatically wider than in either Stage I or early Stage II. Dimensional data begins to emerge, and the threshold is reached for the transition to Stage III. The shift into full Stage III is triggered by aesthetic impact. It is after this point that the true dimensionality of the site may begin to be expressed. This differs from dimensional elements encountered previously, in that Stage II dimensional data is of individual aspects of the site, while Stage III dimensionality is a composite of inherent site aspects. The concept of the Viewer's perspective must, however, be avoided because, in Stage III, the Viewer has not yet reached the point at which complete comprehension and appreciation of the size, shape, and dimensional composition of the overall site can be ascertained.

Generally, Viewers are not precisely aware of their perspective's relationship with the site and therefore not consciously aware of the true relationship of all the dimensional components they may debrief from Stage III. As discussed in various sections to follow, the Viewer must rely on the various tools available in Stage III to obtain and organize the increased information perceived. Although Stage III can provide a great deal of information about any given site, the goal of Stage III is command of structure.

THE METHOD

With the expansion of the aperture in Stage III, you are prepared to make representations of the site's dimensional aspects with pen on paper. This nonanalytic sketching is a rapidly executed, general idea of the site. In some cases, it may be highly representational of the actual physical appearance of the site, yet in other cases, only portions of the site may appear; for example, in Stage III (pages 261–276 of the Sample Session), the Viewer sketched small elements of the target as well as much larger dimensional aspects of the site. The observed accuracy or aesthetic qualities of a sketch are not particularly important. The main function of the sketch is to stimulate further intimate contact with the signal line while continuing to aid in the suppression of your subjective analytic functioning. Sketches allow you to assemble the waveform data relevant to the target site in such a way as to enhance the connection to the site. If you were to develop only verbal data, you would likely lose interest before you produced twenty-six pages of data, as in the Sample Session. Developing the imagery is fun, and I highly encourage the use and practice of it. As I am a visual Viewer, I cannot imagine living without this element in my sessions.

When beginning Stage III, remember that you should have made your decision to leave Stage II for one of the following reasons: (1) the signal line shut down and, after repeated movements within the target, the flow of available data continued to diminish; (2) the verbal and visual data in Stage II began to repeat itself even after repeated movements in the session; or (3) you noticed that the verbal data in Stage II was diminishing and the visual data was increasing.

STAGE III FORMAT

On page 261 of the Sample Session, you can see that the Viewer has moved to Stage III. Remember that, from this point forward, you must take a new sheet of paper to begin a new stage, and you begin by writing the heading at the top of the page. Your sketches will take up most of the page, and you will continue to use the right-hand side of the page for breaks and movements, and to objectify any other experiences, such as AI, EI, or bi-lo.

Track your AOLs, and take a break if appropriate. Know at all times if you are in AOL drive; if you are, declare it and take a break. When you resume the session, move a direction and a distance to clear yourself from the source of the AOL. If the AOL is persistent, you may need to get up from the work area and take a slightly extended break. Walk outside and try to shake the imagery or verbal data prompting the AOL. Keep detecting and decoding the data without analysis or judgment; keep moving forward in the session.

Be prepared for aesthetic impact. It generally follows Stage II dimensional data, but it will continue in Stage III. Its impact need not be pronounced to be present in your session. You cannot ignore it; you must objectify it. When you recognize it, declare it as an AI and objectify (describe) it on the right-hand side of the page. Remember that you are not required to take a break from it the first time it appears—only the second, third, fourth, and so on.

Also, be prepared for emotional impact. Remember, as with aesthetic impact, this is a sudden widening of the aperture. In this case, it brings on an overwhelming abundance of emotional data. It triggers a subjective response in you: sadness, laughter, tears, fear, and so on. It generally follows aesthetic impact, especially AI that is undeclared and not objectified. Emotional impact also need not be pronounced to be present in your session, and you cannot ignore it; you must objectify it by writing "EI" on the right-hand side of the page. Likewise, you are not required to take a break from it the first time it appears—only the second, third, fourth, and so on.

Keep track of your movements when you make them, and move for a reason. Use the movement brackets and write down your movements on the right-hand side of the page. Be careful not to walk yourself out of the target site. It is fine to go exploring in a target, but know where you are off to and how to keep a general sense of where you are in the target. If you move involuntarily, this is all the more critical. If you have no sense of the principal element of the gestalt, you must be even more deliberate and strategic in your movements.

Be aware of the potential for bi-locations. You can begin manifesting the physiological indicators of some aspect of the target site. If you begin feeling something physical in your body, something that is changing during the session—your pulse increases, your temperature falls or rises, your body sweats—take no chances: declare a bi-lo break, and step away from the session for a while. Remember that you will not experience anything that is not in your "experience Rolodex" from the past. Bi-location is nothing to fear; you know that it is possible, you know what is happening, you declare it, you take a break, you resume when ready, and you move a direction and a distance to another location in the target.

DETECTING AND DECODING, PROBING AND LABELING

As you did in Stage II, you will detect and decode the signal line, which theoretically runs down the center of the page. You will begin by placing the tip of your pen into the signal line at the center of the page, approximately two inches from the bottom of the "S3" heading; then you will close your eyes and wait for visual perceptions. In Stage III, you want and need visual data. If you make it your intention to perceive this data, it will appear.

In the Sample Session, on page 261, you can see this visual data appears as a series of circles surrounded by rectangles and various uniform lines. You can see that the Viewer began dissecting the sketch by probing and labeling the various parts: "fluid," "solid," "hard," "transparent," and "amber." You can also see where the Viewer probed other parts of the sketch for more information. During the probing of the sketch, only descriptions of the form developed; no function was assigned to the sketch, so no AOL needed to be declared.

When the sketch is finished—in other words, when you feel the sketch is complete in your session—you move directly down the page, under the finished sketch an inch or so, and place your pen into the signal line to wait for more visual data. Sometimes this information will come to you in a wonderful rapid flow, while other times, you will have to work for it.

One reason you begin decoding data in Stage III by placing your pen in the center of the page is to encourage you to unfold your sketches without constraint. If you have no limits on the page, you can sketch freely and openly, without reservation (within reason—the page is 8½ x 11 inches).

I had a student in England who was a researcher; I will call him Bill. During training, Bill would sketch these tiny, almost undetectable, and certainly indistinguishable, interpretations of the visual data he perceived during the session. When the trainers reviewed his session, they could not distinguish one sketch from another. From Bill's perspective, it was clear that each sketch was different from the others, because he would reference the sketches in his written summary, but no one else could tell the difference. Most of his sketches could be covered with a dime, a few with a nickel, and occasionally you might have to jump up to a quarter to cover one.

After months of training in different classes, including advanced techniques classes, Bill did begin expanding his drawings. The problem with his expanded drawings was that they still never exceeded the size a coffee mug could cover, and he also began framing the sketches, drawing squares around them in order to contain his work. To overcome this handicap, Bill engaged in hypnotherapy. The therapist, a mutual friend, told me that Bill followed this pattern because he had been humiliated in school by classmates laughing at his early artwork. In response to this, he sketched very small pictures that only he could interpret or appreciate.

His learned coping strategy had led him to sketch small so that no one could criticize, then label completely, and, when called upon to do so, to write about what he saw rather than sketch it. His strategy worked, but it was limiting and drastically reduced his effectiveness as a Viewer. Recognizing this, Bill sought help and broke the patterns associated with his sketching. The lesson here is, sketch big, and do not be afraid to express yourself. When imagery comes to you, develop it fully, broadly, and openly.

VISUAL DATA AND SKETCHES

As you develop your visual modality of perception, the imagery will come more quickly. Do not be alarmed if this doesn't happen overnight. If you are not already highly visual, developing the skill will take time, perhaps dozens of sessions. Remember that the best Remote Viewers are balanced Viewers, those who have skill in all modalities of perception. Few, if any, have ever stepped into Remote Viewing with strong ability in all modalities; however, many have trained themselves to very high levels of competence across the board—you can do the same.

You may be nervous at the prospect of sketching even more heavily than in Stage II, but that is unnecessary. Do not wrap yourself up in the sketching part of Remote Viewing; just draw what you see as best you can. It is the flow of the data that is important, not the quality of the sketch; you can always add clarity by probing and labeling every sketch. This way, even if you sketch an airplane that doesn't look anything like one, as long as you label it as such, it will suffice for now. Too many new Viewers shut down when it comes time to capture the images they perceive. Do not worry about what your artistic skills are; just sketch. In time, you will get much better as you come to rely on the right side of the brain to provide your image data and as you learn to sever the analysis of the left side of the brain during sketching.

The painter, sculptor, and writer Frederick Franck said of sketching, "It is in order to really see ever deeper, ever more intensely, hence to be fully aware and alive, that I draw. I draw what the Chinese call 'The Ten Thousand Things' around me. Drawing is the discipline by which I constantly rediscover the world. I have learned that what I have not drawn, I have never really seen, and that when I start drawing an ordinary thing, I realize how extraordinary it is, sheer miracle."

If you are serious about Remote Viewing, I strongly recommend you take a drawing course or purchase Betty Edwards's *The New Drawing on the Right Side of the Brain*, which is the definitive work for encouraging and teaching you to draw well. Practice, practice, and more practice will help you overcome this fear, which you must master if you are to begin decoding what it is you are seeing with the nonphysical eyes of the Viewer.

SKETCHING EXERCISES

Nonanalytic Sketching

You can improve your sketching ability by practicing these simple exercises on a routine basis. Sketching relies on the right side of the brain and, when done properly, is considered nonanalytic. To become a skilled Viewer, you should practice nonanalytic sketching as much as possible. You can do it anywhere and anytime you have a few spare moments. Try this: Purchase an inexpensive drawing notebook and a pencil or pen you feel comfortable using. Clip some photos out of a magazine and keep them in the notebook or an envelope. I used to keep magazine photographs for practice sketching in an envelope that was always with my drawing materials. With this system in place, you can pull out a photograph and begin sketching it, being careful not to look down at what you are sketching. Granted, your sketches will not look anything like the photos at first, but in time, you will get the hang of it. Actually, your right brain gets the hang of it, and your left analytic brain lets go for a while.

Drawing the Negative Space

Another exercise that will help you with nonanalytic sketching is to draw the negative space. Rather than sketching what you think ought to be there, "forget the name," and simply sketch the contours of what you perceive. Find a simple object that is not completely solid, such as a Windsor chair, a stool, a simple houseplant, a half-open pair of scissors. With this object in front of you, draw the holes or empty spaces. Let your pen or pencil follow the boundaries of the spaces where the object is *not*, instead of focusing on the object itself. You will be amazed at the results! This is nonanalytic sketching, and if you practice it as instructed, you will become a competent sketch artist.

ANALYTICAL OVERLAY (AOL) IN STAGE III

Remember that AOL occurs whenever you assign both form and function to elements of the target you perceive. The second sketch on page 261 of the Sample Session does not take on any element of function. The Viewer sketched the dimension of a rectangle and provided some element of texture; see the striated lines on the lower left of the sketch, which were probed and labeled with descriptors of color ("light blue" and "white"). The main rectangle was decoded to be "grey," and then an interesting development is revealed in the sketch.

Notice how the Viewer decoded an element of dimensional data, "taller" and "lower," in the sketch. In your session, you should look for the same kinds of data, as it will likely be available. Notice the angular drop from the rectangle to the lower element of the sketch. Finally, there are indicators of "white" and "curved metal." The description of "curved metal" is a close call; some may argue that since the Viewer assigned a form, "curved," and then identified the material used, "metal," in this portion of the sketch, the entire sketch should be declared as "AOL, curved metal." I would not support this argument, and this decision comes with the analysis of thousands of sessions.

It is important that you grasp this logic. The Viewer was not dancing with an AOL here; "curved metal" does not constitute an AOL. However, if the Viewer had described a "curved metal beam" or a "curved metal handle," or anything of that sort, then an AOL would have had to be declared. As it stands, "curved metal" is only descriptive of a single element of the sketch and does not cross the line to become an AOL.

Now that I've been clear on this, what would happen if you did declare it as an AOL? Nothing! When you are unsure, it is always better to err on the side of declaring an AOL than to ignore the possibility of one. Declaring an AOL is simply categorizing a piece of data; it does not impede your session when you declare an AOL that is not really an AOL. However, if you fail to declare an AOL when present, it is possible that the undeclared AOL will become more pronounced later in the session.

The second sketch on page 262 of the Sample Session is a series of concentric rings intersected by lines radiating from a large, dark-filled circle at the center. The sketch was probed and labeled with color only, but the Viewer declared an AOL on the right-hand side of the page, indicating that the sketch is of patterned concrete, or "pattern in concrete." This is the subtle indicator that, as the sketch was being developed and labeled, the conscious mind assembled the information at the speed of thought and formed the notion of "pattern in concrete" without actually labeling it as such. You should know that, in your sessions, information may assemble in exactly the same manner. Sometimes ideas, notions, perceptions, thoughts, illusions, and concepts will come at you with blinding speed. In many cases, you will not have the slightest idea where they came from; you'll think you are making it all up—but you cannot make something out of nothing. The stimuli must be present in order to develop the decoded data. Thus, what you perceive must be considered data derived from the signal line of the target until proven otherwise in the session feedback and analysis. Remember that, at this point, you are the observer, collecting information without passing judgment; it is only in the session summary that you begin to analyze your data.

I love Ken Wilber's work, in which he says—and I am paraphrasing here—when you have arrived at an enlightened state, you cannot ever know you have arrived and still exist in the enlightened state. In other words, you can be, but you cannot evaluate the sense of being, or even observe the sense of being, and still be. You can only experience without observation or analysis. Therefore, if you continue looking to see if you have arrived, if you are enlightened, then you cannot ever actually be there.

In some ways, this is analogous to being the observer, the experiencer, versus the evaluator in the Remote Viewing endeavor. You can experience a thing and then report on the experience as an observer. Remember, observers do not look for absolutes, and they know there are always other versions of everything—there are no warranted conclusions or judgments, only data that is observed in the moment. This approach and understanding is the most productive and will yield the most usable data. Evaluation comes after the fact, after the observation of the experience. Stepping in and out of the experience to evaluate or question your perceptions disrupts the flow. It is a fear state and not a flow state, and it makes one more vulnerable to AOL, building a false sense of mastery if you will, an invulnerability within the processes of the conscious mind.

Therefore, you must guard against the tendency to censor or make value judgments regarding your perceptions during a session. The act of buying into your AOLs is a common mistake among new Viewers and, unfortunately, some very experienced ones as well. It means you grab on to some version of the target you feel comfortable with, and drive it home from there. This can occur anywhere in the session, but it usually occurs late in Stage II or somewhere in Stage III as you develop the visual data.

Overcome this tendency by letting go of a number of things seemingly inherent in the human condition, for one thing, the strong desire to be right and to win. Remote Viewing is not a contest; it is not a race; nobody wins anything for "calling the target," and even if you did, statistically, you could only do it a limited number of times in any number of sessions. If you make the objective of Remote Viewing to "call the target," you severely limit its potential.

For instance, let us say the target is the dedication ceremony (an event in past time) of the Eiffel Tower. Early in Stage III, you develop a sketch that you interpret to be "AOL, the Eiffel Tower," and you begin driving this point home through the rest of the session by selecting data and naming what you perceive to fit your notion of the Eiffel Tower. From this point on, you have actually compromised the quality and accuracy of your session work. Your job is to detect and decode the data in the moment, based on the concept of the target as it is assigned. If you accept your AOL *as* the target, every piece of data you develop from this point on will likely be driven from your present references, your experiences with the target, what you have read in books, what you have heard, what you have seen in movies.

In other words, you will fabricate data at the speed of thought, standing heavily on a single element in the decoding triad—imagination. In Figure 8.1, you can see a triad of data sources. At the top is the Matrix Field, where raw, pure

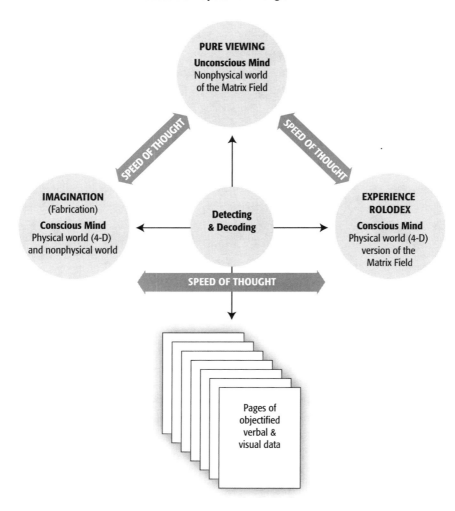

FIGURE 8.1 **Speed-of-Thought Triad**

PURE VIEWING
Unconscious Mind
Nonphysical world
of the Matrix Field

SPEED OF THOUGHT

SPEED OF THOUGHT

IMAGINATION
(Fabrication)
Conscious Mind
Physical world (4-D)
and nonphysical world

Detecting & Decoding

EXPERIENCE ROLODEX
Conscious Mind
Physical world (4-D)
version of the
Matrix Field

SPEED OF THOUGHT

Pages of
objectified
verbal &
visual data

Viewing is conducted through accessing the unconscious mind. On the right is your "experience Rolodex," an aspect of the conscious mind whereby you rely on what you already know to interpret the data derived in the detecting process. This is what allows the decoding of eight-dimensional waveform data into coherent four-dimensional thought forms. If you have no reference for the smell of a rose, if you had never smelled one in your life, you would not be able to decode a sweet, fragrant scent into "AOL, it smells like a rose." You will only recognize and therefore decode what you have references for, and nothing more. Finally, on the left is the imagination or fabrication element of the triad, whereby the conscious mind will take elements of raw, pure Viewing data and, extracting from the experience Rolodex, will build and interpret data at the speed of thought, creating layer after layer of imaginary data. What is important for you to grasp from the model is that all three elements of the triad are critical to the process; all three operate at the same time, all the time. You cannot isolate the imagination element from the other elements; you must learn to use all three in a balanced system of detecting and decoding waveform data.

PURE VIEWING

Right now, the raw, pure Viewing element is likely your least developed aspect. It is by our conditioning in the physical world that this is so. Usually, we get by in the physical world on our ability to recall information and to take action; occasionally, we assemble recalled data to fabricate or imagine, embellishing recalled information to reach a level of creativity. We work the model back and forth between experience and imagination at the speed of thought, and when we do it well, it is labeled "intelligent." When we throw something into the mix that comes from outside ourselves, from this Matrix Field, this unconscious mind, it is labeled "genius." Imagination will always be present, as will pure Viewing and experience; your job as a Remote Viewer is to find balance between the three. You must strengthen what needs to be stronger, and control that which is out of control. If you buy into an AOL, you are empowering the imagination and fabrication element of the triad, giving it more emphasis than the other two elements. If you do this, the system will swing wildly out of control in a matter of moments; remember the model, and keep a balanced flow of decoded data.

Look ahead in the Sample Session. The imagery captured in the sketch on page 269 is repeated on page 270, this time with more detail. You will note there was no declaration of AOL; function was never assigned to either of the sketches. In this example, the Viewer executed "pure Viewing," that is, decoding data without analysis or conclusion—this is exactly what you are trying to do. As a Viewer, you are performing as an instrument, moving at a metronomic cadence, detecting and decoding without too much "thinking" to spoil the effort. The sketch was probed and labeled; you can see new elements of dimension in the sketch, as well as repeating curves and the exact number of clear panels in both sketches (ten panels on page 269 and ten panels on page 270). The Viewer indicated that "solid white metal" was separating the clear elements of the sketch, which adds to the information previously decoded and shows how the aperture was opening for the Viewer.

The second sketch on page 270 of the Sample Session took on absolute form and function as the Viewer produced it. The sketch clearly shows some form of a structure with a glass entryway and people walking in. Outside the Viewer's "field of view," he decoded a jumble of color as "color confusion," meaning he could not distinguish what he was perceiving beyond a mass of color. This, again, is the mark of a controlled and experienced Viewer in that he did not simply make something up because he "thought" it would fit there (such as "colored signs"). He stuck to the protocol, left nothing behind in the decoding process, but worked very diligently to maintain a pure Viewing standard. As soon as he finished the sketch, he accurately declared "AOL, life forms walking inside something." The use of the word "something" is another indicator of nonanalytic viewing: he did not determine what he was looking at based on his perceptions (such as "life forms walking into a sports arena"); he remained nonanalytic.

In another example, at the bottom of page 268 of the Sample Session, you can see a string of color data and a sketch of seven glass cylinders to the left. The sketch is followed by the declaration of "AOL, glasses." The Viewer did a good job of remaining generic; he did not mandate "drinking glasses" or "wine glasses" or anything else. He indicated his perception of seven objects with the function to hold something, most likely liquid, and therefore decoded glasses, and was not specific by design. Are you beginning to get the hang of this? Do you recognize why the Viewer did this? If he had said "AOL, wine glasses" when, in fact, all he perceived were glasses, then he would have self-imposed an AOL drive that would have unfolded for several more pages. If he had let himself say "wine glasses," then he would have produced data to support that. He might have followed that declaration with such things as "a wine cellar," "a wine bottle," "people drinking wine," "a vineyard," or "a party"; you get the idea. It all starts with one unnecessary declaration, and the rest unfolds at the speed of thought. It seems difficult at first, I know, but you will learn this in time and with practice. Do not put words into your session by "thinking what should be there"; decode what comes, when it comes, and as it comes.

Another aspect of the nonanalytic approach of the Remote Viewer is shown on page 275, which opens with a simple textural sketch of a "metal grid" that is "hung between metal bars." The sketch is considerably more simple than most of the Viewer's Stage III sketches. However, it is completely acceptable data and demonstrates, once again, how experienced this Viewer is. You should set your sights to perform in exactly the same manner. Considering the other Stage III sketches, a less experienced Viewer might have omitted this simple sketch in the hope of developing something more complex. Inexperience shows up as impatience with the protocols, a desire to rush to a judgment on the name of the target or to call the target. Patience combined with a methodical application of the protocols will always produce usable data; anything to the contrary is the mark of an amateur.

CHALLENGING THE IMAGE

In your pure Viewing adventure, you will rely on the tools of Remote Viewing to support your role as observer. We've already discussed the use of voluntary movement, using the movement brackets to initiate and note the direction and the distance, as a way of getting away from a source of confusion or AOL drive. You can also use movement to explore a different point of view of an element in the target site, and even move inside an object.

See the second sketch on page 263, which is very detailed. The Viewer did not bother to probe and label either of the sketches on the page because they were both detailed enough to be deemed AOL, which the Viewer declared on the right-hand side of the page. Notice that because railroad tracks appeared in both sketches, he declared "AOL break, a metal bridge over RR tracks." You should understand that the break was declared because of the railroad tracks and not because of the metal bridge—only repeating data requires a break to be taken. Further, because the break had been declared, when the Viewer resumed, he used movement brackets to move a direction and a distance: "[move forward 1000']."

The "move forward" indicates that the Viewer intended to move forward from the perspective indicated in the sketches. It is assumed the Viewer was anchored in an area of the target gestalt that was stimulating this data flow; therefore, from this visual perspective, the Viewer moved across the imagery, over the top of the structures, to see if something was perceivable on the other side of the sketch. This eliminated the AOL of the railroad tracks, the bridge, and the structure.

Look ahead to page 272. A very large sketch developed, encompassing the entire page; this is good Stage III sketching. The Viewer not only captured the dimensional aspects of the target, but he also began decoding energetic data related to the target. He had a hint of energetic data on page 255, decoding "fuzzy energy" back in Stage II, but it unfolded even more on page 272. You can see decoded indicators of "radiant energy" and "bounding or rebounding waves of energy" as descriptors of the energy present. The Viewer's conscious mind finally assembled enough data to generate a specific AOL of "a tower, a radio tower." Again, there is nothing wrong with this—it is a category of data, and the trick is to let go of it from this point forward.

On page 273, the concept of tower repeated during the unfolding of some elaborate visual data. The Viewer sketched what appears to be a tower, with glass and metal and even ribbed concrete as a base for the other components. The Viewer recognized this data as a repeat or carryover from the previous sketch and correctly declared "AOL break, the concrete tower structure."

Upon resuming, the Viewer directed a movement using movement brackets that is called *challenging the image*. Look carefully at the movement directive in the brackets on page 273, whereby the Viewer directed his field of view to "[move inside the object]." The reason the Viewer did this was to challenge what he was perceiving, to test its validity, to see if what was developing was developing because he was unconsciously following the idea of the structure with his visual data, or if the visual data would morph accordingly into data relating to the inside of the structure. This is a kind of test you can execute during your sessions.

The imagery decoded immediately after challenging the image does not necessarily fit any analysis of the sketch of the structure above. This means nothing at this point. Understand that the Viewer may have been perceiving target data related to the inside of the structure from some other elevation or perspective; we do not know this, nor did the Viewer. Thus, the Viewer kept moving forward, decoding what came, as it came, without analysis or judgment. The decoded imagery is unique, appearing tunnel-like and transparent.

The better you become in nonanalytic sketching, the more your work will develop with form and function combined; therefore, almost everything you sketch will be AOL. This is not as bad as it sounds. In time, you will learn to see through AOL to the signal line data. You will learn, in due course, to consciously and unconsciously distinguish between usable AOL and pure analytic fabrication or imagination. Learning to distinguish between these categories of AOL will come during Stage IV training—not right now. However, to plant the seed, in the future, you will be asked to distinguish between analytical overlay (AOL) and analytical overlay signal (AOL/S). The difference between the two comes from your ability to recognize how the waveform data develops in your modality of perception. As you know, AOL is generally considered anything that develops in a fixed, static, lucid, colorful form of imagery. AOL/S is considered imagery that develops as nonstatic, morphing, spinning, dark imagery. Start being aware of how your imagery develops now, so that you can use this awareness in future stages.

DECLARING A HALF STAGE

On page 264 of the Sample Session, the imagery decoded begins with the declaration of "AOL, graffiti words and signs," and the sketch of the area follows this declaration. You can determine this by looking at the start point of the declaration of the AOL, which is well above the sketch itself; the sketch, in this case, is secondary. Why did this happen? It is important that you understand why this develops. The Viewer, in this case, turned the page after moving in the target and theoretically dropped back into the target from a slightly different perspective than before. As the aperture opened, he perceived, most likely in visual form, a montage of imagery that appeared to him to be "graffiti words and signs." Because the imagery was rapid and complex (this is my analysis since we cannot actually know the mind of the Viewer), the Viewer chose to declare the imagery as an AOL rather than sketch the complex words and signs—this was a very logical step. What the Viewer was doing was making a decision not to bog himself down trying to unravel all the details of the graffiti; instead, he relied on the verbal descriptor. What I would like you to make a mental note of is the fact that verbal data was building in the Viewer's mind that was not objectified fully in a sketch, and it was not fully explored verbally. All the Viewer did was to declare it in a few short words, "graffiti words and signs." This is a prelude of something to come in a couple more pages.

After the Viewer developed the first sketch on page 264, he probed and labeled it as "metal link fence" and "pipes overhead," which was quickly declared as an AOL of a chainlink fence. As previously mentioned, the Viewer was feeling some level of data building up that had not yet been objectified. Recognizing this, he decided to use a Stage III and a half (S3½) protocol to objectify his perceptions. All the imagery perceived to this point had led him to conclude that he was "underground or near something underground," which was a piece of verbal data that had not yet been objectified in the session. He went on to describe "trash and graffiti" as well as "paint, oil, and grease," even to say that "this place is filthy"—all of which he had not yet described in those terms.

This is the purpose of the S3½: to use this kind of language to purge what you are feeling is present in the target without trying to call the site. The incorrect procedure for this would have been to say something like "I think I am looking at the railroad station in downtown Washington, D.C., because I think I recognize some of the graffiti or surroundings." To declare the S3½ in this manner would have done nothing to purge data; it would only have served to prompt more AOLs now anchored in Washington, D.C. The manner in which it was declared actually leaves it wide open: an urban area with graffiti, trash, filth, metal fences, railroad tracks, bridges, and structures. This keeps it as good data that has not been corrupted with an assignment of a geographic location.

Use a Stage III-and-a-half (S3½) if you want to. Do not be afraid to pause in the session and write two or three sentences allowing you to objectify what you are feeling about the target site. This is a tool to clear the conduits into the unconscious, to objectify information that is building in the subconscious mind. You can feel it building, but the CRV structure does not permit any decoding of this category of data, hence the Stage III-and-a-half (S3½). It is analogous to draining the garden hose before repositioning the sprinkler. Do this as often as you like, but be careful not to decide what the target is. Use this tool to describe in generic terms what your perceptions of the target site are, always remembering to forget the name of what it is you are looking at. If you are at all confused by this statement, look through the Sample Session at all the S2½, S3½, and S4½ comments to see how the Viewer carefully worded them. You will see that each declaration was crafted so as to be descriptive rather than definitive.

MOVING FORWARD BY GOING BACK TO S2

Go back to Stage II if you need to. Know why you moved to Stage III, and do not be afraid to go back to Stage II if you moved prematurely to Stage III. You are in charge of the session; therefore, if for any reason you feel the need to back up, do so. On page 261 of the Sample Session, the Viewer moved to Stage III, and on page 266, the Viewer made the decision to move back to Stage II to purge the data; on page 267, the data was purged and the coordinates were taken to reestablish signal line contact. Remember, taking the coordinates again is not a requirement. In this case, the Viewer chose to do it because he felt he needed to reconnect to the signal line, and taking the coordinates again is an excellent way to do that. In this example, he could just as easily have continued the Stage II process on page 267 until he felt he had exhausted the flow of verbal data, at which time he could have moved forward to a new page and begun Stage III sketching again. Taking the coordinates again was an option, not a mandate.

On page 265, the Viewer developed a large sketch of a cylinder that was described in the probing as "concrete" and "hollow." As the sketch unfolded, the Viewer perceived what appears to be a base, as it can be interpreted as angular from the sketch, and it was labeled as "concrete." Combining all the visual information, the Viewer declared the sketch an "AOL a concrete cylinder." More accurately, the Viewer could have described the AOL as "AOL, a hollow, concrete cylinder." This would have included all the descriptors used in the decoding and labeling of the sketch. However, this Viewer had been leaving verbal data in a number of areas, not intentionally; nonetheless, there was a great deal of information piling up in the Viewer's subconscious mind, data that did not have any place to be objectified in Stage III. Sensing this, and already having made one attempt at purging the data using S3½ on page 264, the Viewer decided on page 266 to move forward into Stage II again to purge the verbal data from his subconscious mind. This is a rare situation, but it can occur, and when it does, this is the correct course of action.

On page 267, the Viewer reengaged Stage II, detecting and decoding a string of eight pieces of verbal data. It is my analysis at this point that he did not feel he successfully purged the data from the subconscious or was disappointed in the string of data he produced. Therefore, he decided to take the coordinates again, to reestablish target gestalt contact and to control the opening of the target aperture once again. This practice is more common among experienced Viewers. Something does not seem right, you may not be able to pinpoint the problem, so you take the coordinates again, and reenter the session. The Viewer quickly decoded the A/B/C component as "manmade" and "structure," and moved back to a new Stage II near the bottom of the page. This decoding was no change from that produced back on page 249, but even if it had been, the Viewer would have had to move forward in the session from this point. Remember, you should never look back during the session, especially if you take the coordinates again.

On page 268, the Viewer produced several elements of olfactory data—"burnt smell" and "sweet smell"—only to have them prompt the AOL of "food smells," which he declared on the right. Back into the signal line, the Viewer decoded a list of colors, textures, and dimensional data that prompted a sketch made appropriately on the left. Immediately following the sketch, the Viewer declared an "AOL, auditorium or theatre seats," which analytically matches the sketch made on the left.

On page 269, the Viewer moved forward to Stage III once again. Immediately he began sketching wide across the paper, labeling the sketch with indicators of "outside" (if there was an outside, it implies there was an inside). The sketch was also labeled to include a "solid column" and something that was "polished," "linear," "patterned," and "grained." Looking at the sketch, it is not clear what the descriptors "linear," "patterned," and "grained" pertain to, so in the analysis, I would assume they reference some aspect of the top sketch. You should learn from this observation that listing verbal data without drawing an arrow to what is being described may cause some confusion.

PROGRESSING THROUGH STAGE III

Sketch like crazy; leave nothing in the Matrix Field, nothing in the conceptual illusion of the conscious mind. Objectify everything you perceive, and be grateful for all that you perceive. In Stage III, if you do not write it down, you will miss half of your session. And if you do not write it down, it does not count. Sketch everything, and probe and label everything.

Even if you are an excellent sketch artist, you can often sketch objects that are incomplete. The best way to open the aperture on a piece of visual data is to place your pen directly onto the sketch and probe it. Probing within the sketch, on the lines of the sketch, and around the sketch intensifies the signal line, developing additional textural, energetic, mass, and density data, among other things.

If it has form and function, it is an AOL. No judgment, no analysis, no decision about anything being target data or not—if you verbally or visually develop anything that has form and function combined, it is an AOL. In Stage III, you are asking for visual data. Obviously, the better you get at decoding and objectifying the eight-dimensional waveform data, the more AOLs you will have. Even if you declare the AOL for something you give form and function to, probe and label everything to let yourself and everyone else know exactly what you are perceiving.

On page 271, the target's visual data began expanding rapidly into a sketch the Viewer declared as "AOL, metal escalators." The sketch was well-made, simple, complete, and it was probed and labeled. The second sketch on the page was unique in the session. From an analytic perspective, it seems to assemble dimensional elements already captured in sketches on pages 269 and 270, although the point of view in this sketch appears much farther away, perhaps even from the outside. Some portion of the sketch was labeled as "red metal," and the Viewer declared the entire sketch as "AOL, a red metal structure." Look closely at the sketch to see the probe marks, which are an indicator that the Viewer worked himself all over the sketch before determining it was some form of "structure."

On page 274, the Viewer began sketching a curved surface, a "wall" that was decoded to have several large maps hanging on it. This labeling, "large map on walls and floor," should have been declared as an AOL, but the Viewer failed to do this, most likely because he was mentally preparing to objectify his perceptions in another S3½. Structurally, this failure to declare the AOL of the maps, wall, and floor is not good; however, it is understood that the Viewer's mind was engaged in stitching together a number of previous sketches from pages 258, 260, and 269–273, depicting circles or circular structures. Recognizing this building up, the Viewer wisely used the S3½ to purge this data and move forward in the session. The second sketch on page 274 zeroes in on an element of the interior of the structure, decoded as "AOL, a table and chair." What is interesting about this sketch is the Viewer's attempt at some distant perspective; notice the arrows showing something "far away outside."

The second sketch on page 275 depicts a curved-wall structure composed of glass panels with life forms looking through them. There is a structural pillar in the sketch, on the right-hand side of the curved wall. If you look closely, you can see that the Viewer probed all over the sketch for more information, but settled on the declaration of "AOL, a gathering of people looking out a set of windows."

TRANSITION FROM STAGE III TO STAGE IV

Let us review the bidding thus far. Look back at the Stage II and Stage III pages of the Sample Session (pages 249–276) to see the flow of the visual data. What trends do you see? Do you understand why the Viewer made the decision he made on page 276. Clearly, the signal line was not shutting down for this Viewer; the visual data just kept coming.

However, the data was beginning to repeat itself. The elements of circular structures, glass, people, wooden tables, chairs, maps, walls, and other dimensional indicators were repeating in various forms. It was a subjective call by the Viewer—he was in charge of his session, and he had developed fourteen pages of Stage III data to this point; it was time to move to the next stage and begin opening the aperture to the next widest level of perception. As such, the Viewer finished his Stage III data by once again declaring S3½, indicating his sense of this target as "a place for tourists, with places to eat, purchase, and observe." He continued to objectify "there is some other purpose to this target as well" and finished the page with a note to himself that he was moving forward to Stage IV.

Your decision to move from Stage III to Stage IV must follow some logic. While time is always a factor in completing a CRV session in ninety minutes, it is not generally considered a suitable criterion for moving to Stage IV. This said, there might come a time when you experience an overwhelming abundance of data in Stage III such that you could go on sketching almost indefinitely. If you sense this is the case, you may have to end the stage and move forward in the session. The understanding would be to save the additional visual data for the widest opening of the aperture in Stage VI. Since eight to ten pages is the goal in Stage III, should you exceed this number by three or four pages, you may want to look at moving forward to Stage IV. This situation will likely be the great exception rather than the rule. For most, the signal line data will begin to slow down or darken; you will have to work harder and harder to keep the flow of visual data moving. This diminished data flow manifests itself in a number of ways in the session.

For some, the imagery perceived will become smaller and smaller. It is as if you are zeroing in on smaller aspects of the gestalt rather than looking at the bigger picture. Your sketches will become smaller and more focused. Instead of sketching the entire structure or object, you may begin sketching a corner of it or a place where two different materials join together. When every sketch takes on this perspective, it is time to move to Stage IV.

Others will find that the material they are sketching begins to repeat. Initially, it may seem as if the sketches are changing in size or content; however, in a few pages, they will begin to repeat with limited shift in angle of perception. When this condition occurs, it is time to move to Stage IV.

Every condition listed may have its variations as it applies to your session; you are always in charge of the session, and as such, you must have a system for deciding exactly when it is time to move to the next stage. What is provided here is a guideline to be followed by new Viewers. In time, you will know when it is time to move to the next stage, and it will not matter to you if you have ten pages of visual data or not. You will know it is time to open the aperture to the next level and begin decoding data beyond the surfaces of the target. The conditions listed are decision points, navigation aids for those who need them. There are many rules for you to follow right now. Learn them, and you will move smoothly through the sessions. Rest assured, you will find your own level in all of this and fly through the sessions easily and accurately.

9

The Journey Inward Continues:
Coordinate Remote Viewing—Stage IV

*Sit down before fact like a little child, and be prepared
to give up every preconceived notion. Follow humbly wherever
and to whatever abyss Nature leads, or you shall learn nothing.*

T. H. Huxley

Stage IV is a verbally driven stage much like Stage II; the unique difference is the Viewer's quest to detect and decode data that is linked to information contained beyond the surfaces of the target site. This does not imply that the decoded data will refer to an underground site or facilities; it implies the nature of the data that is to be decoded by the Viewer: intangible, emotional, and aesthetic data, rather than textures, contour, colors, and other data of this ilk. Figure 9.1 is a graphic representation of the notion that we perceive the many dimensions or layers of existence through progressive levels of awareness.

In Stages I through III of Coordinate Remote Viewing, you are asked to detect and decode waveform data relevant to what you would find if you were to stand in a target site and look around. You would be able to smell, taste, and hear; you could feel texture and temperature, perceive dimension, and feel energetic data. However, in Stages I through III, you are not required to look for waveform data pertaining to aesthetic aspects of the target or emotions present in the target; you are not required to seek out abstract intangible data relating to the target. As such, your work in the early stages of CRV is considered Level 1 Viewing. Stage IV begins your journey beyond the visible surfaces of a target

FIGURE 9.1 **Seeing in Layers**

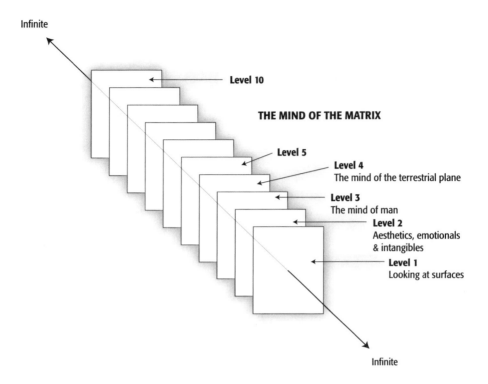

Infinite

Level 10

THE MIND OF THE MATRIX

Level 5

Level 4
The mind of the terrestrial plane

Level 3
The mind of man

Level 2
Aesthetics, emotionals
& intangibles

Level 1
Looking at surfaces

Infinite

to see into the 99.9 percent space we all are. Here, at Level 2 Viewing, you will detect the kinds of data you would not be able to touch in the physical world. If you move beyond your Coordinate Remote Viewing training into the world of the Extended Remote Viewer, you will begin Viewing, at Level 3, into the collective mind of humanity, the electrostatic field of the planet, and beyond. At Level 4 Viewing, you begin knowing the mind of the terrestrial plane, the mind of the planet, also known as the Gaia or Earth energies. Levels 5 through 10 of Viewing span the different levels of the Matrix Field of all creation, and end at Level 10 only because we then stand at the edge of knowledge, without the language to describe what we perceive beyond this conceptual boundary. Standing at this illusionary veil, we share a common ignorance—no language, no reference, only the communal intention that the journey must continue. Your journey has just begun; work hard so that you may know the way to the edge of knowledge and beyond on the return to the eternal return.

THE METHOD

To review, you will move forward in the session from Stage III to the next widest opening of the aperture, Stage IV, upon experiencing any of the following conditions, either independently or in consonance with others, in Stage III. If you are spending too much time in Stage III, to wit, you have developed pages well beyond the required eight to ten pages—move to Stage IV. If you find it is taking you more than thirty minutes to complete eight to ten pages of sketches—move to Stage IV. If the visual data sketched is shrinking, or if your perspective is closing in to very narrow fields of view in the target—move to Stage IV. If you feel the imagery you are sketching is repeating endlessly, and despite multiple movement exercises, the imagery is not shifting—move to Stage IV.

In Stage IV, you will be detecting and decoding signal line data from an array of signal line categories that form the Stage IV matrix. This format is illustrated in Figure 9.2 and will be further described shortly, as will each of the eight signal line categories. The method of progressing through the signal line

FIGURE 9.2 **Stage IV Matrix**

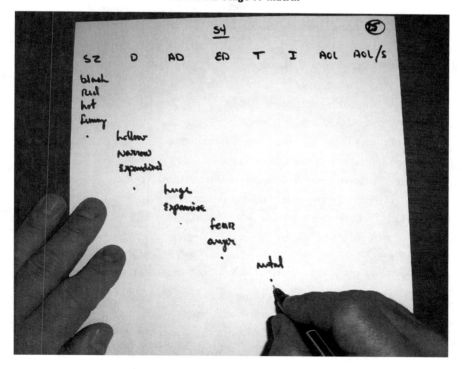

categories is designed to facilitate and heighten the perception of nonphysical information in the target site: the aesthetic, emotional, and intangible aspects present. You begin detecting data by placing the tip of your pen in the first signal line category, S2, and you decode the data you perceive in a descending vertical line down the page. Any time your pen is touching the page in the signal line category, you are considered in signal line contact or in the detect mode on the page. Lifting your pen from the page is analogous to breaking signal line contact. Therefore, working in Stage IV requires that your pen is on the page and your eyes are closed to facilitate the detecting of waveform expressions of data. You detect and decode data in S2 until the flow of this data stops. When it stops, you move your pen laterally to the right and place it in the next signal line category, D, to begin detecting and decoding data.

Movement from left to right across the page changes the categories of data you will perceive. You permit only the decoding of data that is perceived in the signal line category you are working in. In other words, if you are decoding data in the dimensional category and you suddenly begin perceiving intangible data, you ignore it until you move forward to the "intangible category, I." If the data is significant, it will be present when you get to that category; in fact, it is often the very first piece of data you decode when you arrive at that category. Data arriving out of category is the most common pitfall of Stage IV. As long as you remember that you do not step out of the category to list data that is not part of the category you're working in, moving neither forward nor backward between the categories, then you will be fine. If data belonging in another category drops onto the page (for instance, a dimensional is decoded in the tangible category), all you do is parenthetically enclose the category abbreviation (D) next to that piece of data, and keep working.

In every category, you maintain a metronomic cadence, eight to ten seconds between elements of data decoded. If the time between decoded elements of data exceeds ten seconds, you should remove your pen from this signal line category and move it laterally to the right, to the next category of data. Failing to follow a suitable pacing through the matrix will prompt the unnecessary development of AOL. Figure 9.3 illustrates the process, which is called *movement through the matrix* of Stage IV. You keep this process of movement through the matrix until you complete "one pass" through the matrix. One pass is defined as the complete movement through all signal line categories of data from top to bottom and left to right. This means from S2

FIGURE 9.3 **Beginning Another Pass through the S4 Matrix**

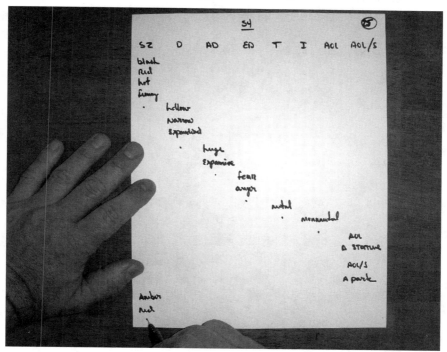

to AOL/S, whether or not you detect data in all the signal line categories. Upon completion of one pass through the matrix, as shown in Figure 9.3, you reenter the first signal line category, S2, on the left-hand side of the page, and start making another pass through the matrix. You continue making passes through the matrix for eight to ten pages, or until the signal line data shuts down in all the categories.

Remember that before you consider your Stage IV complete, you logically make several attempts to move within the target site, just as you did in earlier stages. Moving should change your perspective enough to allow you to detect and decode additional elements of data in the various signal line categories. However, the aperture of the Stage IV lens is not the widest of the CRV structure, and therefore, you will only be able to see what the unconscious mind can present through this aperture, no matter how many movements you make.

Everything you have learned up to this point in the CRV protocol remains the same. You still keep track of AOL, AOL drive, AI, EI, all movements, bi-locations, miscellaneous breaks, such as confusion breaks, too-much breaks, and rest breaks, and any other condition that may arise in the conduct of the session. You are in charge of your session; keep track of everything, keep moving forward, and be meticulous in your structure. As you read this chapter, refer to pages 277 through 294 of the Sample Session to see what a complete Stage IV can look like.

STAGE IV FORMAT

You begin Stage IV, as any other stage in CRV, by numbering the page and indicating that you are working in Stage IV by writing "<u>S4</u>" at the top center of the page. As in the previous stages, you will sketch on the left and write or declare breaks, AOL, and the like, on the right of the page. However, in Stage IV, the Stage IV matrix will also prescribe the layout of your work on the page and the order of your detecting and decoding as you progress through this stage. You can think of the Stage IV matrix as being

FIGURE 9.4 **Sketching in Stage IV**

superimposed over the general page layout of sketching on the left, declaring breaks and such on the right.

SKETCHING IN STAGE IV

In Figure 9.4, you can see how the Viewer, working in the tangible data category, stopped and moved slightly to the left to complete a form-and-function sketch. Notice where the image is placed on the page. Because Stage IV is a verbally driven stage, there is limited space for sketches. Ideally, you purged all the major visual data in Stage III; therefore, remaining visual data should be minimal but will undoubtedly be present. If you feel an overwhelming desire to sketch large and this desire returns frequently in Stage IV, you may need to move forward into Stage III again and purge this data. I have discussed this several times before, and the option to move forward into the previous stage is always with you in CRV.

The Stage IV sketches should be simple contour and textural sketches that are, as always, probed and labeled to maximize the amount of information you

FIGURE 9.5 **Declaring AOL**

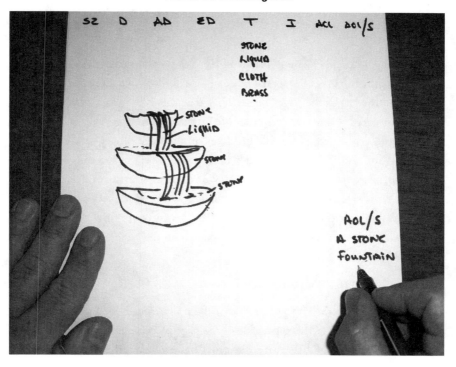

FIGURE 9.6 **Structural Spacing and Order**

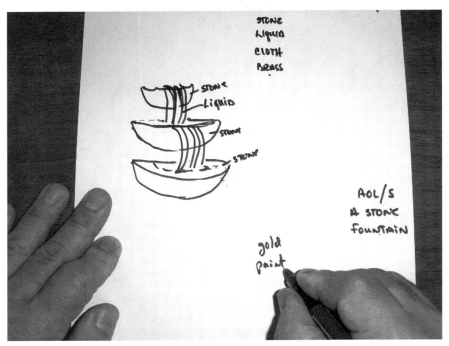

can extract from them. There is a spacing issue when you sketch. Notice that the sketch in Figure 9.5 takes the spatial place of decoded verbal data in the signal line category on the left of the page. The same is true across the board in all stages of CRV; this structural spacing and order are critical to the protocol. Without this sense of order, there would literally be chaos on the page. When you look at the Sample Session and the figures provided here, you can see the neat and orderly appearance of the data; you should try to mirror these in your work. In Figure 9.6, the Viewer has completed the sketch on the left, declared the AOL on the right, and is now rejoining the signal line in the category he was working in before he left it to sketch. Notice the clear and readable spacing on the page.

THE RIGHT-HAND SIDE OF THE PAGE IN STAGE IV

A special note about the right-hand side of the page in Stage IV (and this will be true in Stage VI as well): the entire side of the page is considered a "free zone," for lack of a better phrase. This means the structure recognizes there can potentially be so much data filling this area that it would be impossible to keep AOL and AOL/S listed in their separate signal line categories on this side of the page and still make room for the orderly listing of everything that can find its way here, such as AI declarations, AI breaks, EI declarations, EI breaks, bi-location declarations, bi-location breaks, miscellaneous breaks, resumes, and movements. Because it can get crowded here, you keep AOL and AOL/S signal line categories separated by labeling them with their designations of "AOL" or "AOL/S." You can see on the Stage IV pages (278–293 of the Sample Session), how much information is listed on the right and how the category designations serve to identify them for analytical use.

SIGNAL LINE CATEGORIES IN THE STAGE IV MATRIX

The word "matrix" in this context refers only to the signal line categories used in the Stage IV process of CRV. The matrix format is shown beginning on page 277 of the Sample Session. You create the matrix format by listing each of the abbreviations for the signal line categories from left to right across the top of the page as follows: S2, D, AD, ED, T, I, AOL, and AOL/S. This format must be across the top of every page in Stage IV for as many pages as you develop data, which will be up to eight to ten pages. You will work top to bottom and left to right across the matrix.

Signal line categories refer to each of the categories of data you will detect and decode. They are Stage II verbal sensory data (S2), dimensional data (D), aesthetic data (AD), emotional data (ED), tangible data (T), intangible data (I), analytical overlay (AOL), and analytical overlay signal (AOL/S). Each of the categories of data is considered to have an imaginary vertical line dropping from the abbreviations, flowing to the bottom of the page. Each time your pen enters one of these imaginary vertical lines (probing), you are theoretically asking for data pertaining to that category to be made available to you from the Matrix Field of the unconscious mind.

Stage II Verbal Sensory Data (S2)

This category of signal line data contains exactly the same subelements of data required in Stage II, with one exception—dimensional data. As you place the tip of your pen into this signal line category, you may begin decoding data relevant to color, taste, temperature, sound, smell, texture, and energetic data pertaining to the target gestalt.

In the Sample Session, the Viewer began Stage IV on page 277; he completed the heading and began decoding S2 data at the top left of the page. He developed a string of verbal sensory data and included olfactory descriptors. If he had decoded "natural" and left it at that, it would not have been clear whether he was decoding a smell, a taste, a texture, and so on. Being complete in this manner is the mark of a skilled Viewer. The string of data prompted a form-and-function (AOL) concept of a restaurant, and it was objectified on the right. Notice the spacing in the page where the Viewer rejoined the signal line category in the S2 column. Another string of verbal data was detected and decoded, and then a sketch was developed on the left-hand side of the page. As the sketch was probed and labeled, the Viewer developed a form-and-function concept of the sketch, declaring "AOL, a doorway or main entrance."

Next, the Viewer moved to page 278. Understand that the Viewer had not completed the flow of data in S2; instead, he ran out of room on page 277. Therefore, he was still working in the S2 signal line category of data and had to rejoin the same signal line category until the flow of data from that category was exhausted. Also remember that on each new page, you must write the Stage IV matrix of signal line categories across the top under the S4 heading.

Farther down on page 278, two elements of energetic data were decoded, and the Viewer moved to the right to objectify "AOL, electromagnetic energy associated with this structure." Recognizing that the "structure" elements combined with "energetics" had appeared before, the Viewer declared "AOL break, the tower structure," probably related to the tower sketched on pages 255 and 272, and perhaps page 273 as well. Remember that you are tracking AOL drive, the same AOL repeating itself, for the entire session and not just within the stage you are currently working in. Upon resuming the session, the Viewer logically moved, and then reentered the same signal line category he was working in before the break. He decoded two additional pieces of data, and then the signal line ran dark; notice the small dot on the page where the Viewer rested his pen in the detect mode. He waited here for three to five seconds without detecting any more S2 category data, so he moved laterally to the next signal line category of data—dimensional data (D).

Dimensional Data (D)

In Stage IV, dimensional data is separated from the S2 verbal category of data. It is a freestanding category in Stage IV because it helps initiate the flow of nonphysical information about the target in the signal line categories that follow. There is no change in the definition from previous Stage II data. It is, however, a continuation of this data, looking through a much wider lens than before. You place your pen into this signal category and ask for data that can be detected and decoded into mass and density, contour, verticals, diagonals, horizontals, curves, and arches.

On page 278 of the Sample Session, beginning with "tall," three elements of dimensional data were decoded, and then something different occurred. The Viewer decoded a piece of data, "compartmentalized," and wrote parenthetically "(I)." This piece of data was decoded out of signal line category. It was not placed here intentionally. It was instead decoded quickly, and after it was on the page, the Viewer recognized that it belonged to the intangible category. This may happen to you, and it may happen frequently, especially as you increase your detecting and decoding cadence. When it happens, and you catch it, do as the Viewer did here and indicate your awareness of it by parenthetically enclosing the abbreviation for the relevant signal line category. The Viewer continued at the top of page 279 in the dimensional category and decoded a string of data until the signal line ran dark. He then moved to the next category of data.

Aesthetic Data (AD)

In earlier chapters, I discussed the notion that dimensional data prompts aesthetic evaluation, and that an aesthetic evaluation will usually prompt an emotional response. The purpose of Stage IV is to begin looking beyond the surfaces to the nonphysical aspects of the target. To facilitate this, the signal line category of dimensional data is separated from the normal Stage II categories of data. This will prompt a heavier signal line flow of aesthetic data. In Stage IV, you are asking for aesthetic data that is present in the target site. This means data relating to a sense of beauty, awe, artistic quality, inspiration. Notice in the Sample Session, on pages 279, 280, 284, and 288, the kinds of words found in the AD category: "ornate," "stunning," "beautiful," "uniform," "breathtaking," "modern," "balanced."

You are not asking for aesthetic impact, and you must understand this. Aesthetic data will be present all over the target (depending on the target and your response to it). For example, there will be distinctly different levels of aesthetic data for an art museum and a sandbar in the middle of a river. However, if you begin responding to the aesthetic data in such a way that it "impacts" you, then you must move to the right-hand side of the page and declare an aesthetic impact (AI) before moving on in the session. If this impact is a continuation of one that developed earlier in the session as bleed-through data, you must declare an AI break and follow the protocol from there, which should include a movement exercise complete with a direction and a distance after you resume.

You can see on page 280 that the Viewer developed a string of aesthetic data, "comfortable, formal, uniform, crisp, pleasing," and declared "AI, I feel like I am very high up—like I might fall." It is interesting to note that the verbal descriptors used in this session do not correspond with the "impact" the Viewer experienced. This can happen, and you should not expect a series of decoded data to prompt any predictable kind of impact. This kind of response is subjective, and each session will be different, as will each target. If you look for patterned responses to certain kinds of words, you will begin self-imposing impact in your sessions, and this would not be desirable.

After declaring the impact on the right, the Viewer rejoined the signal line category and decoded one more piece of data before the signal line ran dark, and he shifted to the next category of data.

Emotional Data (ED)

Remember that dimensional data prompts aesthetic data, which prompts emotional data, the natural sequence in human interpretation. Emotional data is defined as emotions that are present in elements of the target site or are present in the inhabitants of the target site.

In the book *Psychic Warrior*, I recount a story of working a military training target. In the session, I began weeping because I became overwhelmed by the emotions present in the walls of the Nazi death camp at Dachau. This was not a decoding of "spirits" present or of leftover "heavy energy"; it was the remembrance of the structures, the grounds, the earth, the trees, and so on. It was as if the buildings themselves were sad and they could not forget.

There is another kind of emotional data that can be present. It relates to the inhabitants of the site, but you need not assume it comes from the currently living inhabitants of the site. Emotional data can be indicative of the spirit of those who departed from a specific place or those who were somehow called together in another place to be remembered. If you visit the black granite wall of the Vietnam Memorial in Washington, D.C., you may have the sensation of decoding emotions present in a seemingly inanimate object.

I have walked this wall several times, and I included the experience in several Remote Viewing classes I taught in the D.C. area. It begins with the dimensional data: you descend below the visible surface of the Mall while following a black wall lined with the names of the sixty-five thousand honored dead. The latter is an aesthetic element of data, which prompts the flow of emotional data. You are carried deeper with each step, and with each step, the emotions present become heavier. When you exit the other side, it is rare to see a dry eye in man, woman, or child. Even those who know nothing of the war sense the emotional energy present, and it is so pronounced that you rarely, if ever, escape the emotional impact of the site. That is how the detecting and decoding process works in a target distant in space-time as well. It does not matter if the target is five thousand miles away or if it is in the next room; it works the same, since it is all from the Matrix Field.

Tangible Data (T)

Tangible data in Stage IV refers to objects in or characteristics of the site that are "touchable." This category of data represents waveform expressions of target data that could be touched if you were physically present in the target site.

Think about how exceptional the CRV structure is at this point. Look at what is happening. You have been led on a journey to detect and decode waveform expressions of target data that is far distant in space-time. You have decoded distinct sensory elements, such as colors, textures, and sounds; visual elements; then dimensional data; aesthetic data; and the emotional data that follows.

Essentially, at this point in the session, you should be completely stretched as a Remote Viewer. It can be said that you are "strung out" in the session, and you will need to be grounded before you can effectively assemble other elements of data in the session. For those of you who are technophiles, being "strung out" in a session is a bit like having a bad ground or ground loop.

You "ground yourself" in order to eliminate the "ground loop" and hum in your decoding abilities. The brilliant men who created most of the CRV structure recognized the need for grounding at this point, and in Stage IV, they placed a grounding mechanism: detecting and decoding tangible elements of data in the target site. You do this by energetically touching objects in or characteristics of the target site that can be considered physical, thereby reconnecting with the physical aspects of the target site and thus staying balanced in the RV process. I am continually amazed by what the early Remote Viewers and researchers came up with. It is especially astonishing considering that, at the time, they did not really understand why they were coming up with it.

I want to add a little more on this subject to clarify the difference between AOL and tangible data in Stage IV. Let us say I am perceiving my office chair, and I decode such tangible data as leather, metal, brass, plastic, glue, chrome, aluminum, paper, and wood. As long as I continue perceiving the chair this way, I am accurately listing tangible data. However, if the tangible data springs together into a form-and-function image of "office chair," then it is no longer only tangible data; it is now "AOL, an office chair." Again, there is nothing wrong with this. It would not be considered unusual for you to list a string of tangible data as I did and have a corresponding AOL generate quickly behind it. It could also work in the reverse, whereby you have the AOL of the office chair, for example, and then you dissect the image into the long list of tangible data supporting this AOL; both are acceptable means of decoding data.

Once you have detected and decoded signal line data in the tangible category and the signal line runs dark (see page 281 of the Sample Session), you move to the next category.

Intangible Data (I)

In Stage IV, intangible data is considered a use of language that is broad and abstract in its description of the various elements of the target site, such as "military," "industrial," "enforcement," "artistic," "religious," "honorary," "academic"—and about a thousand other words that can be used to describe intangible aspects of the physical world around us. How this category of data unfolds in structure is in consonance with the rest of the Stage IV strategy. By the time you get to the intangible category of data, you have been "strung out" and "grounded," and now you are asked to figuratively rise up above it all and decode some major conceptual elements of the target that tie the entire process together. If you have a strong command of language, this process is a welcome challenge; otherwise, you may find your strings of intangible data are short. On page 281 of the Sample Session, you can see the kinds of words that describe intangible data: "entertainment," "demonstrate," "inspire," "communication," and so on.

Analytical Overlay (AOL)

There is no change to the definition or understanding of AOL that you have learned thus far. However, in Stage IV, you are asked to divide it into two different categories of AOL based on your understanding of how the imagery appears to you. To be sure, this is a highly subjective process, but it is of tremendous value for you to know how the imagery comes to you, especially in Stage VI, when you begin assembling imagery into detailed renderings.

Any imagery data you perceive in this signal line category that is fixed, static, lucid, nonchanging, and colorful, or various combinations of these, is considered AOL. This category of AOL is heavily weighted as imagination or fabrication. It can also be said that data appearing in two-dimensional postcard form, as if you are looking at a picture, should be decoded as AOL.

Analytical Overlay Signal (AOL/S)

AOL signal is defined as imagery that is broken, fleeting, spinning, morphing, dark, grainy, or fragmented. This decoded form-and-function imagery seldom appears as a seamless image. Instead, it appears much as the imagery in the movie *Minority Report* appeared to the "precognitives" looking into the future. If you saw the movie, you may remember how the imagery was fragmented and fleeting. The role of police chief Anderton, played by Tom Cruise, was to assemble the imagery and interpret it analytically so that it could be acted upon to stop a crime before it was committed. In this regard, it was an excellent Remote Viewing movie. The police required at least two of the three Viewers (precognitives) to agree on the imagery, and all data was subjected to analysis before sense could be made of it. The Viewers did not play any analytic role in their sessions; they just did the Viewing and left the analysis to someone else—pure Viewing.

Throughout Stage IV, AOL and AOL/S are decoded on the right-hand side of the page anytime they appear, as on the bottom of page 281 in the Sample Session. They are also separated out as unique signal line categories of data that you will deliberately detect and decode. On page 283 of the Sample Session, the Viewer declared "AOL, a security guard or policeman." Notice the small dot indicating he placed his pen back into the AOL/S category of data, and this time, the signal line ran dark.

This was the first completion of a run through the matrix, and the data showed no signs of slowing down. To begin his second pass, the Viewer executed what has been called a "carriage return," analogous to the mechanics of a typewriter, before decoding S2 data again. Notice on page 291 that the Viewer began a fourth pass through the Stage IV matrix, and on page 293, a fifth. This is the process you will use until it becomes obvious that it is time to move on to Stage V.

Notice in the Sample Session that previously discussed tools showed up in Stage IV. On page 290, the Viewer decoded an AOL/S of "a crown," but he did not attempt to sketch it. Instead, he used a familiar tool, declaring S4½: "I have a sense the target gestalt is linked to a large structure that serves multiple purposes; tourism, communications, national pride, and corporate interests." Next on the page, he declared a bi-location break because his "head is hurting—vibrating like I am near a microwave oven." This is a good example of how a bi-location manifests the physiological indicators in the Viewer's body of something taking place in the target site. The Viewer had been repeatedly decoding high levels of energy throughout the session. As he continued decoding this data, his body began manifesting the physiological indicators for which he had a past reference: a headache relating to ambient energy radiating from a microwave oven at home. Acting wisely, the Viewer wasted no time in taking a break from these sensations and temporarily terminated the signal line contact that was causing the pain.

TRANSITION FROM STAGE IV TO STAGE V

On page 293 of the Sample Session, the decoded data became sparser as the Viewer quickly moved across the categories. He decoded a total of four tangibles and one intangible before completing the fourth pass through the matrix and beginning the fifth. A string of S2 data completes page 293, and page 294 actually terminates the Stage IV segment of this session.

Be aware of how the signal line will manifest its completion in Stage IV. As in Stages II and III, you must come to understand when it is time for you to move to the next stage. Sometimes the data in each of the signal line categories will repeat itself, meaning it is time to move to Stage V. Other times, the data will change each time you move, but it will change only slightly and will continue at a trickle, slowing you down in the session. Still other times, the signal categories will simply dry up and produce no further data. When you place your pen into the categories, nothing comes. You will move laterally to the next category, and again, nothing comes. You may make several passes through the matrix, producing nothing, and when this happens, you should move to Stage V.

You will notice that the Viewer in the Sample Session produced a great number of pages of data in Stage IV, eighteen, to be exact. This is a very long Stage IV, but as long as the data is coming, and you are moving at a solid metronomic cadence, continuing is fine. The recommended time you should spend in Stage

IV is approximately fifteen minutes, keeping in mind that your total time for the CRV session is ninety minutes. However, the time limits are guidelines and not rules. If the data is coming strong, then keep decoding it. If it is interrupted, if it is repeating, or if it stops, then move to Stage V.

10

The Journey Inward Continues: Coordinate Remote Viewing—Stage V

Lulled in the countless chambers of the brain,
Our thoughts are linked by many a hidden chain;
Awake but one, and lo, what myriads rise!

Alexander Pope

Stage V is a relatively simple stage to understand and to implement. It deals with language as a tool for extracting the hidden data locked into the biological brain of the Viewer. As such, the technological approach itself is straightforward; there are not a lot of moving pieces to the structure of this stage. However, it is imperative that you understand what you are doing and why you are doing it, and this chapter will cover this objective as thoroughly as possible.

In this chapter, you will come to understand the deep mystery of the human brain and the miracle of language in understanding what lies beneath the surface in each of us. I have to say, when I was trained in the Remote Viewing unit, I was not given explanations for many of the elements of structure presented. If I asked the why or how for much of the structure of Coordinate Remote Viewing, there was often no answer of any substance. It was clear to me that much of what we did, as military Remote Viewers, was not yet fully understood or explained in plain language. Therefore, when I asked a question and no suitable answer was provided, I did my own investigations into the nature of the phenomenon. Such is the case with Stage V.

Understanding Stage V, the brain, cognitrons, linguistics, logic, language, and all the other considerations in this protocol is a bit like understanding the classic argument between science and technology: Where does the one separate from the other? Is science applied technology or is technology applied science? To understand this timeless argument completely would require another book; however, parallels can be drawn between this argument and the mechanism of Stage V. Does the signal line connection support the biological brain's ability to unlock data, or does the brain's ability support the signal line's ability to manifest infinite data?

To address this argument from the scientific and technological perspective, we explore, as we have throughout this book, the notions of quantum physics. Research into quantum computers has implied that matter itself processes information, leading to the controversial claim that the universe itself is governed by the laws of computation and is, therefore, a finite computer. This theoretical perspective does not stop with physics. Biologists are also drawn into the computational worldview. Ever since Erwin Schrödinger suggested in 1943 that genes carry a "code-script" similar to Morse code, biology has focused on understanding how genes control and regulate life. Today, the burgeoning field of systems biology is explicitly predicated on a computational model.

Ironically, the most significant consequence of the view that the natural world is computational may be the death of the notion that technology is applied science. If both the physical universe and the biological world are best understood in terms of information and computation concepts that arise from the artificial world of technology, it no longer makes sense to think that technology results from an application of science. Indeed, if computation is the basis of all nature, then science is just applied technology.

If this is the case, then science becomes less purely contemplative and purposeful; it finds itself fraught with social and political goals on an equal standing with technology. Scientific theories are more properly viewed not as discoveries but as human constructions subject to interpretive observation. It is already happening in physics. Take the mysterious quark, for example. Quarks only exist inside hadrons, the latter being particles made up of quarks, because they are confined by the interdependent force fields. Therefore, we cannot measure their mass by isolating them. If we cannot separate them out, how do we know they are there? How do we know they are real? The answer is simply that all our calculations depend on their existence and, when considered, give the right answers for the experiments. Therefore, the accumulation of results for which experiments match predictions based on quarks convinces scientists that quarks are real. However, philosopher of science Andrew Pickering suggests that the quark, which cannot be isolated and observed, should not be regarded as scientific fact; rather, it should be understood as scientific invention. All of this deals with another perspective on how we think, why we think, where our thoughts come from, and so on. Know that because we are constantly discovering, there is always another perspective, always another version. You cannot trust just one take on anything to give you complete knowledge. Even the Matrix Field can be considered a computational model. You can accept this when you remember that this is only one of many possible ways to make sense of it.

THE SPEED OF THOUGHT

There is a great deal of information locked into the biological brain. Every experience in this existence embeds itself into neural and glial cell patterns within the biological brain. Our experiences and our ability to record them occur at the speed of thought, considered faster than the speed of light.

A brilliant nuclear physicist from the University of California at Berkeley, Dr. Elizabeth Rauscher, has written extensively on this subject, exploring complex Minkowski space and relating it to the nonlocal concept of thought. Her conclusions in a 2001 paper, "The Speed of Thought: Investigation of a Complex Space-Time Metric to Describe Psychic Phenomena," indicate that the speed of thought is transcendent of any finite velocity. Further, she states that the speed of thought is instantaneous, not defined in units per second as the speed of light is. What is defined in Minkowski's eight-dimensional space as being contiguous is also existent with no apparent space-time distances. Space-time distances are nonexistent for mind-to-mind or mind-to-target awareness; separation of consciousness is an illusion. Without temporal or spatial correlation, then, in this state, you are omnipresent, or as Dr. Deepak Chopra puts it, you are nonlocal. As you have learned, this is the Matrix Field, the Akashic Record, the global mind, the collective unconscious, the universal supercomputer, nirvana, the mind of God. *Nonlocal* defines a concept of nonseparation, meaning you are neither here nor there, but everywhere. As a Remote Viewer, you must imagine, and you must accept, an unbounded, infinite space that curves back on itself. You cannot blink in your understanding of this, or you empower Kant's suspicion, explained in his 1781 *Critique of Pure Reason*, that human consciousness is resigned to eternally haunt its four-dimensional world.

Mathematics defines a new world for us; our task is to reorient our understanding of the richness of this new world and to devise a new manner of piercing the imaginary veil dividing this world from our own. We exist awash in a nonlocal domain with access to infinite information in waveform. It should be clear at this point that you have access to an infinite level of data as you work through the structured protocols of CRV. In such a condition, there is no separation of consciousness; there is no time in the detecting and decoding process. At the speed of thought, you are experiencing the target during all stages of Coordinate Remote Viewing—except in Stage V.

COGNITRON FORMATIONS

In Stage V, you ignore the nonlocal connection (obviously you cannot disconnect from it, not even temporarily) for the purpose of accessing the biological brain and extracting everything that was detected at the speed of thought but did not make it to the page in Stages II, III, and IV. This iceberg of data remains in the biological brain until you initiate the protocol to mine it or uncover it.

You will select a critical intangible from the data you decoded in the previous stages and use a protocol of reverse engineering to extract from your biological brain the hidden content of the intangible. The content of the intangible goes well beyond the thought it expresses. Your interest is to understand the possibility that remains locked in your brain and to use the Stage V method of extraction to realize this possibility.

What is the mechanism for extraction? Call it lexical research, language evolution, morphology, grammar theory, linguistic analysis, or symbolic logic. The protocols rest upon the work of many great linguists, theorists, writers, and others who, unwittingly in many cases, have provided an analysis of language, which I now place in a new application to unlock neural pattern data. If you wish to learn more about linguistic analysis, study the work of these two notables: Nobel laureate in literature Bertrand Russell and the German mathematician, logician, and philosopher Friedrich Ludwig Gottlob Frege, whose work on language logic helped form the protocols that follow.

Stage V is an odd duck in an otherwise sophisticated structural procedure. As I have stated, it does not rely on the previously vital signal line contact; it does not employ movement techniques, either voluntary or involuntary. No breaks of any sort are permitted, such as too-much, confusion, aesthetic impact, emotional

FIGURE 10.1 **Recording Data from the Biological Brain**

FIGURE 10.1 **Recording Data from the Biological Brain**

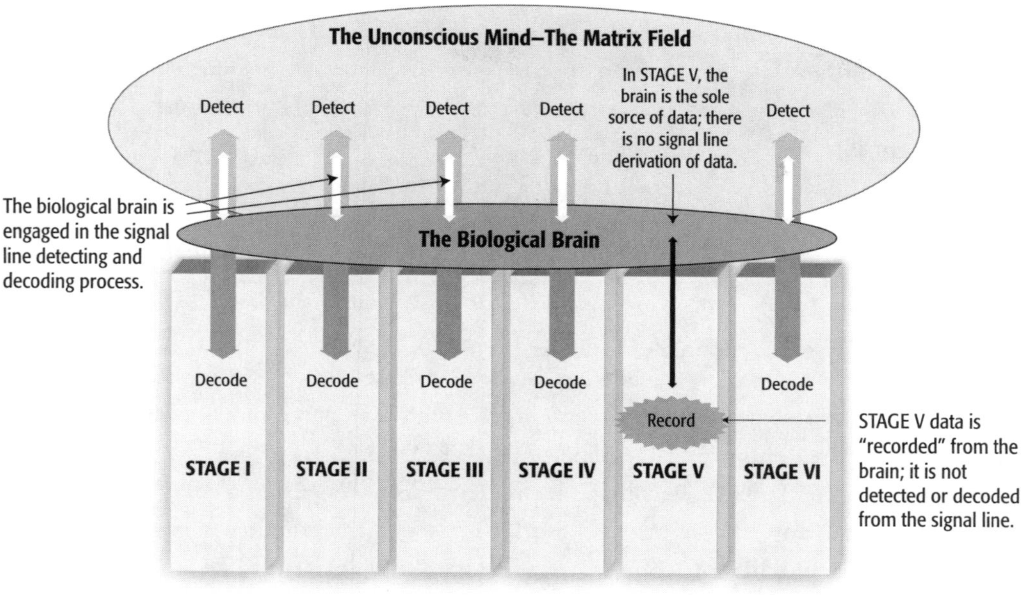

impact, bi-location, and so on. There are no analytical overlay relationships in Stage V; in fact, no data is permitted except that which is understood to be derived from the biological brain.

Thus the peculiar mechanism of Stage V: it *does not* rely upon signal line contact (see Figure 10.1) but relies on data already burned into the biological brain because of previous signal line contact. Such data is considered to be cognitron data.

Cognitrons are networks of neurons and glial cells involved with learning or memorization, or the unconscious logging of experiences derived from existence within the Matrix Field. The word "cognitron" is not a medical or scientific word. It was invented in the Remote Viewing community circa 1984 to connote a combination of neural patterns; at the time, the medical community considered glial cells to be nothing more than the matter in which neurons existed. Glial cells are now considered an intrinsic part of the brain's cognitive functioning, and when combined with neurons relating the combined data to a specific target, a cognitron formation is said to exist. There is no empirical data to support a possible number of cognitrons in the human brain. One can only speculate as to the billions of cognitrons that would make up an individual's patterns of memory and at what levels these patterns would function. Be that as it is, in the lexicon of the Remote Viewer, cognitrons are an everyday manner of speaking, especially when related to the subject of Stage V. The construction of the word "cognitron" comes from "cognition" and the acronym TRON.

Cognition—The process of knowing in the broadest sense, including perception, memory, and judgment, or the result of such a process.

TRON—The acronym refers to the project that originated with Dr. Ken Sakamura of the University of Tokyo in 1984. The initials stand for "The Real-time Operating-system Nucleus." This project introduced the notion of a future world where computer technology embedded in common everyday objects would allow them to instantly communicate with each other and also interface seamlessly with human beings. The current TRON Association (see www.assoc. tron.org) continues to encourage high-tech industry engineers and academic intellectuals to work together on worldwide standard computer architecture. The goal is to achieve a "computing everywhere" environment where our world is full of computer-embedded "smart objects" that link up and collaborate with each other.

Back in the 1980s it was a fascinating concept, especially considering the only computers anyone had were Atari or some other really basic models. The internet existed only for military use or university research—so linking computers across the world for instant access was a strange, futuristic concept that explained in a unique way how the human brain stores information used in "perception" for recall. You can see the TRON project's results today, for example, in cell phones for which the TRON operating system quickly became the standard in Japan, linked with the internet, linked with the Global Positioning System, linked with real-time television broadcasts. Science-fiction buffs will agree that what was a fringe vision in the mid-eighties is now a reality we fully own.

In the same way as the TRON project seeks to allow computers to communicate with each other in vast networks, the concept of a cognitron in Remote Viewing is that information from the Matrix Field is communicated through the signal line resulting in the formation of neural networks in the brain. The structures of these neural networks constitute the cognitron formations, which contain that information in the brain related to all perceived categories of data in RV (color, texture, taste, smell, temperature, sound, dimension, energetic,

FIGURE 10.2 Cognitron Formations Yield Sketch in Stages II–IV (Neural Maps)

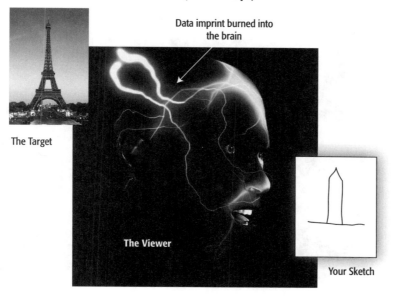

Data imprint burned into the brain

The Target

The Viewer

Your Sketch

emotional, intangible, et cetera). Every element of data—an infinite series of data waves—are linked at the speed of thought into cognitrons that are objectified in the form of recorded data during the session. In Stage V, we recall these cognitrons and break them into component pieces (objects, attributes, subjects) to better understand the total target picture. Essentially every detail of the target is locked into the biological brain in these neural maps. That information is accessed and brought to conscious awareness through the Stage V process.

Look at Figures 10.2 and 10.3. They depict the reasons for Stage V. Figure 10.2 illustrates the process of detecting and decoding data related to the complex gestalt of the Eiffel Tower in Stages II, III or IV. The Viewer has access to the total gestalt data; however, when this gestalt data passes through the brain's inherent distillation and filtering process, the sketch manifested is a simple contour, dimensional, or textural snippet objectified on the page. In Figure 10.3, which pertains more to Stage IV data, the Viewer detects total gestalt data, again of the Eiffel Tower, but this time the data is decoded in broad, abstract elements (called *intangibles* in Stage IV).

In Stage V, you are interested in the "lighting bolt," which represents the data that is burned into the biological brain during the detecting and decoding process.

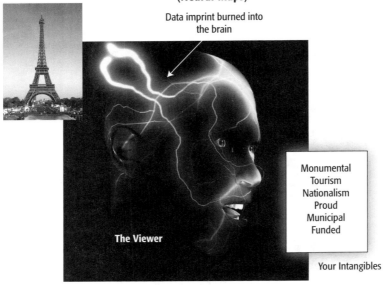

Data imprint burned into the brain

The Viewer

Monumental
Tourism
Nationalism
Proud
Municipal
Funded

Your Intangibles

The mechanism for extracting this data focuses on cognitron formations in the brain. From a more scientific perspective, these cognitrons are formed each time stimuli are applied to the brain, which is constant (remember the speed-of-thought and Matrix Field concepts). Each neuron and glial cell connects to others within its specific class of cells via an enzymatic response we do not yet fully understand. This enzymatic trigger causes small fila to "shake hands," forming the cognitron. This neural "handshake" never lets go, ever. Thus, you *cannot* forget anything; you may well bury it under layers of additional data, but you cannot unlearn or misplace something indefinitely.

Various parts of your brain designed to handle specific tasks expand and contract in physical size and neural makeup as they are tasked to increase. For example, London taxi drivers are required to learn the streets of London and are tested on that knowledge prior to obtaining their Green Badge, which authorizes them to work as taxi drivers. Testing has determined that these driver candidates actually build those areas of their brain required to support such gross memorization; the regions of the brain responsible for this function grow larger than before the memorization was required.

WORD ASSOCIATION AND MIND-MAPPING EXERCISES

Sigmund Freud, eighty years ago, used hypnosis to uncover his patients' unconscious feelings and conflicts. This was not entirely satisfactory, so he switched to the notion of free association. In this process, the psychoanalyst instructs the patient to lie on a couch and talk about whatever comes to mind, regardless of whether it is logically connected to the previous topic or seems related to their troubles, or not. The patient is "free" to say anything. Under these conditions, the theoretical internal "censor" of the unconscious mind relaxes, allowing data to emerge, at least, some would say, symbolically. Free association through the use of language is said to unleash a flow of verbal data from the unconscious mind, a veritable iceberg of data relating to a more obvious neurosis or issue within the patient.

Mind Mapping

In 1942, Karen Horney, a psychotherapist noted for her pioneering work on theories of neurosis, advocated self-psychoanalysis by recording free associations. Called *mind mapping* today, I would equate it with purposeful daily meditation or even prayer. Either process—word association or mind mapping—can be considered letting the physical body as the decoding instrument speak, or rather, allowing the biological brain to emanate or evoke that which is hidden. Becoming familiar with mind mapping and word association will help you understand how the Stage V protocol works similarly to call forth data that would otherwise remain hidden in the cognitron formations in your brain. To practice mind mapping, you first pose a question to yourself on a specific aspect of your life. Once the question is overtly developed, the next step is to internalize the listening process in the altered brain-wave state required for meditation or prayer. As information comes to you in sentence form or in simple single words, you record without judgment or analysis. Figure 10.4 shows an individual using a nonlinear mind-mapping technique to record the answer to the question "What is the most important thing for me to know now about the direction of my life?" In mind mapping, you write your associations, which are manifesting first as thoughts, at the speed of thought. You objectify these thoughts into written words describing not the direct and scripted memory of events, but rather the vast inner mountain, the iceberg, of data supporting the memory or the thought.

FIGURE 10.4 Free-Association Self-Questions

The individual in Figure 10.4 produced eighty-nine elements of data relevant to the focus question. Is the answer somewhere on the page? You bet it is. However, it may not be visible yet. In this case, the mapper may have to look at the data developed in the mind-mapping process, review the links and similarities, and select various pieces of data to consider in meditation or prayer once again. Each time the process is followed, you will sequentially narrow the focus, and eventually the answer will be obvious. Theoretically, in psychoanalysis, this process would allow emotions and forgotten memories, buried deep beneath layers of protective thought, to surface. Looking through the associated and linked words, you would be able to see objectified elements of neural patterns and thoughts that would otherwise have remained in the realm of conceptual illusion. You cannot work with illusion; you can, however, work very effectively with objectified data.

Word Association

As more background for Stage V, I would like to explain briefly another aspect of this psychoanalytic process, a word association "test," not because Stage V is a psychoanalytic process, but because there are definite parallels between the science and the mechanism. To perform a word association test, you will need someone's help; in Remote Viewing terms, this would be a monitor. The monitor presents single words to you. You are blind to the nature of the words (you do not know what the words will be), and you respond as quickly as possible with the first word that comes to your mind. Since we are proposing this structure in a nonanalytic posture, you can write the words as fast as they come to you, or you can have the monitor record them for you, or you can make an audio recording for later transcription. Words thought to be emotionally, spiritually, or directionally significant to you are scattered among

FIGURE 10.5 **Mind Map**

common words. The significance of your response is judged subjectively—a sort of clinical conjecture about the specific word you blurt out.

This process and the result could be looked at as another form of mind mapping—that is, freely associating random thoughts, without analysis. While the technique of mind mapping is not part of the CRV protocols, mind mapping is used in the more advanced Extended Remote Viewing process. In Figure 10.5, a Remote Viewer used a mind map to capture all perceptions made during a sixty-minute Extended Remote Viewing session. The three focus questions used during the session were to describe the target gestalt, to describe any and all life forms present in the target, and finally, to describe the purpose of the target. Using the mind-mapping method, the Viewer produced 120 additional pieces of data relevant to the target. What is unique to this process is the fact that this additional data was produced in a matter of minutes and on one page, much the opposite of a structured signal line detecting-and-decoding process.

THE METHOD

As a Remote Viewer, you know that what you produce on the page in the session is your version, in the moment, decoded from your unconscious mind using the protocols of Coordinate Remote Viewing. In Stages I through IV, we perceive vast quantities of data in waveform, without expressing the majority of this data in any language. The structure of CRV slowly opens the viewing aperture, allowing larger quantities of waveform information to be perceived, and we do our best to objectify this data. We move systematically through the process—gathering, collecting, objectifying, albeit imperfectly and incompletely due to the infinite nature of the unconscious mind. However, deep within the neural circuitry of our brain, something is happening. The waveform interpretation of this data is being assembled into packages of linked data in accordance with our "experience Rolodex," our history, our references, our life—this life and, theoretically, others. Quietly, behind our eyes, the biological brain is interpreting, "decoding," this data, stitching language to these interpretations at the speed of thought, yet only a small portion of this language will ever make it to the page.

Stage V is about language. Simply, it is about what we perceive and what we actually objectify on the page in the form of intangible concepts, words used to describe abstract concepts related to the target distant in space-time. More completely, it is about understanding how we think, how we form ideas at the speed of thought and express them verbally or in writing. The latter serves as the beginning of our exploration of the mechanism of Stage V.

LANGUAGE AND THE MATRIX

It should be clear at this point that you have access to an infinite amount of data as you work through the structured protocols of CRV. You have been introduced to mind-mapping and free-association examples that illustrate the fact that we often objectify using a minor word when there is a mountain of data supporting this objectified word. You understand that you detect at the speed of thought every possible element of data, without regard to space or time. You experience this level of awareness, yet you produce simple verbal descriptors. Humans are clocked at one quadrillion thought processes per second, but what does that mean in terms of actual conscious thought? Do you have a sense that your conscious thoughts outrun your ability to speak or write? That your mind can run at seemingly unlimited speed, but you often cannot remember what your perceptions were? Considering language, do you think in the language you speak? Understanding the nonlocal concept, perhaps you are detecting the Matrix Field in every possible language simultaneously, or perhaps there is no language at all in the Matrix Field except that which is distilled down by those present, communicating, each in their own way, within their various tribes. This would mean that we all understand a language of waveform within the Matrix Field, a language consistent with the speed of thought.

Language is the most glorious of all our human inventions, incomparably the finest of our achievements. Noam Chomsky, longtime political activist, writer, and professor of linguistics at MIT, maintains, "When we study human language, we are approaching what some might call 'the human essence,' the distinct qualities of mind that are, so far as we know, unique to man." We marvel at the fact that, as you pass your physical eyes over the pages of this book, you experience ideas similar to those I am thinking as I write this, in another place and time, moving my fingers across the symbols of my keyboard. Because I write and you read, we can both extend ourselves beyond the physical, four-dimensional limitations others accept as inevitable. This is the miracle we call language, and it is the stuff of Stage V.

For most humans, language is like the air we breathe. It is all around us, but we take it for granted. However, without realizing it, we spend most of our waking hours inventing language. Incredibly, practically every sentence you speak and write has never been spoken or written before in human history. This extraordinary human that is you has the ability to constantly invent new ways of expressing your perceptions and also to comprehend the verbal and visual inventions of others. Consider, for example, an exercise conducted at Wesleyan University in Middletown, Connecticut, by Dr. Richard Ohmann. He asked twenty-five students to look at one simple cartoon and write a caption describing it in one sentence. The cartoon depicted a traveler and a bear in a telephone booth on a country road. As you would expect, Dr. Ohmann received twenty-five different versions of the situation. These results are discussed in his essay on grammar, published in *The American Heritage Dictionary*, first edition, 1964. He then analyzed the results to see how many grammatical sentences in English could be generated using the words his students produced. The material generated 19.8 billion other sentences! Mind-boggling, is it not? Think about what this means in relation to your task as a Remote Viewer—being infinitely connected to a Matrix Field of infinite possibilities and taking on the assignment to translate its meanings to your page using finite language.

I often hear in new Viewers how little information they believe they are detecting. The point of this chapter is that you are not restricted in any manner as to the amount of available information. The structure of CRV is designed to control and organize the flow of information; however, you are never short of data. By now you should begin to understand the magnitude of your task and the miracle of your accomplishment! In your ninety-minute session, you will likely describe elements of the target in several ways, and others working the same target will describe it in their terms—this is exactly what makes Remote Viewing such a precious and usable tool. There is no shortage of data, and Stage V provides a mechanism for further extracting the data.

CHOOSE AN INTANGIBLE

The first thing you must do in Stage V is to prepare a list of all the words in the category "intangibles" that you have decoded or listed in the Remote Viewing session thus far. From the list, you will choose one word to work with in Stage V. It will be the seed concept upon which you focus your intention and thereby call forth the abundance of data, unlocking it from the cognitron networks in the biological brain. You can work with what you produced in Stage IV, or you can go all the way back to Stage II (if you produced any S4 intangibles there) and use these as well. It is your call. You can go back to Stage II and review the entire session all the way through Stage IV. You may find intangible data in Stage III as well, so look carefully.

Take a clean piece of paper and label it "Intangibles" at the top (see Scratch #1 and Scratch #2 immediately following page 296 Stage IV in the Sample Session). Notice that these two pages are not numbered in sequence with the session. That is because the list of intangibles is considered a "scratch list" and is not part of the session; it is a work page, a compilation of intangible data decoded in the session thus far. You will look through your session and list every intangible you can find. If you cannot find very many, you can look at your AOL/S's and AOL's from the session and develop intangibles for those. This is not the most desirable approach, as it adds a layer of interpretation to data that is already highly interpreted; however, some new Viewers have trouble decoding intangibles and are forced to apply this method. You cannot skip Stage V; it is a requirement of the structure of CRV.

For example, the AOL/S of "a crown" on page 290 of the Sample Session could be turned into the intangibles "monarchal" and "valuable." You would add these to your list and continue to do this until you developed a list of ten to twenty intangibles. This method is a guarantee that you can and will develop intangible data for Stage V. This may be necessary when you are learning, when you negotiate your first couple of sessions, but it is not likely to occur after a little experience.

Look at the long list of intangibles developed from the Sample Session (see the Scratch list following page 296 of Stage IV). They number thirty in all. Remember, these thirty words represent billions of pieces of data; this is all that made it to the page. These are the thirty points of the Matrix Field of data that distilled themselves down during the CRV process. Now you are going to reverse the tree of data in your brain and record more data. Before you can do this, you must select one intangible to work with in Stage V. You only have to work with one of them, not all thirty. In CRV, you are on the clock, and you do not have the time to work with every one of them. Therefore, you have to determine which one is in your subjective interpretation, the "juiciest" intangible, the one with the most hidden data. As stated, this is a highly subjective process, so there are a couple of ways you can do this. These are only suggestions; they are not hard-and-fast methods.

FIGURE 10.6 **Visual Dowsing for Intangibles**

The Page of
Intangibles

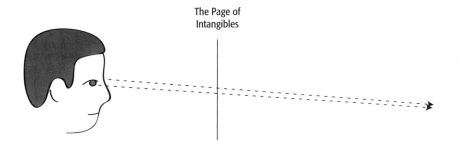

Visual Dowsing

The first is a form of visual dowsing. It is a rapid selection process, particularly suited to visual perceivers. In this process, you join the two scratch pages together so that all the intangibles can be seen. Make it your intention to find the most productive intangible in the list. Do not just stare and see what happens. Everything in life is governed by intention, so begin with this. Say to yourself, "I would like to find the most important intangible in this list that pertains to the target." Then relax your eyes and look softly into the center of the page, letting your eyes rest on the center line of the list of intangibles. Keep your gaze fixed there, but let it be the kind of gaze you might have if you were looking at one of those stereo images composed of dots. Your gaze need not be cross-eyed; it is better to let your focus cast beyond the page (see Figure 10.6).

While holding this focus, you may begin to notice that some of the intangibles appear darker than others; in some cases, they may appear more brilliant or lighter than others. This is not an exact process. The object here is to develop an ability to visually dowse the page for information. If you make it your intention to find the best possible intangible, you may find it using this process. Sometimes several choices may appear, and if this happens, circle the choices or list them on a separate page, and visually dowse the page again until one appears more prominent than the others. Work as quickly as you can; this time still counts against your ninety minutes. In the beginning, this may take more time than you want it to; not to worry, you will become very fast at this process. In fact, many experienced Viewers will know which intangible is the most important while they are recording them on the scratch paper—they just feel it as they are writing the list.

Sensory Perception

The next method is sensory perception. In this method, you build your list of intangibles on the scratch paper, but you make it your intention to be aware of the most prominent intangible as you are preparing the list. If you establish your intention before you build the list, you may be able to determine which intangible is loaded with hidden cognitron data.

Tactile Dowsing

If you do not perceive the "best" intangible while building the list, you can try tactile dowsing, running your finger down the list with your eyes closed. Try to "feel" as a tactile perceiver might feel; you might feel heat or cold, or you might feel an energetic bump or rise in the page where the best intangible is. Again, until you perfect this method, or if the intangibles are closely related, you may develop multiple choices. Record them on a separate page, and repeat the process until you can make a single selection. Do not second-guess yourself; there are no wrong answers.

Analysis

The final method I will share with you is for those of you who are logical and heavily left-brained. You may find discomfort with the visual, sensory, and tactile methods for selecting intangibles. For you, there is an analytical process, but you must move quickly and without remorse in your choices. In this process, you look at the list and link similar or mutually supporting intangibles together. For example, you might link "pride," "national," "monumental," "heroic," and "inspired" together. When I use this method, I draw brackets and connect the linked intangibles (see Figure 10.7). Then, I search the list for other intangibles I can link, for example, "entertainment," "tourism," "guided," and so on, until I have linked everything I can. Now look at the list; there will likely be some intangibles that are not linked to any others. Draw a line through them; they are no longer considered usable.

These "lone wolf" intangibles do not carry enough weight to be considered for Stage V. If they were significant, they would be linked to other intangibles. If the intangible is alone, it is likely an anomaly and not linked to a powerful string of data in the brain. You next look at your list of linked intangibles and begin a rapid and deliberate process of eliminating the small branches, linkages of two or four words; draw lines through them, and keep moving. Eventually you will come to the largest linkage of intangibles. The reason you work backward, and do not simply jump to the biggest linkage, is that you may find you are intrigued by one of the intangibles even though you did not link it to a larger branch. You want to allow yourself this option, so work backward from smallest to largest.

Once you begin working on the largest linkage, look for the "most important" intangible. This intention will help, even if your logical mind doesn't understand why. Keep thinking that you have to find the intangible that has the most "objects," "attributes," and "subjects" related to the target. This *will* help you make your selection. Eventually you will come to a final selection, an intangible you feel, by way of elimination, has the potential to unlock the largest number of objects, attributes, and subjects for the target.

FIGURE 10.7 **Analysis for Intangibles**

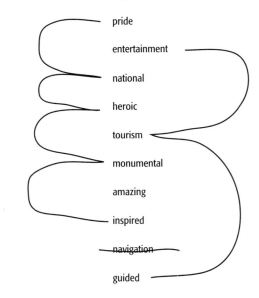

STAGE V FORMAT

As always, indicate that you are beginning this new stage by writing "<u>S5</u>" at the top center of a new sheet of paper. After you have chosen one intangible to work with, you begin at the top left of the page and write the intangible to be processed. You can see on page 297 of the Sample Session that the Viewer chose "communication." You will be eliciting three categories of information from the intangible you have chosen: objects, attributes, and subjects, which are further defined below.

Objects

An *object,* for your purposes, is a thing that can be seen or touched. For additional understanding, an *object* can be a material thing that occupies space or, grammatically, a noun or other substantive that directly or indirectly receives the action of a verb or is governed by a preposition. Philosophically, an object can be anything that can be known or perceived by the mind. Notice on page 297 of the Sample Session the kinds of words in the category of "objects" elicited by the intangible "communication": "towers," "platforms," "microphones," "wires," and so on.

Attributes

An *attribute,* for your purposes, is a characteristic or quality of a person or thing in the target site. For additional understanding, an *attribute* can be thought of as belonging to, produced by, resulting from, or originating in; assigned or ascribed to, for example, "the play is attributed to Shakespeare"; or ascribed as a quality or characteristic, for example, the degree of excellence that a thing possesses. Note the attributes under "communication" on page 298 of the Sample Session: "single source," "monopoly," "purposeful," "accountable," and so on.

Subjects

Subjects, for your purposes, are the nature, purpose, function, and activities of the inhabitants of the target site or of some aspect or all aspects of the target gestalt. I am aware this sounds confusing, so I will elaborate by defining *nature, purpose, function,* and *activities,* as well as further clarifying *subjects.* A *subject* can be considered something dealt with in discussion, study, writing, painting, and so on; the theme, originating cause, reason, or motive; any of the various courses of study in a school or college; a branch of learning; or, grammatically, the noun or other substantive that is one of the two immediate constituents of a sentence and about which something is said in the predicate. Speaking philosophically, *subjects* are the actual substance of anything, as distinguished from its qualities and attributes—the mind or ego that thinks and feels, as distinguished from everything outside the mind. Below are terms that further characterize the kinds of words you'll look for in the "subjects" category.

Nature—The quality or qualities that make something what it is—its essence. The essence or nature of a water bottle is that it is a container—it holds stuff. It can hold anything that is malleable enough to fit into the bottle without destroying it: sand, water, paint, paper, nuts, paper clips, and so on. Further, *nature* can be understood as the essential character of a thing; the inborn character, innate disposition, inherent tendencies of a person or the vital functions, forces, and activities of the organs, often used as a euphemism; or any or all of the instincts, desires, appetites, drives, and so on, of a life form—from the macro, a person or animal, to the micro, such as a paramecium or microorganism.

Purpose—The point, aim, goal, intention, or objective for which something exists or is done. The purpose of the water bottle in this discussion is "to hold water"; it is not to hold sand, paint, and so on. How would you know the difference? Remember what I said many paragraphs ago. As you read the words on this page, you are connecting energetically to my intention, as it is set into the organization of the symbols on this page. By virtue of your inherent and timeless connection to the collective unconscious, the Matrix Field, you may know my thoughts. The same is true when working a Remote Viewing target, and it is again a reason for Stage V. Each time you begin Stage V, choosing an intangible and looking for the subjects related to that intangible, cognitron data will always be linked directly to the purpose of the subject of that intangible in the target site. That is how you will know that the water bottle's purpose is to hold water and not something else. Cognitron formations are created from specific target information being detected from the Matrix Field. The Stage V process allows further details to unfold. Just as a fingerprint is linked to an individual, the details that unfold will naturally be specific to that particular target.

Function—The normal characteristic or action of anything; special actions of a system or a structure. For example, the function of a water bottle is to allow you to drink or pour from it.

Activities—The quality or state of being active; energetic action; liveliness; alertness; the normal function of body and mind; an active force, or any specific action or pursuit. Some examples of the activities associated with the water bottle in this discussion are that you can store water, transport water, drink water, and refrigerate water.

SETUP AND INTENTION

After you have written your intangible at the upper left of the page, underneath it you write "objects," followed by "data" and a question mark. This is called the *setup,* and it is done for each aspect or category of Stage V. It is a ritualistic process of structure designed to trigger the release of cognitron subelements of data. Before you begin recording (not decoding) the cognitron subelements of data, remind yourself what this phase of Stage V is about. Using the Sample Session as an example, you would say to yourself, "Okay, I am looking for communication objects related to this target." You must establish your intention in order to prepare your brain for the release of subelements of data. If you were recording data for the "attributes" category of communication, you would say to yourself, "I am looking for communication attributes, characteristics, or qualities of life forms present in the site, or of objects present in the site." Repeat this as necessary, until you feel ready to begin. Then, open your eyes and place pen to paper, to begin recording the string of subelement data. Remember, this is called *recording* and not *decoding,* because decoding implies signal line contact, and that is not what Stage V relies upon.

BREAKS

As I've mentioned, in Stage V there are no AOLs, no breaks, no sketches, no reliance on signal line contact to produce data—all you have to do is to shake loose the subelements of data already burned into the biological brain. Imagery, bi-locations, or other session-related problems can develop, even though they are not supposed to in Stage V. Well, you are human, so anything can happen. If anything of that sort happens, stop what you are doing and breathe. You will find that forgetting to breathe usually precedes any difficulties that appear in Remote Viewing. You cannot take a formal break in Stage V, but you can put your pen down, breathe, close your eyes, and refresh your intention and conviction in the process. When you feel ready, pick up your pen and rejoin the string of subelement data you were working on before you felt the need to stop. You can "break" like this as often as necessary; there is no requirement to record the break on the right of the page; you just stop and restart as often as you deem necessary.

PROGRESSING THROUGH STAGE V

In the Sample Session, beginning on page 297, you can see that the Viewer selected the intangible "communication" as the focus of his Stage V. This means the Viewer felt that the intangible concept of communication related heavily to this target, that it was the richest intangible. He then evoked cognitron data related to "objects of communication" or "communication objects." After all the related communication objects were recorded, he moved to the next category of data, "communication attributes," specifically, characteristics or qualities of a person or thing in the target site. Once all communication attributes were recorded for this target, he moved to "communication subjects," specifically, the communication nature, purpose, function, and activities associated with this target. It is critical to the process that you embed this intention into each step of the Stage V process.

On page 297, the Viewer established his intention, "communication objects" related to this target, and immediately opened his eyes and began recording the cognitron subelements of data without judgment, analysis, or interruption of flow. He kept producing subelement data as long as the flow was steady and smooth. If he slowed down, hesitated, or found himself digging for words, it was time to move on to the next phase of Stage V, "communication attributes."

The reason for this trigger switch is due to the theory that as long as the metronomic pacing is held, you will produce reliable cognitron data; however, slowing down or hesitating implies depleted or lost subelement data, meaning you are now crafting from logic. It means the tree of information is not being followed; instead, you are likely making it all up from pure memory and not from evoking the subelement data related to communication objects.

Look at the flow of data produced by the Viewer on pages 297 and 298. With a cadence of three to five seconds for each word, the Viewer moved through the objects phase, producing twenty-four additional elements of data before the string was broken. When you work in your session, you must be careful to follow this cadence rule. It is okay to pause when a word is right on your tongue and you are struggling to pull it out of your head; there is a distinct difference between this and a blank stare waiting for something to show up. If you take the latter position, your conscious mind will engage and begin crafting words, pulling from memory instead of recording words embedded as a result of previous signal line contact with the target. Further, if you slow yourself down by analyzing the recorded data, the same can occur. You write whatever comes, as fast as it comes. Subelement data can repeat itself, it can manifest in no specific order, and it is all good as long as you maintain a cadence throughout the process. Just as in all other phases of CRV, when the data stops flowing, you move to the next category of data—in this case, "attributes."

Notice how the setup appears on page 298. As in previous stages, the process is top to bottom, left to right; however, there are some differences in Stage V.

While the setup appears to move directly to the right on page 298, the reason is only to facilitate the flow of subelement data. Remember, there is no signal line present in Stage V; therefore, there is no requirement to stay in signal line on the page, as you do in any other stage. In other words, as a Viewer you will move from top to bottom and then from left to right when beginning a new category, as long as you are working on the same page. Whenever you begin a new page, regardless of the subelement category, begin again at the top left-hand corner.

For example, if the string of subelement "communication objects" data on page 298 had run all the way to the bottom of the page and terminated there, the Viewer would have moved to page 299 and, at the top left-hand corner, would have written the setup ("communication," "attributes," and "data?"); he would not have moved the setup to the right on the page. In Stage V, you only move to the right when you finish a category on a page and there is enough room for you to continue on that page in the next category (see pages 298 and 301 in the Sample Session for examples of this).

Sometimes elements of data from "objects" can show up in "attributes"; it is not a problem. Somewhere in the neural tree, they overlap, connect, and branch; it is the way we link and process memory and stored data. You record the data as it comes, again, without judgment or analysis. Data may repeat and look and sound similar—this is all normal and appropriate; just record what comes, as it comes. Look at the Stage V data in the Sample Session to get a feel for the type of language used to convey characteristics and qualities of objects and life forms in a target.

It is not unusual to begin with very minimal strings of data. The more you practice manifesting the subelements of data, the more you will amaze yourself with what you are able to produce. Remember, this is all about potential and not competition. You will get what you commit to in the process of Remote Viewing. You are dealing with one of the most complex, detailed, yet powerful protocols for seeing beyond the physical. Master this, and doors will open for you in life. Mastery of anything requires tremendous effort and passion; therefore, be passionate about anything that offers you an expanded awareness within the moment. Master the moment, and you master life.

In the Sample Session, on page 301, the Viewer set up the next category, "subjects." You may want to review the definitions for nature, purpose, function, and activities before you begin this phase of Stage V. This is usually not a problem for native English speakers; however, this can be challenging for nonnative speakers. For example, most Scandinavians do not think of "nature" as the essence of something. Ask a Scandinavian what communication subjects are related to the nature of the target site, and he will likely not be able to make the connection; to him, "nature" means outside. It means life; it means trees, snow, mountains, animals, air, water; it does not mean the essence of something, or its quality—it is simply a word to describe the great world around us. How does one who is not a native English speaker cope with these conditions? Well, per my experience training thousands in Scandinavia, they simply adopt our meaning of the word. They say to themselves, the English word "nature" means the quality or qualities of something, its essence. Likewise, you can use the definitions provided to help you focus your intention.

On pages 301 through 305 of the Sample Session, notice the types of words the Viewer recorded for communication subjects related to this target. Eliciting "subjects," he recorded sixty-three additional elements of data from the selected intangible. He recorded words like "resourceful" as a quality and "information" as a purpose. Activities associated with the site were described with subelements of data like "reaching out," "increasing," "growing," "getting higher," "watching over," and so on. Carefully explore the list to see how this data lends more clarity to the abstract, intangible aspect of this target. I get a distinct sense it is about energy—broadcasting, focused energy of a very high level. What is your sense of the recorded data as you read it? Remember, Stage V is designed to search out cognitrons and break them apart in order to extract more information about the intangible aspects of the target—those aspects that are not easily defined, formulated, or grasped during the Stage I-through-IV process.

Have fun with this—see you in the next chapter.

11

The Journey Inward Continues:
Coordinate Remote Viewing—Stage VI

A mosaic reveals an entire society, just as a skeleton of an ichthyosaur suggests an entire creation. Everything is deducible, everything is linked.

Honoré de Balzac, *The Search for the Absolute*

Having just completed Stage V, you begin the final stage of the Coordinate Remote Viewing protocol—Stage VI. It may seem, in this chapter, as if I am winding down, and in a sense, I am. Stage VI is the simplest to teach because you already know everything you need to know in order to complete the flow of data in this stage. Originally this was considered "the modeling stage," whereby the data derived by the Viewer was applied to clay or some other suitable material in order to create a three-dimensional model of the target site. Viewers would roll clay to form fence lines, gates, towers, aircraft wings—anything and everything perceived in the target. The objects would be assembled into elaborate models depicting, for example, a suspected chemical munitions plant in Libya. Constructed on plywood sheets of varying sizes, these models would make their way to intelligence agencies for analysis and photographing.

Modeling is not limited to the construction of clay representations of target data. As Viewers verbally objectify what they perceive in a target, they will often move their hands in the shape of dimensional elements of the target. They are routinely not aware that they are "talking with their hands," and if you mention it to them, they will likely become conscious of the movement and lessen it or omit it from the explanation. However, years ago, this desire to "model" the major dimensional aspects of the target was not only encouraged, it was a requirement in Stage VI.

Difficulties in the use of clay and other modeling materials, such as hobby foam, heavy construction paper, cardboard, balsa wood, and the mix of glues and paints, to complete the models eventually resulted in the elimination of the actual modeling required in Stage VI. During my time in the unit, Stage VI involved the capturing of visual data in the form of detailed sketches, called renderings. Models were done only upon special request. The mission was to capture the data as a detailed drawing, fill in the textures and the like, and assemble the data in as complete a form as possible. The method used since the late 1980s has been this "rendering" with pen and paper.

Stage VI was developed to support a mosaic concept. Its purpose was to combine the final perceptions of a number of Viewers into a "complete" picture of the target site. This combined effort, which includes the assemblage of every piece of available visual data, could be used to form a type of composite mosaic of the target, which the analyst could ultimately use to build a three-dimensional model. Imagine the picture that can be developed using five, ten, or fifty Remote Viewers working on the target. I have observed the work of over three hundred Viewers working on the same target, and the intricacy and detail of the data is astounding. Assuming you will be practicing your first few sessions alone, you will use only your data to create this overall image of the target. It just means that the image may not be as elaborate and complete as one developed using multiple Viewers.

Stage VI is the process of allowing the aperture to open to its widest point, and it is the "objective" of Remote Viewing. This is the stage you have been waiting for, this is where you want to be, and this is where Remote Viewing really measures up. Most of all, this is where the discipline of having controlled the opening of the aperture will pay off. If you lose control of the session early on, you will be driven by AOL into oblivion. However, if you are disciplined, if you control the session cadence, the direction, the volume of verbal and visual data derived via your perceptions throughout the session, the reliability of your data here will likely be much higher.

Many students expect the ability to "see" target elements immediately, or they assume their perceptive ability will naturally open to this level at will and at the earliest opportunity. This is not desired, nor is it the norm, because it would overload the Viewer with data that cannot be categorized or managed. Many Remote Viewing students engage the protocols of Remote Viewing just to have a system available that will help them manage the flow of information that appears constantly in the quiet moments of their life, in their thoughts and dreams. They often feel overwhelmed, beaten down, and exhausted by the amount of information forced upon them, with no trained ability to control the flow, sort the data, or assemble it for application and integration in life. For these individuals, the control offered by CRV is a blessing.

THE METHOD

Stage VI is a visually driven stage. Upon completion of the recording protocols of Stage V, the Viewer reengages the signal line and once again begins the process of detecting and decoding the flow of verbal and visual data. Because the target aperture is now open to its widest point, you can expect the visual sensory data to be abundant. This stage uses a verbal sensory matrix, exactly like that learned in Stage IV, to stimulate or trigger visual data, which will be more complete than the data found in Stage III. The visual data developed here is carefully stitched together, filled in, combined, and completed to form a detailed image of the target from the Viewer's perspective.

In Stage VI, visual data is developed into renderings. This means three-dimensional perspective drawings—final and finished drawings depicting every possible detail in perspective and proportion. For example, in architecture, a rendering would represent the architect's conception of a finished building or bridge. In Stage VI, the rendering is a detailed drawing of the target site, which includes probing and labeling of colors, cardinal direction, light source, distances, heights, widths, energetic data, and anything else sensory-related that is derived from the session. From the data included in the Viewer's renderings, another person might be able to assemble a three-dimensional model of the target, which becomes highly accurate when the modeler uses multiple Viewers' data.

You take time with your renderings, working them until the flow of data slows down or stops, before returning to the verbal matrix to prompt the flow of more visual data. Regardless of the possible austere nature of the target, visual data is available to the Viewer, and this is the time to detect and decode it. Even a target of a crater on the moon would be rich with visual data, especially if you committed to not filtering your perceptions. Trust the structure, trust the signal line, and the data will flow. Stage

VI is all about opening the aperture to the widest point and beginning the process of assembling the details of the target in the most complete manner possible.

In Stage VI, you still track AOL. You can still experience AI, EI, bi-location—anything and everything you have learned thus far applies here. The only difference is the use of the page-numbering system. Since this is a visually driven stage, and since verbal data is only used to prompt the development of visual data, the page numbering shifts radically to support your strengths. For example, if you are highly verbal, the numbering system allows you to stack the pages of verbal sensory data without jumping over the visual data (more on this in a moment). On the other hand, if you are highly visual, you can move from rendering to rendering, in sequence, without having to abandon or lose your position in the verbal sensory matrix. It is a beautiful system once you understand it, that allows you to develop fully in any direction.

STAGE VI FORMAT

You work with two sets of pages simultaneously in Stage VI: one for verbal descriptors and the other for visual renderings. Begin by setting two blank pieces of paper side by side. Indicate that you are working in Stage VI by writing "S6" at the top center of each page, and number them in sequence, beginning with the page immediately following your last page from Stage V. For example, if your last page was 56 (as was the case in the Sample Session, per the Viewer's page numbering; it is page 307 of this book), then you would number these two pages 57 and 58. From there, you would number subsequent verbal pages using alpha indicators, for example, 57a, 57b, and so on. Likewise, your first page of visual renderings, page 58, would be followed by 58a, 58b, and so on. This is called *stacking* the data or the pages of data. Your stack of pages for verbal sensory data will be on the left, beginning with page 57 of the Sample Session, and your stack of pages for visual sensory data will be on the right, beginning with page 58 of the Sample Session. You detect and decode, beginning on the verbal page, working just as you do in Stage IV. However, as visuals develop, you move to the visual page, the page on your right. This is the basic flow and structure of Stage VI.

THE STAGE VI VERBAL SENSORY MATRIX

This is the exact verbal matrix taught and used in Stage IV of the CRV protocol. You write the abbreviations across the top of the page and follow the sequence of

signal line categories as you work your way through Stage VI. Only slight procedural changes are made to facilitate the development of visual data. As in Stage IV,
you probe the signal line categories and write down verbal descriptors in the vertical columns assigned to each category on the page, working from top to bottom,
left to right. You continue to use the right-hand side of the page to declare breaks,
movements within the target site, AOL, AOL/S, and so on. The difference in Stage
VI is that you use separate pages, the visual sensory matrix, for developing images
into detailed renderings. When verbal data prompts a visual rendering, you move
to the visual sensory matrix to do your drawing, and you reference the drawing by
writing its page number on the right-hand side of the facing verbal sensory matrix
page. You can see this at the bottom of page 57 (306) of the Sample Session.

THE STAGE VI VISUAL SENSORY MATRIX

Here you use the method taught in Stage III, but the visual data will be more
fully developed. The Viewer spends more time with the images, completing
them, shading them, filling them in with texture, color, and so on. As in Stage
III, images begin in the center of the page and expand outward symmetrically.
Images are probed and labeled, and the Viewer spends time looking, "perceiving," beyond the working image to what may lie beyond, to the right or to the
left, of the existing image.

In Stage VI, when a new image is perceived, you look at what you have
already rendered and ask yourself if this new image can fill in the background
of an existing image or if it should be added to the side or front of an existing
image. Doing this will help you create the full concept of the image. You are
trying to give a complete, panoramic view of the target, if possible. Every image potentially connects to another. Therefore, you must consider each image
as a part of the whole first, and then render it separately only when no other
association is possible. You can see on page 58 (313) of the Sample Session that
you continue to use the right-hand side of the page to make declarations and to
reference further sketches that may develop.

THE DANCE BETWEEN THE VERBAL AND VISUAL MATRICES

You can see the entire process of Stage VI in Figure 11.1. The arrows indicate the
flow of data from verbal to visual, from visual to visual, and back to verbal again.

Using the Sample Session (pages 306–321), augmented with this illustration, you can trace the flow of data. The Viewer began verbally on page 57, and this prompted an image that was carried to page 58 and rendered. While on page 58, another image developed that was carried to page 58a and rendered.

FIGURE 11.1 **The Stage VI Dance between the Matrices**

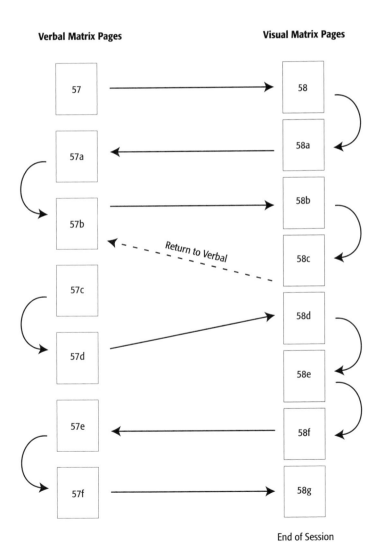

End of Session

REMOTE VIEWING

When the visual signal line ran dark, the Viewer moved back to the verbal page; however, it was full, so he began another on page 57a. Page 57a flowed into page 57b, and on this page an image was encountered that was carried to page 58b and rendered, and so on.

Thus, the flow is seamless; it is a dance between pages, taking time to fully develop renderings before moving to the next rendering or before returning to the verbal matrix. Remember, you are using the verbal data to prompt visual data—this is the purpose of Stage VI. Your intention should be to detect and decode visual data even if being visual is not your strongest modality of perception. You can make do with strong auditory data, as well as tactile and digital perceptions, as long as you make every effort to translate your perceptions into visual interpretations. In time, you will find that you are developing more visual data than you ever thought possible. I have trained thousands of students who claimed they could "see nothing" or they are "not visual," only to find that they are as visual as anyone else, in time and with practice. As with all things in life, your intention is the key; intend to record visual data, trust and work with the structure, and the data will come.

PROCEEDING THROUGH STAGE VI

The following section gives a detailed account of the Sample Session Viewer's progress through the "dance" of Stage VI, alternating between verbal and visual data, beginning on the verbal sensory matrix page, then switching to the visual sensory matrix page to sketch, probe, and label images, and back again to the verbal. The discussion of the visual data is in italics to help you keep track of the two stacks of data. You will begin to get a sense of the rich abundance of information that shows up in this stage, the beauty of the structure, and how the structure supports the Viewer in bringing forth what he perceives onto the pages.

Let's begin with a view of the use of the verbal sensory matrix, which begins on page 57 (306) of the Sample Session. This page looks exactly like a beginning page for Stage IV, with the exception that the stage heading is S6, not S4. The matrix across the top is the same, and the flow of detected and decoded data in the signal line categories is just as if you were working in Stage IV, top to bottom and left to right. At the bottom of page 57 (306), you can see the first indication of Stage VI. There is a reference to a sketch on another page, which reads "(sketch p. 58)," followed by the declaration of an AOL, "a machine digging earth." Notice that no attempt was made to move left on the page to sketch the image; instead, it was placed on a page in the visual matrix.

On page 58 (313) the Viewer rendered a sketch of earth-moving equipment with as much detail added as possible. Looking at the rendering, you can see there is a wind direction (note the direction of the exhaust of both machines). Further, there is shadow, indicating a possible light source (note the shading on the exhaust stack of the machine in the foreground). There is elevation: one machine appears higher than the other, operating on a small ridge of what one assumes to be soil. What is missing is an adequate probing and labeling of color or indications of temperature; the Viewer omitted a good deal of information, and you can learn from this. In failing to probe and label, the Viewer may have assumed anyone looking at the sketch would be able to know about 50 percent of the data from the recorded image—this is not an assumption I want you to make. Don't get me wrong—it is a great sketch with lots of detail, but it can be improved.

The analyst will look back at the verbal sensory data and use it to fill in the gaps, to augment what is omitted from the rendering; however, you can be more complete in your work by sparing nothing in the rendering. Probe and label the image until the data stops or repeats significantly. Take the time to master the structure, even exaggerate the requirements, and provide as much information as you can possibly gather.

Now look at the note at the bottom of page 58 (313), where the Viewer encountered an image inside of the image. What this means is that you can have another AOL or AOL/S while you are developing the present rendering. This should come as no surprise. Visuals will prompt visuals, and those visuals will prompt more visuals; again, that is the purpose of the structure. Therefore, when you are developing one image and another image comes to you, procedure dictates that you ask yourself, "Does this new image fit with, or attach itself to, the image I am currently working on?" Or, "Am I looking at the same thing, or is this a piece of the same thing, or is this new image part of something else in the target?" In this example, the Viewer saw a "star-shaped hole in ground," and even though the present image is of earth-moving equipment in action, this new image is from a different perspective.

Look at page 58a (314). The image that came to the Viewer is completely different from the one on page 58 (313). In fact, the earth movers may be working inside of the image sketched on page 58a (314), but that determination is the responsibility of someone wearing an analytical hat—the Viewer just knew it was a different image. Because the image was sketched on another page, in this case, 58a (314), the Viewer made what is called a "housekeeping note" on page 58 (313), directing the reader to page 58a (314) to find a rendering from the image perceived on page 58 (313). Do this in your session as well; it will help you find your way through the session after months or years. You can read the verbal pages to see what strings of data prompted what visual data and where this visual data was recorded. Further, you can look at various renderings to see where other visual data was prompted and follow the notes to the pages where it was recorded. At this point, you should understand why the numeric-alpha system works so well. It would be nearly impossible to logically follow, at a later date, these pages in numeric sequence.

Page 58a (314) includes four major elements of data: a set of [railroad] tracks, a cross-shaped hole fifty to eighty feet deep, a rounded illustration labeled as a structure in progress, and a hard-surface road. If you consider this information as it is presented, you may assume the Viewer perceived the target from an elevated position, in essence, looking down on the target. Notice the indications of soaked earth as "soft & muddy" or simply "muddy." Also, pay particular attention to the declaration of an AOL/S, "a construction site w/structures," followed by the note "no sketch." What is taking place here is the development of a concept by the Viewer. He felt he was perceiving a construction site, and this analysis came while developing the rendering. He did not have additional visual data; he sensed what it meant, or he developed a "knowing" of the image, as he was working with the image.

Once all the available visual data was objectified in the rendering, the Viewer may have probed the images, trying to prompt more data; however, once the signal line ran dark, he returned to the verbal matrix where he left off, and began decoding verbal data in an effort to prompt more visual data—this is the structure and method of Stage VI.

The Viewer returned to the verbal sensory matrix at the bottom of page 57 (306), picking up where he left off. Because he was out of space for working yet still in the AD (aesthetic data) column, he moved to the next page, 57a (307). He again began decoding data in the AD signal line column.

Several substantial strings of data were produced until the Viewer declared a too-much break at the bottom of the page. Remember from earlier chapters that this break means the Viewer was being overwhelmed by data and was using the structure to control and objectify the sensation. This break was declared as the result of "emotions present" that were "too fast and all over the place." This was a wise call by the Viewer because, even at this late stage of CRV, emotions can morph into overwhelming sensory data, as emotional impact that disrupts or degrades the session, or they can develop into bi-locations that erode the experience for the Viewer. Thus, even in Stage VI, you must remain in control of the session.

After declaring the break, the Viewer placed his pen on the table, sat back, and breathed; the purpose was to disengage from the out-of-control feeling and prepare to move back into the session powerfully. Out of working space, the Viewer prepared the next page, 57b (308), by writing the verbal matrix at the top. The Viewer began the page by resuming the session and noting "no movement," which is a sort of note to self or to whoever looks at the session, so that they will know that the Viewer did not feel the need to move after resuming.

The Viewer began in the same signal line category he was working in at the time of the break. The string of data flowed into the tangible (T) category; at the end of this string of tangible data, note the probe mark. The Viewer perceived image data that he declared as an AOL/S, "a large wooden wall." To complete the task, a note was made to see the sketch on page 58b.

Remember that in Stage VI, you address each image as it appears and compare it with the existing renderings. You look at what you have rendered and ask yourself if this new image can fill in the background of, or be added to the side or front of, an existing image. The Viewer assigned page 58b because he felt that the new image did not fit the image on page 58 or 58a; thus, the new image was placed on a separate page.

The rendering on page 58b (315) carries elements of life form; humans were included in the sketch. This addition gives proportion to the rendering. Further, there are indications of underground, aboveground, climbing, soil, length, height, width, wooden texture, and metal or iron. From an analytical perspective, one might call this a "retaining wall" or a "foundation" of some type. Given the size of it, it would be for a very large project. You can see that analytical thinking, meaning the assemblage of data in Stage VI, is a natural tendency. You still want to be careful to forget the name of what it is that you are looking at, even though you can barely contain the desire to begin fitting the pieces together. At the bottom right of the page, the Viewer declared another piece of AOL/S visual data, "a rising structure." Because the new image was determined not to be a part of the present image, the new image was developed on a new page, in this case, page 58c (316), and the housekeeping note directing the reader to the sketch was included in parentheses.

The rendering on page 58c (316) is beginning to give a better sense of what was happening. Looking at it, you can still easily forget the name of what you are seeing, but it was clearly being perceived by the Viewer as a construction site or a structure under construction or men working. Look at the rendering; pay attention to the labeling. When I study it and close my eyes, I can almost smell the wet earth and hear the rumble of machines. Note the declaration of an AOL (meaning the Viewer did not trust the data as much as an AOL/S would have indicated, and it appeared in a fixed manner): the dimensional aspects of the rendering prompted an AOL of "a rocket bottom," likely from the analysis of the shape of the structure where three life forms are depicted. Because the "rocket bottom" did not involve an actual image, in and of itself, the data was not carried to another page; it was simply declared as being present. Just as on page 58a (314), it was an analytical call and not a new piece of visual data.

When the Viewer returned to the verbal matrix, at the bottom of page 57b (308), he understood that he had completed his first run through the verbal matrix, meaning he had to begin again in the S2 signal line category (just as in Stage IV). Beginning in S2, on the left of the page, the Viewer developed a small string of data before exhausting the work space and moving to another page.

Work began again on page 57c (309). A very long string of S2 data was decoded before the Viewer shifted into the dimensional category. He worked downward, decoding "tubes," "rolls," "cylindrical," and so on, waiting for visual data—in fact, using this verbal data to try to prompt or trigger more visual data. The page was completed, and the Viewer moved to page 57d (310) and developed three more pieces of dimensional data before experiencing a bi-location and declaring a break. He felt "nauseous," as if he had been "inhaling something"; one assumes inhaling something toxic.

Note that when he resumed the session, he decided to "[move up 500']." This was wise, since he had declared two breaks while detecting and decoding in this portion of the target. He was voluntarily moving to another location to avoid further difficulties that might have resulted in additional forced breaks. After he resumed the session, he reentered the signal line category he was working in when the bi-location occurred—the dimensional data category. The Viewer continued the string of data for another six elements before a visual AOL/S developed. The AOL/S was declared as "suspended/stacked boxes," and the housekeeping note "sketch page 58d" was made.

Page 58d (317) exhibits a great deal of detail; however, once again, the Viewer created an assumptive rendering. Missing are measurements of height, mass, and density and other critical pieces of data that would help us understand the rendering. When you do your sessions, always keep in mind the mission of Stage VI—renderings let us see the total picture of the target. Since all images in CRV are two-dimensional, it is up to the Viewer to include dimensional labels in the rendering; without these, we cannot grasp the concept of the target. The details are critical. You want to include everything available to you. Leave nothing to the conceptual illusion of your mind: objectify, objectify, objectify—write it down.

Note that at the bottom of page 58d (317) the Viewer declared an AOL/S, a visual of "men connecting metal." This visual did not attach to any other previously developed rendering; thus, it was given a separate page, numbered 58e (318).

Page 58e (314) is a rendering of two men attached to or standing on a platform that surrounds a vertical column. It was not labeled as such by the Viewer, so this is pure analysis. Again, it is an excellent sketch, with quality and quantity of data; however, you should consider the following: What is in the distance or the background, if anything? Are the two men above something? What is the color, the temperature, the texture, and so on? So much can be omitted by Viewers who are highly visual and who sketch quickly and well—you must be deliberate in your effort to objectify all that your mind perceives. Observers know nothing more than two dimensions of the rendering unless you tell them in your words. The bottom right of page 58e (318) indicates an AOL/S of "a cable and hook mechanism," which was sketched independently on page 58f (319).

Page 58f (319) does include a statement of distance in two instances: the labeling of "structures below" and the AOL declaration, in which the Viewer is analytical of the rendering, indicating "buildings/structures of glass and steel in the distance." Other details in the rendering ascribe "remote controlled" and "rotating" elements to the sketched "hook." Further, labeled data describes a "resistant, thin, & bolted surface" present, which appears to be connected to the "hook" and appears to be in perspective, above the AOL "buildings/structures." As soon as the signal line ran dark in the rendering, the Viewer returned to the verbal matrix to begin again.

Beginning again on verbal page 57e (311), the Viewer entered the signal line category he was working in when the AOL/S developed—the dimensional data category. A string of two more elements of data was produced, the signal line ran dark, and the Viewer moved to the right, entering the aesthetic data category. A string of six elements of data was produced—"creative," "complex fabrication," and so on—and the signal line weakened, so he moved to the emotional data category and decoded five elements of data. The emotional data signal line ended, and the Viewer moved to the right, entering the tangible category. Note the probe mark, in the tangible category with no data, meaning no tangible data was perceived. The Viewer moved right, entering the intangible category, and finished the page. The Viewer's final verbal page was numbered 57f, and he began detecting again in the intangible category. Five elements of data were decoded before an AOL/S moved him to another visual page, where he developed the rendering for "a vertical object of metal receiving energy (sketch page 58g)."

When additional visual data manifested, the Viewer checked to see if the image fit any existing renderings; this image was new and existed separately from all other renderings, so it was given a separate page, page 58g (320). The Viewer developed the sketch and described a flow of energy very well. In fact, there was a sense of source, "AOL, lightning strike," as well as motion and direction, "energy flow" and "pulsing outward and downward." These are excellent descriptors of something likely not visible in the target. Even if the Viewer perceived lightning striking an object, to carefully observe the motion and wave or pulse of the energy in relation to the object is the stuff of pure viewing—well done, in this case.

Note that the Viewer ended the session by ritually writing "End of Session" and including the time. To complete the ritual, you go to the front page of the session (see page 321), to the heading, and below the start time, you fill in the end time (ET:____), thereby completing the Coordinate Remote Viewing session.

END OF SESSION

You should now have a sense of how to navigate Stage VI to the completion of the CRV session. In these training sessions, your session ends because the ninety-minute time limit has been reached. You write "End of Session" to symbolically disengage from signal line contact and formally conclude your Remote Viewing session. Remember to record the time. At the end of the session, take a moment to "change set" and reorient yourself to your current surroundings. Breathe, stretch, take a sip of water, and then proceed to complete your session summary.

Next up is the session summary—see you in Chapter 13.

12

Sample Session

This chapter contains the work produced from a single Coordinate Remote Viewing session. It is provided to you as an expert example of how to record your raw data, correctly following the CRV structure, during a session from beginning to end. Throughout the text of this book, you will be instructed to refer to the Sample Session. The handwritten numbers in the upper right-hand corner of these sample pages are the Viewer's page numbers.

Mark
27 June 04
ST: 1300
ET:

AV - Yes
A SERIES OF IMAGES
AROUND A MARINA

PI - Yes
TIRED

3345
129

A. ACROSS, RISING
   SLOWLY, UP
   SHARP, peaking
   sloping down
B. MAN MADE

C. NO C

3345
129

A. ACROSS, flat,
   swooping up,
   VERTICAL up,
   Vertical down
   ACROSS

B. MAN MADE

C. AOL break
   A MARINA w/
   SAIL boats

Resume

3345
129

A. ACROSS,
Rising sharply,
vertical down,
Across, spin up
drop, flat across

B. manmade

C. STRUCTURE

SZ
gray
Amber
black
green
white
gray
Silver
muggy
warm
refertime
Reddish
misty
fuzzy texture

SZ ③

chipped

Silver

Red

copper

honking sound

clacking sound

Rushing sound

ROTTEN smell

WET

STEAMY

hazy

bright

glowing

golden

Rushing sound

VIBRATING ENERGY

MOVING/Swirling Energy

hot

AGITATED ENERGY

THERMAL ENERGY

RADIANT ENERGY

LIGHT BLUE

White

S2

black

ORANGE

yellow

grey

green

brown

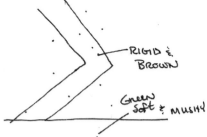

RIGID &
BROWN

Green
Soft & MUSHY

White

WET TASTE

fumes

ACRID smells

dirty / unclean tastes

GREASY smell

AOL
A GREASY
SPINNING
PIECE of
metal

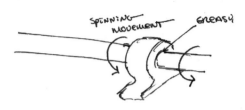

SPINNING
MOVEMENT   GREASY

S2

Reflective
gold
polished
Smooth

Stacked
Verticals
sharp
Edged
Creased
Wet smell

WATER smell

AOL
A SEA
SMELL

NATURAL smell
Sweet smell
Reddish brown
STRIATED

flat across movent
fluid
moving this way

AOL
SOME SORT
of fluid moving

S2

grainy
sloping
NARROW
pocked
squared
green
grey
SPARKLY

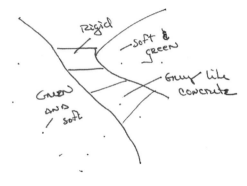

rigid

→ soft & green

→ grey like concrete

GREEN AND / soft

AOL
A CONCRETE
side walk

WARM

BLUSTERY

FLAPPING SOUND

HISSING SOUND

SQUEAKING SOUND

LAUGHING

AOL People
LAUGHING
& TALKING

S2

red

Blue

Flashing ENERGY

DARk clouds

AOL
DARk clouds
Like diesel
smoke

black

STRUCTUR

SLOPE

SLOPE

AOL
GRADED
NATURAL SLOPES
SURROUNDING
A STRUCTURE

blAN texture
NEUTRAL COLORS
heavy ENERGY

AI -
I feel VERY
put upoN -
AGITATED

S2
circular
Tall
Angled
hollow
sunken
curved verticals
Monumental (S4)
PRIDE (S4)

— Fuzzy
Energy

— white metal

AIRY

AI BREAK
I am feeling
overwhelmed by
some energy.
I feel small, even
engulfed by
something big.
— Resume
[MOVE up 500'
& Look down]

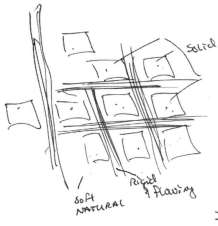

Solid

Rigid
& flowing

Soft
NATURAL

life (S4)
INANIMATE (S4)
high

CONFUSION
Break
I can't lock
ON — seem
to be unfocused

Resume

[down 500']

[RIGHT 500']

CUBES
SOLID
DENSE

STEEP

VERTICAL

heavy

RAPID ENERGY

MOVING ENERGY

heat

INTENSE heat

BRIGHT

Reflective

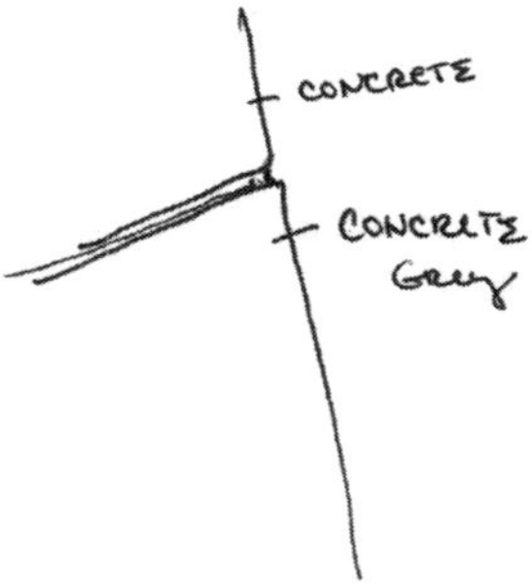

CONCRETE

CONCRETE
Grey

grey
flat

AOL
STACKED oR
FORMLESS CONCRETE
Blocks

AOL BREAK
CONCRETE
SIDEWALKS

RESUME

[RIGHT 100']

ANGULAR

RIBBED TEXTURE

FORMED (S4)

CIRCULAR

TRANSPARENT

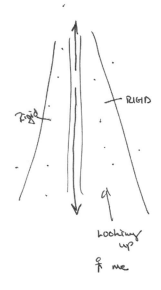

Rigid

RIGID

Looking up

ↂ me

AOL A
STRUCTURE
TALL & VERTICAL

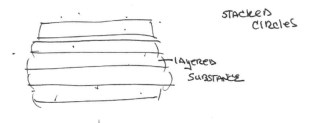

STACKED
CIRCLES

LAYERED
SUBSTANCE

AOL like
A STACK of
PANCAKES

S2

flexible
grey
black
white

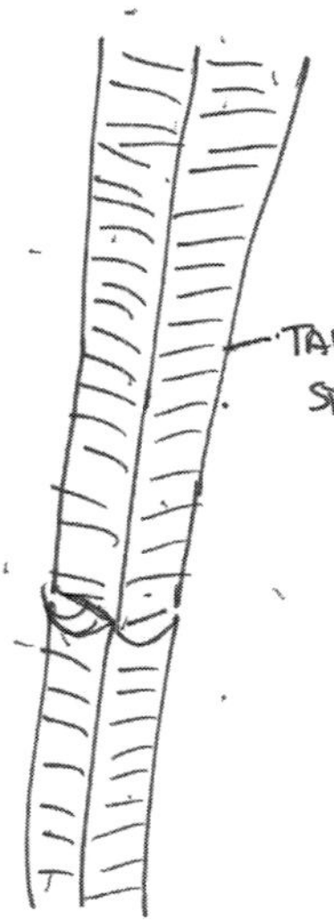

TALL AND
STACKED OR
IMPRINTED

AOL A
LADDER-LIKE
STRUCTURE

[MOVE BACK, LEVEL
1000'

BLUE
white
Red
BROWN

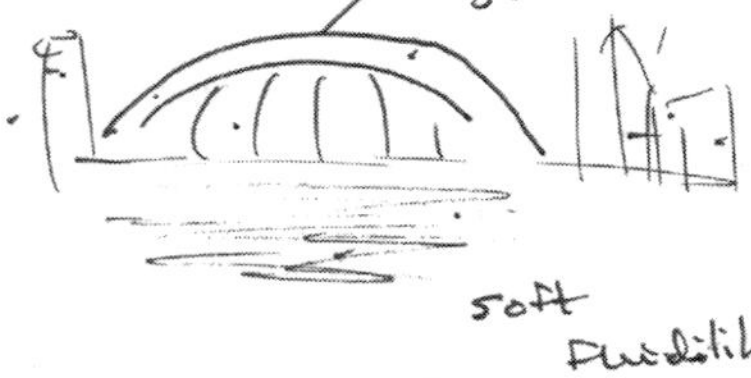

white
SOLID

soft
fluidilike

AOL A
CITY SKYLINE

S2

BLACK
SLICK
TALL
LINEAR
hollow
horizontal
    STRIATIONS

SQUARES
COLUMNS

              — Reddish
               Brick

             — Black glass

      — life forms

AOL BREAK
A BRICK
AND GLASS
    STRUCTURE
w/ life forms
moving IN & AROUND
RESUME

· fluid
blue

AOL
A body of
    water
wind blown

AOL
Chicago

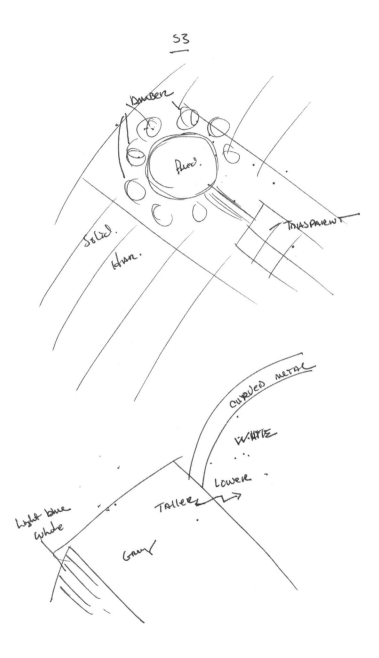

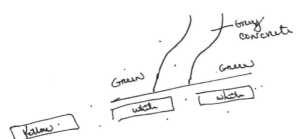

Grey concrete

Green   Green

Green

white   white

Yellow

AI - I am
up high looking
down - feels
WEIRD.

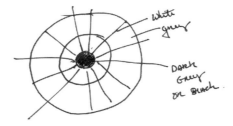

White
grey

Dark
Grey
or Black.

AOL
PATTERN IN
CONCRETE

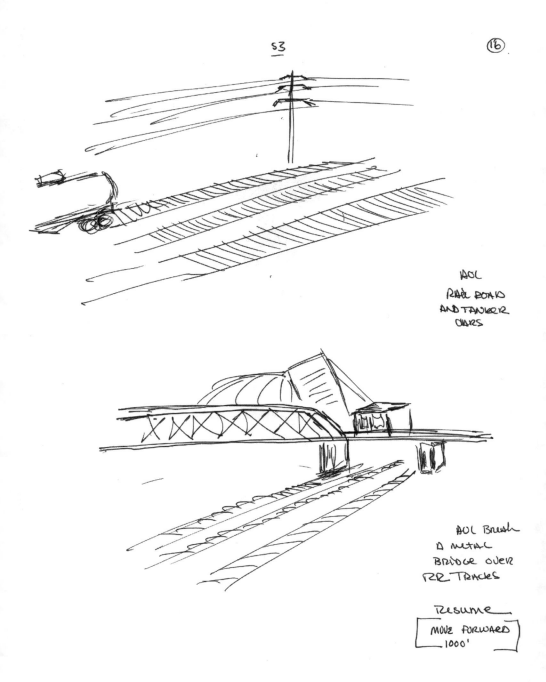

S3

⑯

AOC
RAIL ROAD
AND TANKER
CARS

AOC Bridge
A METAL
BRIDGE OVER
RR TRACKS

Resume
[MOVE FORWARD
1000']

AOL
GRAffiti
WORDS AND
SIGNS

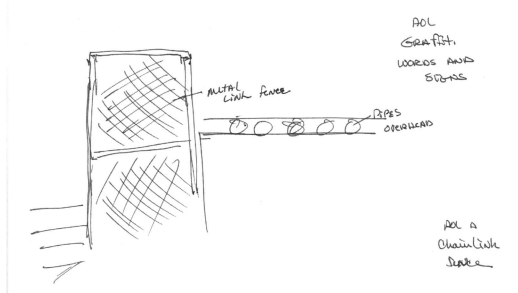

METAL LINK fence

PiPES
OVERHEAD

AOL a
Chainlink
fence

S3½ – I have a sense
I am underground or near
something underground. There is
trash and graffiti everywhere, paint,
oil and grease. This place is filthy.

AOL AN
OLD ORNATE
BRIDGE IN
URBAN
AREA.

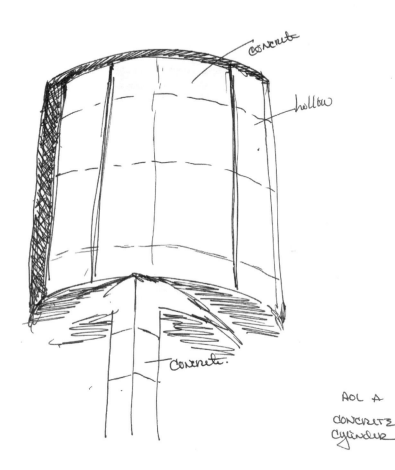

concrete

hollow

concrete.

AOL A
CONCRETE
Cylinder

S3   (19).

* MOVING BACK
  TO S2 to
     PURGE
  VERBAL data

S2

ROTTEN SMELL
ROTTEN TASTE
FILTH (S4)
decay (S4)
darkness
SPRAWL (S4)
UNEVEN TEXTURES
BLOCKED

AOL
URBAN
CAVES

3345
129L

A. CURVING UP
to VERTICAL. Vertical
down to curving
WAVY ACROSS.

B. Manmade

C. STRUCTURE

S2
grey
VERTICAL
STEEP

burnt smell
sweet smell

AOL Food
Smells

blue
Red
Leaning Verticals
Smooth
Small circles
curved horizontals

SILVER

grey
plastic

AOL
AUDITORIUM
OR THEATRE
SEATS.

Purple
grey
Red
MAROON

GLASS

AOL
GLASSES

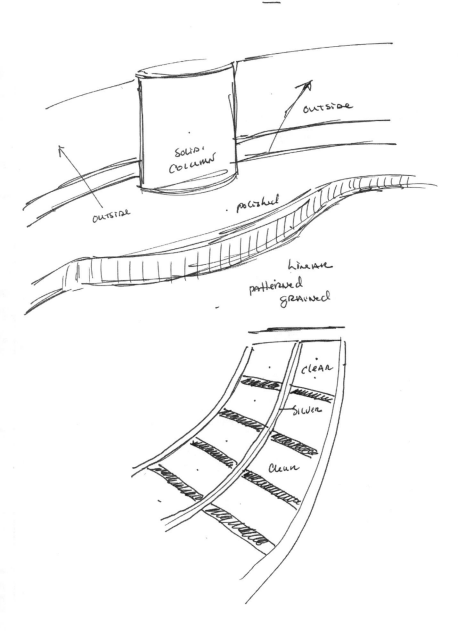

OUTSIDE

SOLID COLUMN

OUTSIDE

polished

LINEAR patterned grained

CLEAR

SILVER

Clean

CLEAN

CLEAN

SOLID WHITE METAL

CLEAN

CLEAN

SOLID WHITE METAL

COLOR CONFUSION

GLASS

WALKING IN

AOL LIFE FORM
walking Inside
something

(24).

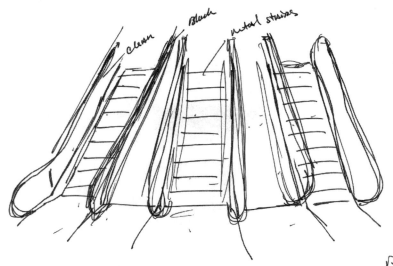

clean   Black   metal stairs

DOL
metal
ESCALATORS

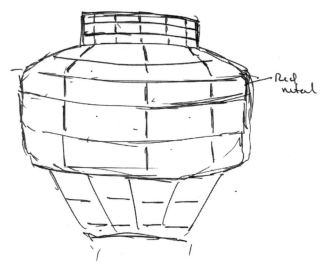

Red
metal

DOL A
Red
metal
STRUCTURE

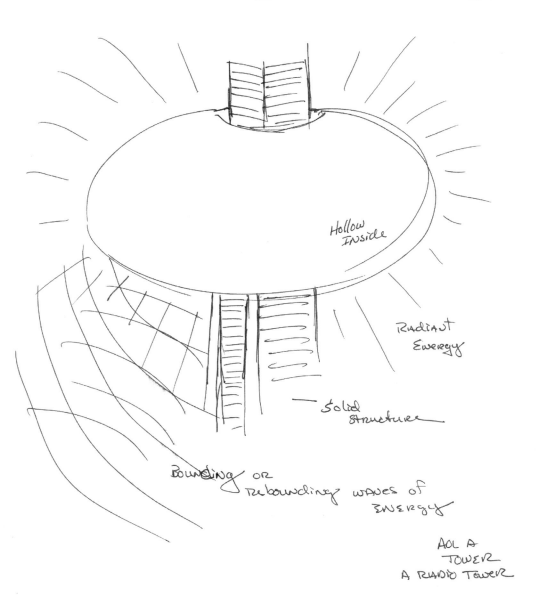

Hollow Inside

Radiant Energy

Solid Structure

Bounding or Rebounding waves of Energy

AOL A TOWER A RADIO TOWER

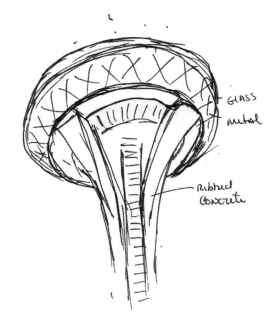

GLASS
metal

Ribbed
Concrete

AOL BREAK
The concrete
Tower
STRUCTURE

RESUME

[MOVE INSIDE
THE OBJECT]

AOL Δ
GLASS TUNNEL
INSIDE THE
STRUCTURE

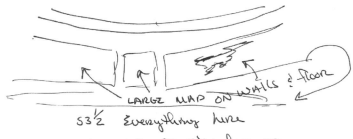

LARGE MAP ON WALLS & floor

S3½ Everything here

appears to be circular or

related in some way to

circles or circular objects.

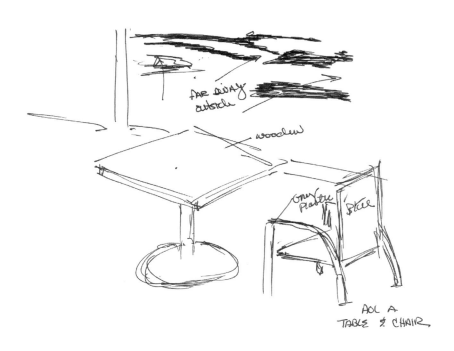

FAR AWAY
outside

wooden

only
plastic
steel

AOL A
TABLE & CHAIR

Some sort
of metal
grid
hung between
metal bars

glass

AOL A
gathering of
people
looking out
A set of
windows

S3½   I have a
sense this is a place
for tourists, w/ places to
eat, purchase and observe.
But, there is some other
purpose to this target as
well.

* Data repeatedly
— moving to STAGE
IV

54   ③0.

SZ   D   AD   ED   T   I   AOL   AOL/S

gray
red
blue
orange
green
natural smell
food smell

AOL/S
A RESTURANT

beige
white
fluffy
gleaming
brilliant light
red
yellowish

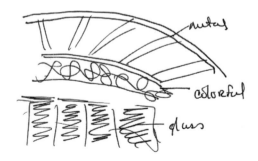
metal
colorful
glass

AOL
A doorway
or main
entrance

S2   D   AD   ED   T   I   AOL   AOL/s

hot
bright
muggy
stinky
stale
cool

RADIANT ENERGETICS
ELECTROMAGNETTC

AOL
AIR CONDITIONED

AOL
Electromagnetic
Energy associated
with this structure

AOL BREAK
the tower
STRUCTURE

Resume

[MOVE right
100']

Blue
Dark blue
        .
            TALL
        squares
        long
        COMPARTMENTALIZED (I)

SZ   D   AD   ED   T   I   AOL   AOI/s

Angled
Sloped
Curved
TALL
AIRY
Shaped or notched

.
         GARGANTUAN

         MASSIVE

         Complex

         ORNATE

         STUNNING

         Beautiful

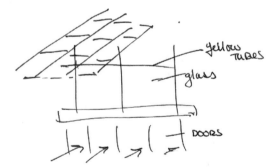

Yellow TUBES
glass
DOORS

AOL BREAK
4 glass
door way
again

S2   D   AD   SD   T   I   AOL   AOL/S

RESUME

[MOVE UP
     1000']

comfortable
formal
uniform
CRISP
pleasing

AI - I
feel like I
am very high
up - like I
might fall

open
    .
        Agitated
        Relieved

        worried.

        happy

        together

        Celebrating

            .

S2   D   AD   ED   <u>S4</u>   T   I   AOC   AOL/s   (34)

metal
glass
brass
steel
Rubber
Cloth
wood
plexiglass
fiberglass

Entertainment
demonstrate
INSPIRE
TRANSFORMED
COMMUNICATION
problematic
NAVIGATION

AOL/S
Break A
Large Tower
Again

Beaming waves
In and out

Concrete

H2O

Resume

[MOUZ INSIDE
THE IMAGE]

Amazing

casual

observation

NATIONAL

MONUMENTAL

HEROIC

Recognized

AOL
TURNSTILES

AOL
BINOCULARS

regulated movement

Polished
metal

BRASS

SZ   D   AD   ED̄ (S4)   T   I   AOL   AOL/s   (36).

AOL - A
SECURITY
GUARD OR
POLICEMAN

.

Yellow or
Blue

gold

silver

humid

~~flapping~~ sound

humming sound

.

No smell
.

AOL/s
AN ELECTRIC
MOTOR

BOXED

MOVING SQUARES

NARROW

POINTED

SPINES

S2	D	AD	S4 ED	T	I	AOL	AOL/S

POINTED

TALL

white
metal

AOL A
church
steeple

Square

shaped

slope of concrete

VERTICAL

.   breath-taking
         fine
         thrilling
         RACING/OR RACY

S2	D	AD	S4 ED	T	I	AOL	AOL/S

STRONG

' AFRAID

fear

COURAGE

.

glass

copper

cable

wood

flexible
MATERIAL

carpet

AOL
A CARPET
ON A FLOOR

glasses

AOL
wine & water
glasses

—GREY
EVERY

dishes

AOL/S
Grey Every
Capturing
dishes

S2   D   AD   <u>S4</u>   ED   T   I   AOL   AOL/S   (39)

wire

broadcasting

CONSTRUCTION

FINANCIAL

TARGET

REVOLVING
          INTEREST

ASCENDING
          INTEREST

ORANGE

AOL
A Helicopter
AN old
helicopter
style

AOL/S
spired and
horizontal
metal
          structure

54

S2   D   AD   ED   T   I   AOL   AOL/S

AOL/Break
A dining
Room filled
w/ people.

resume

[MOVE IN
50']

AOL/S
A circular
STAIRWAY
of metal and
stone

AOL/S
polished
stainless steel
walls, doors
AND RAILINGS

.

S2	D	AD	54 ED	T	I	AOL	AOL/S

blustery
blue

grey
polished
smooth

· curved

[curved AND flexible]

CIRCULAR

TILTED

· modern
incredible
Enclosed
MASSIVE
Extreme
Spectacular
Precision
balanced
proportioned

·

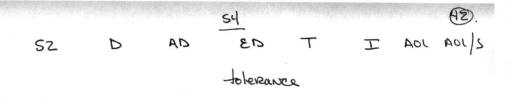

S2   D   AD $\overset{S4}{ED}$ T   I   AOL   AOL/S

tolerance

'   .

ENGINEERED

NATURE

SAFe

guided

controlled

driven

purposeful

.

AOL Break

A COMMUNICATION

TOWER

Energy

Energy

S2   D   AD   ED̄   T   I   AOL   AOL/S

54

AOL/S

A CROWN

54½ - I have a sense
the target gestalt is linked
to a large structure, that
serves multiple purposes; tourism,
communications, national pride
and corporate interests.

Bi LOCATION
Break
my head is
hurting —
vibrating like
I am near
A MICROWAVE
oven.

Resume

[MOVE DOWN]
1000' to
surface again]

S2   D   AD   S4/ED   T   I   AOL   AOL/S   44.

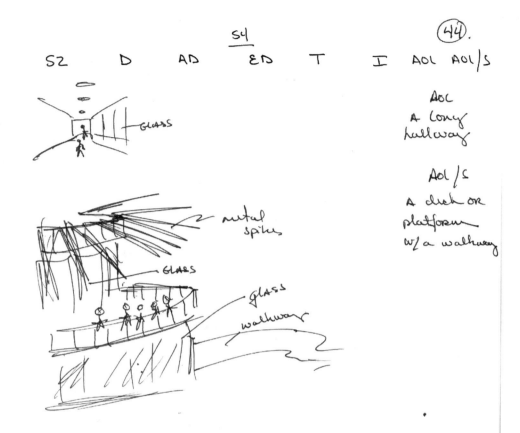

GLASS

metal spikes

GLASS

glass walkway

AOL
A long hallway

AOL/S
A deck or platform w/ a walkway

silver
glowing, gleaming
bright
hot
fresh smell
chattering sounds

S2	D	AD	S4 ED	T	I	AOL	AOL/S

whooshing
Sound
RAchet of
Soundes

AOL/S
Lots of
different sounds
playing in
backgrouncl
from televisions
and recorders.

blue
Silver

.   sloped down
       curved

.

AOC
A whulchair
Ramp in
blue and
Silver .

AOL
blue carpet

.

bottom heavy
thick
buried
Secured / fastened

SZ	D	AD	S4 ED	T	I	AOL	AOL/S
	base						
	.	.	.				
				grass			
							AOL S A grass field.
				glass			
							AOL/S glass doors and windows
							AOL/S FLAGS IN the wind
				white cloth			
				brass			
			.	pride			
				.	.		

white
brown
greenish blue
red
blue

S2	D	AD	S4 ED	T	I	AOL	AOL/S

.   .   high
                         ~~tall~~
                         thick
                         crossed

                                         EI-Break
                                       I feel
                                     Agitated or
                                     Angry from
                                     Something

                                       Resume

                                   [move inside
                                       the IMAGE]

                              UNEASY

                                         * Moving to
                                           STAGE V

INTANGIBLES

Entertainment
PRIDE

TOURISM

NATIONAL

CORPORATE

ENGINEERED

NATURE

SAFE

GUIDED

CONTROLLED

DRIVEN
PURPOSEFUL

BROADCASTING

CONSTRUCTION

FINANCIAL

TARGET

Revolving - Interest

Ascending - Interest

Amazing

Casual

OBSERVATION

Monumental

Heroic

Recognized

DEMONSTRATE

Inspire

NAVIGATION

Intangibles (cont.)

Transformed
Problematic
Communication

COMMUNICATION
OBJECTS
DATA   ?
_____

Towers
platforms
Microphones
Wires
Antenna
Speakers
dish
Cones
Scanners
Amplifiers
Loud speakers
Lecturns
phones
television
Radio
cellular phones
microwave dish
boosters

COMMUNICATION
OBJECTS
   DATA   ?
---

transmitters
re-transmitters
SATELLITES
COMPUTERS
Handhelds
data links

COMMUNICATION
ATTRIBUTES
   DATA   ?

Single source
Monopoly
purposeful
ACCOUNTABLE
CHOKE-POINT
DRIVEN
ORIENTED
Focused
CONSCIENTIOUS
GREEDY

COMMUNICATION
ATTRIBUTES
DATA ?

thorough
PAINSTAKING
Assidous
diligent
Meticulous
EDUCATIONAL
useful
helpful
INFORMATIVE
NARRATOR
Capitalist
ENTREPRENEUR
CORPORATE
Political
following
supporting
biased
INfluenced

COMMUNICATION
ATTRIBUTES

DATA ?

SUBJECTIVE
PREJUDICED
MANAGEMENT
direction
Regime
COMMAND
SUPERVISOR
Authority
LAW
Rule
ADMINISTRATION

IN CHARGE
ORGANIZE
MONITOR
Regulate
INspect
Limit
RESTRICT

COMMUNICATION
ATTRIBUTES
DATA ?

hegemony
domination
Power
sway
Influence
dictate

.

COMMUNICATION
SUBJECTS
DATA ?

boost
direct
Limit
charity
SORTING OUT
INCREASING RANGE
REACHING OUT
growing
getting higher

COMMUNICATION
   SUBJECTS
     DATA   ?
_____

   INCREASING

   INTENSIFYING

   GROWING

   EXPANDING

   BROAD

   EXPANSIVE

   ESCALATING

   A LARGER PIECE

   UPWARD

   CAPACITY UPWARD

   ENERGY

   ENERGY INCREASING

   MUSCLE ENERGY

   MIGHTY

SS

COMMUNICATION
SUBJECTS
DATA ?

Increasing Technology
Intensity
Forcefulness
Potential
Increased potential
Select talent
facility
Imagination
Prospective
Promise
Creativity
Captured energy
React
Ability

COMMUNICATION
SUBJECTS
DATA   ?

FAR REACHING
WORK
RANGE
DESIRE
POTENTIAL
KNOWLEDGE
data
facts
Details
INFORMATION
ESSENTIALS
Specifics
Thoughts
CONCENTRATION

COMMUNICATION
    SUBJECTS
        DATA   ?
_____

AWARENESS
CONSTANT ATTENTION
Watching Over
ATTENDING
CARE for
focused Intellect
Precision
Attention
Carefulness
Artistic
INVENTIVE
Resourceful
Ingenious
INNOVATIVE
Technological
Unlimited
.

* COMMUNICATION =
    144 Additional
    Pieces of data.

56

(57).

SZ	D	AD	ED	T	I	AOL	AOL/S

UNEVEN
    Texture

Not level
    Texture

Irregular
    Texture

bumpy

Jagged

Sweet smell

pot holed texture

Pocked texture

Rutted

.

        big

        giant upright

        lofty verticals

        Erect

        upright columns

        plumb verticals

        parallel squares

                A symetrical

                ENORMOUS

                gigantic

                Cosmic

                Incalculable

(shetch p.58)

AOL – A MACHINE
digging earth

56

SZ	D	AD	ED	T	I	AOL	AOL/S

huge
complex
STRIKING
EXTRAORDINARY
STUNNING
gorgeous
INTRICATE
difficult
.

EXCITED

ENTHUSIASTIC

Willing

FERVENT

PASSIONATE

NERVOUS

Apprehensive

Fearful

ENERGIZED

Too much Break
_____

Emotions present are
too fast and all over
the place.

S2   D   AD   ED   T   I   AOL   AOL/s   (57b).

Resume
(No movement).

thrilled
agitated

    fabric
    MATERIAL
    sludge
    dirt
    MIRE
    steel
    bracing
    Synthetics

AOL/s
A large
wooden wall
(sketch 58b)

HAZY
WARM
STILL

CALM ENERGY

SZ   D   AD   ED   T   I   AOL   AOL/S

grey
black
dark-brown
Earthy smell
Neutral taste

Wet

Soggy

mushy

Sodden

moist

bright

Salubrious

.

       Tubes
       Rolls
       clyndrical
       bowed
       curled
       Rounded
       warped

SZ   D   AD   ED   T   I   AOL   AOL/S

Octagonal
poly-Angles
MANY Angles

BI-LOCATION
BREAK —
I feel NAUSEOUS.
Like I have
been inhaling
Something.

Resume.

[Move up 500']

hexagonal
cylindrical
boxed
IRREgular
              surfaced
ATTACHED

CONNECTED

AOL/S
Suspended / STACKED
boxes (Shitch pg. 58d)

SZ   D   AD   ED   T   I   AOL   AOL/S

Affixed
~~fastened~~

creative
complex ~~fabrication~~
Elaborate
metaphorical
flamboyant
ORNAMENTAL

thrilled
delighted
overjoyed
blissful
Elated

ATTRACTION
INTERESTING
Seeing
historic
significant
Important
EPIC

SZ   D   AD   ED   T   I   AOL   AOL/s

famous
celebrated
Notable
Remembered
EMINENT

AOL/s
A VERTICAL
object of metal
RECEIVING ENERGY
(sketch pg. 58g)

58.

(Sketch Pg 58a)

AOL/S
A STAR SHAPED
Hole IN
GROUND

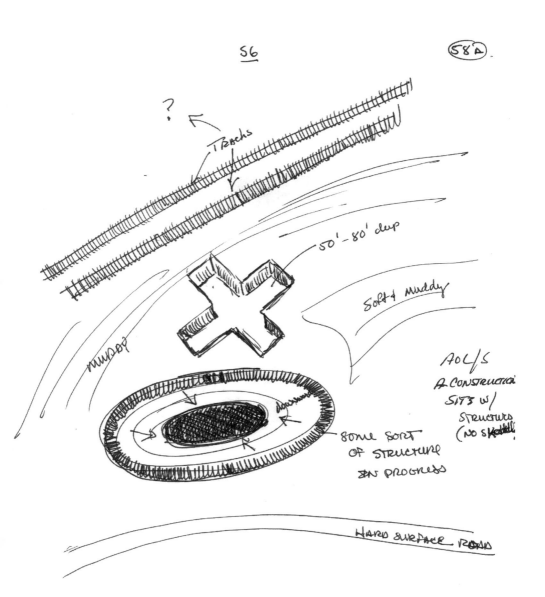

?

Tracks

50' - 80' deep

Soft & Muddy

MUDDY

AOL/S
A Construction
Site w/
Structure
(no structure)

Some sort
of structure
in progress

Hard surface road

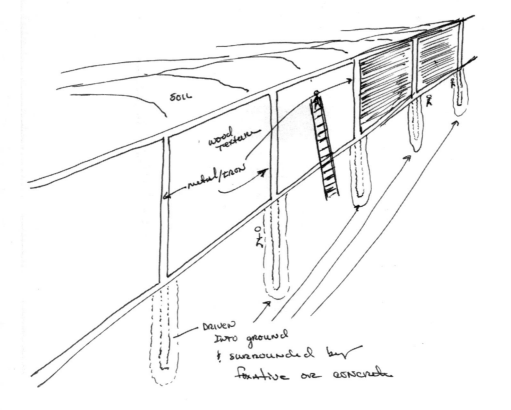

SOIL

wood
Texture

metal/IRON

DRIVEN
INTO ground
& surrounded by
fixative or concrete

AOL/S
A RISING
STRUCTURE
(Sketch 58c)

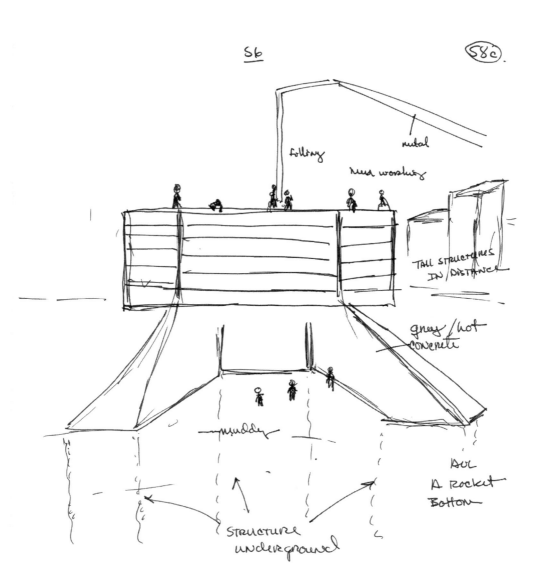

metal

falling

men working

TALL STRUCTURES
IN DISTANCE

grey/hot
concrete

muddy

but
A Rocket
Bottom

STRUCTURE
underground

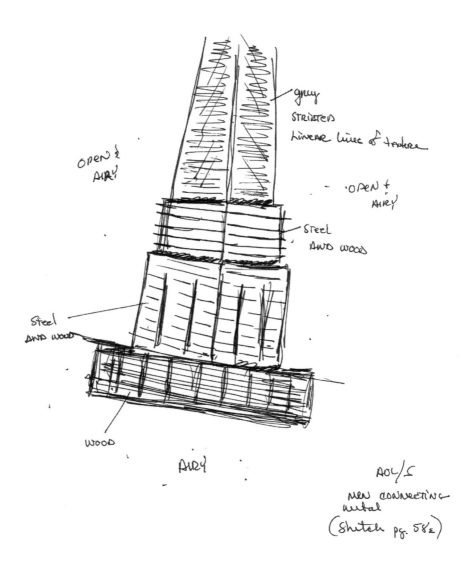

grey
STRIATED
linear lines of texture

· OPEN +
AIRY

OPEN &
AIRY

STEEL
AND WOOD

STEEL
AND WOOD

WOOD

AIRY

AOL/S
NEW CONNECTING
METAL
(Sketch pg. 58c)

S6

58e

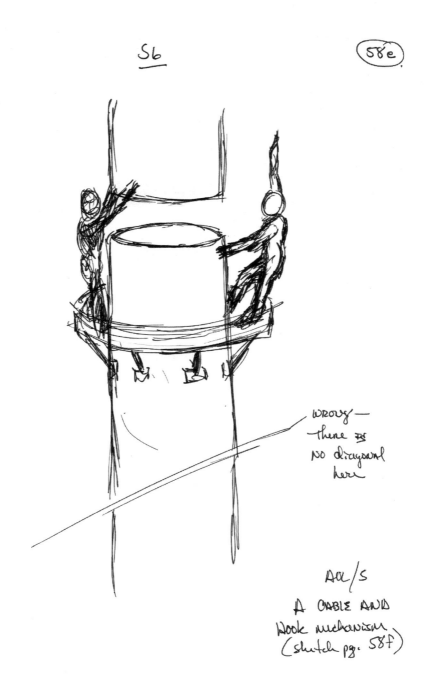

WRONG —
There is
NO diagonal
here

ALL/S

A CABLE AND
Hook mechanism
(sketch pg. 58f)

S6

RESISTANT
Thin &
Bolted
Surface

Rotating hook
Remote controlled

STRUCTURES
BELOW/

AOL-
BUILDINGS/
STRUCTURES of
glass and steel
IN the distance

S6

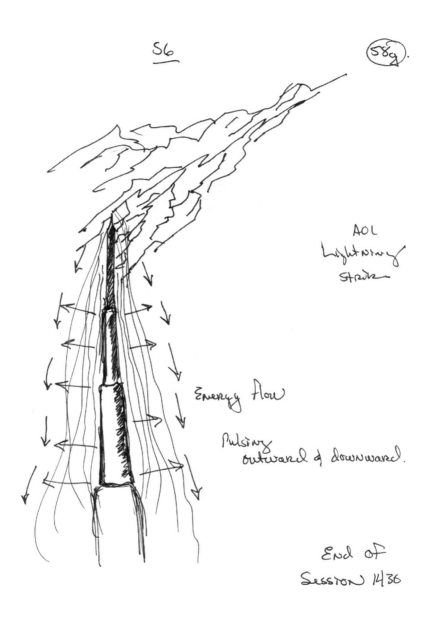

58g.

AOL
Lightning
Strike

Energy Flow

Pulsing
outward & downward.

End of
Session 1436

Mark
27 JUNE 04

ST: 1300
ET: 1430
73 pages

AV - Yes
A SERIES OF IMAGES
AROUND A MARINA

PI - Yes
TIRED

3345
129

A. ACROSS, RISING
SLOWLY, UP
sharp, reaching
sloping down

B. Man made

C. No C

3345
129

A. Across, flat,
swooping up,
VERTICAL up,
Vertical down
ACROSS

B. man made

C. AOL break
A MARINA w/
sail boats

13

Session Summary and Analysis

Direct your eye right inward and you'll find a thousand regions in your mind yet undiscovered. Travel them, and be expert in home-cosmography.

William Habington

This chapter discusses the "art form" of the session summary in detail. It provides you with a tool that guides you through the process from start to finish. You may want to begin by looking at the Summary Template (pages 336 and 337) and reading the Sample Session Summary at the end of this chapter (pages 338–343), which resulted from analyzing the Sample Session we've been working with throughout this book. Become comfortable with the summary process. Like everything else you have done so far, the session summary is part of the CRV protocol, and it is important that you grasp the structure of the summary. You must be able to translate your session experience into the summary effectively so that others will understand your work. The main responsibility rests with *you* in telling the story of the journey in the most usable and credible fashion.

To be successful in the summary process, you must stay in the observer role, developing your session data without judgment. It is never your mission to decide what it is you are viewing or to "call the target." New Remote Viewers have a tendency to leave valuable data in the session because they believe it "doesn't fit" or it's "not important." The cost of this judgment is the quality of the summary; therefore, the template and the process used to analyze and harvest data from your session are designed to make the summary easy for you. The structure here helps drive and pull the maximum amount of data from the session, and presents it in its most usable form as a list of critical verbal data and a narrative of your journey to and from the target site.

Consider it a procedural mandate to complete the summary immediately upon completion of the session. Plan time to do it in your session schedule, and never break the habit. Delaying summaries was a common error in the old military Remote Viewing unit. The program manager for the unit was constantly tracking down Viewers and asking them for their summaries, often of a target viewed days earlier. We could find all sorts of reasons not to do it in the moment. While you are preparing this summary, you should maintain the sanctity of your Remote Viewing environment, which means you should not drive to your favorite coffee shop to work on your summary, nor should you put it off until after dinner or after a movie. You are considered to be in residual signal line contact during the session summary; in other words, data is still flowing from the session. The summary process is the final mechanism for objectifying the data. To be clear on this point, the session is over; however, signal line data is still in the subconscious mind, your random-access memory, and it wants to be objectified. You should give yourself every opportunity to clear this data from your mind. In the residential classes, I never let students retire for the evening until they have completed their summaries—make this your practice as well.

PREPARE FOR THE SUMMARY

It is important for you to do all that you can to maintain an atmosphere of peace and quiet during the session summary. You should schedule a minimum of thirty minutes to complete an average session summary. If you have an extremely high volume of data, or your session was lengthy, as was the Sample Session for this text, then it may take you considerably longer to analyze the session and write the summary. Therefore, on occasions when you need more time, take the time to do a thorough job on your summary. Put on some peaceful music, preferably instrumental music, as vocals tend to disrupt your concentration and often skew your ability to focus properly on the summary. Keep your intention pure, remaining the observer.

ANALYSIS

Before you can write the summary, you must analyze the session and harvest the data you will use to cover the points in the Summary Template. In the following paragraphs, I identify several techniques used by experienced Viewers to analyze their sessions. You can use whichever you feel most comfortable with; however, I am partial to the process of listing elements of data on a separate worksheet and counting them to establish a numerical weight. I have found this technique helpful and accurate in establishing "clustering" of data.

Data clusters are present when colors, temperatures, or any other textural, dimensional, energetic, taste, smell, or sound data repeat. You can find data clustering by looking through the entire session rather than looking for groupings of words on one page. For example, you may find the texture of "spiky" in various forms: words like "sharp" and "pointy," a sketch of something that is labeled as sharp, narrow, pointed, or spiked. These constitute a cluster of textural data.

You will use the statements in Paragraph I of the Summary Template to look for the three dominant data clusters in each of twelve different data categories. One technique I have used involves highlighting elements of data with different-colored highlighters. You form your own color key and highlight or place a check mark next to each verbal indicator in the color assigned to its category (for example, use a blue marker for verbal elements of data indicating the color blue in all its shades and variations—light blue, cobalt, violet, pale blue, deep blue, sky blue, blue water, icy blue, bluish, and so on). When finished, you simply page through the session, count the check marks in each color, and record the totals on a separate page.

Obviously, in any session, you can perceive and describe every color imaginable within the light spectrum; therefore, you need a system to group them for measurement. Using the ROYGBIV acronym gives you seven major categories of color (red, orange, yellow, green, blue, indigo, violet) in which to group all color data. This framework keeps it simple and keeps the analysis moving at a manageable pace. Using the same technique, the Viewer can group dimensional data, separating all elements of data into vertical, horizontal, diagonal, tubular, arched, curved, mass and density. Each dimensional category is assigned its own color, and the Viewer works through the session, highlighting or placing a check mark next to each dimensional characteristic. Finally, the dimensional data is tallied by color, and the totals are recorded.

When writing Paragraph I of the summary, where the template calls for the respective principal elements of the data categories, you simply use the numerically superior subcategories of data to complete the sentences—for example, "The principal elements of dimensional data are tall verticals, curves, and heavy density." After you complete a few session summaries, you will know what colors, textures, dimensional data, and so forth are dominant without having to methodically count them all. After a few sessions, say five or six, the details will begin to emerge during the session, and you will easily move through the session analysis and determine what the principal elements are.

Among other techniques, some Viewers prefer to circle clusters of data with their black pen, while others simply indicate dominant clusters of data by placing a check mark, an asterisk, or a line through, while still others draw an arrow next to the clusters they are tracking through the session. It is your choice how you mark clusters of data, but you must do so in order to know what to list in the session summary.

The analysis technique used by the Viewer of the Sample Session involves moving through the session listing the verbal data in their respective signal line categories on a separate sheet of paper. This "initial analysis" is similar to the listing of intangibles for the Stage V process. These worksheets are not considered part of the session and they are not numbered to be included in the session; however, they are valuable analytic notes, and you should save them with the session summary for your reference and training.

In the "initial analysis" page for the Sample Session, shown in Figure 13.1, you can see how an analysis of a session is conducted. Working as quickly and thoroughly as possible, the Viewer harvested data from his session and assigned it among the sensory categories itemized in the first paragraph of the Summary Template. The data was then organized into a more usable format. Figures 13.2 through 13.5 illustrate the "summary analysis" pages, on which the data is totalled so that it can be "weighted" to determine the three dominant data clusters per category. Note that the third and fourth pages of the summary analysis include both the assigning and totalling of data for four of the twelve data categories itemized in the first paragrapsh of the Summary

FIGURE 13.1 **Initial Analysis**

Template, as well as qualitative analysis of the AOLs and AOL/Ss. Note that, as the Viewer counted the elements of data, he lined through what he counted so as not to count anything twice. These worksheets are sequentially numbered and serve as a reference to be used when writing the summary.

If you apply this technique, give it your best effort, but do not expect perfection. You *will* miss elements, double-count, omit, and so forth; however, knowing this,

FIGURE 13.2 **Summary Analysis, Page 1**

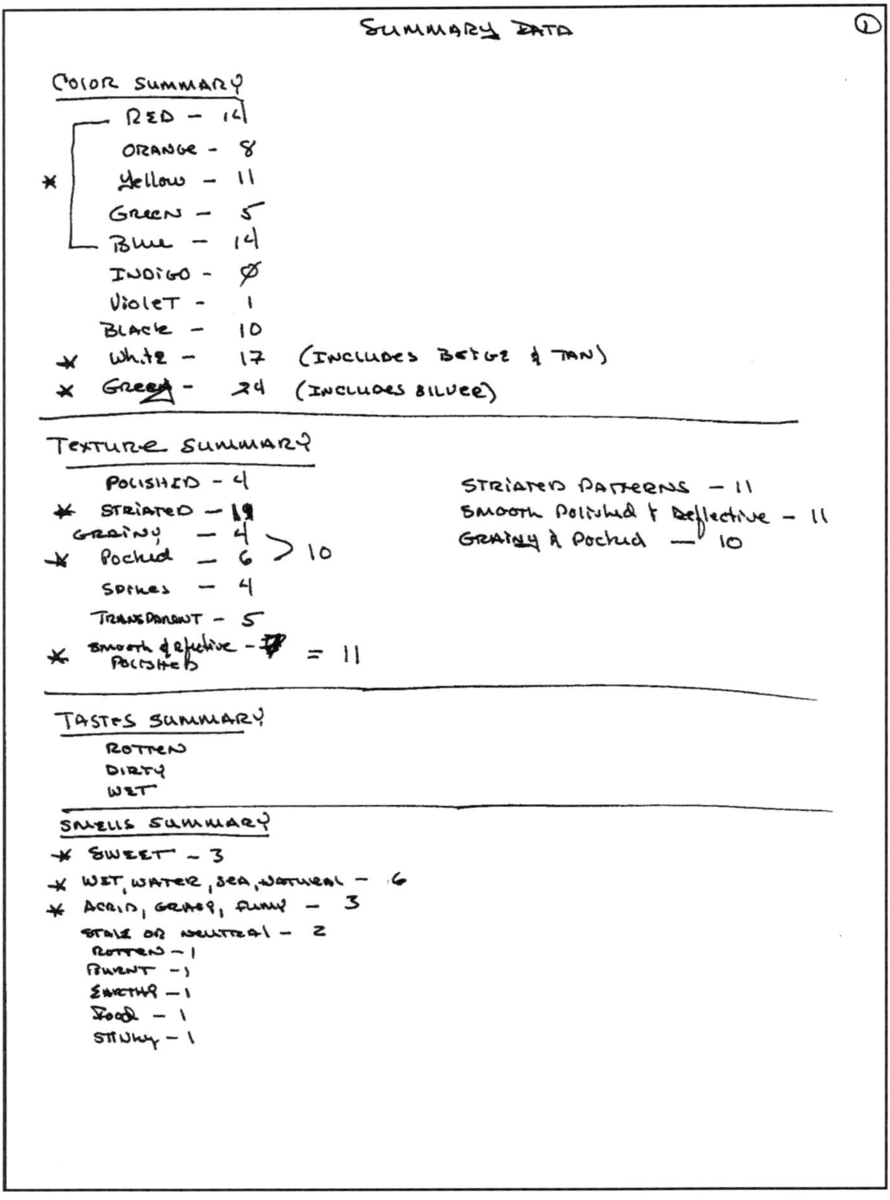

SUMMARY DATA ①

COLOR SUMMARY
- RED — 14
- ORANGE — 8
- * Yellow — 11
- GREEN — 5
- BLUE — 14
- INDIGO — Ø
- VIOLET — 1
- BLACK — 10
- * White — 17 (INCLUDES BEIGE & TAN)
- * Green — 24 (INCLUDES SILVER)

TEXTURE SUMMARY
- POLISHED — 4
- * STRIATED — 11
- GRAINY — 4
- * Pocked — 6 } 10
- SPIKES — 4
- TRANSPARENT — 5
- * smooth & reflective — 7 = 11
  Polished

STRIATED PATTERNS — 11
SMOOTH Polished & Reflective — 11
GRAINY & Pocked — 10

TASTES SUMMARY
- ROTTEN
- DIRTY
- WET

SMELLS SUMMARY
- * SWEET — 3
- * WET, WATER, SEA, NATURAL — 6
- * ACRID, GRASS, FUNNY — 3
- STALE OR NEUTRAL — 2
  - ROTTEN — 1
  - BURNT — 1
  - EARTHY — 1
  - FOOD — 1
  - STINKY — 1

FIGURE 13.3 **Summary Analysis, Page 2**

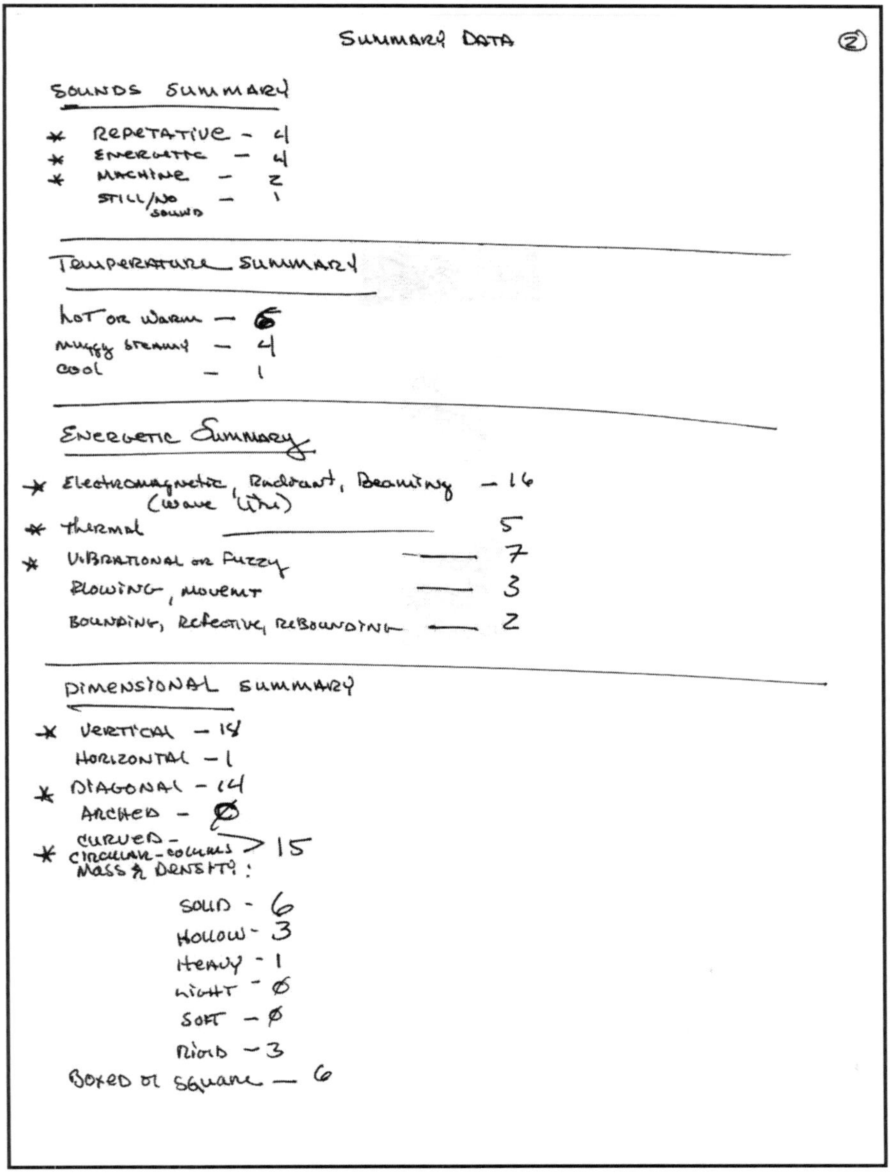

SUMMARY DATA ②

SOUNDS SUMMARY

* REPETATIVE – 4
* ENERGETIC – 4
* MACHINE – 2
STILL/NO – 1
SOUND

TEMPERATURE SUMMARY

HOT OR WARM – 6
MUGGY STEAMY – 4
COOL – 1

ENERGETIC SUMMARY

* Electromagnetic, Radiant, Beaming – 16
(Wave 'like')
* Thermal _____ 5
* ViBRATIONAL OR FUZZY ———— 7
BLOWING, MOVEMENT ———— 3
BOUNDING, REFLECTIVE, REBOUNDING —— 2

DIMENSIONAL SUMMARY

* VERTICAL – 18
HORIZONTAL – 1
* DIAGONAL – 14
ARCHED – Ø
* CURVED –
CIRCULAR-COLUMNS } 15
MASS & DENSITY :
SOLID – 6
HOLLOW – 3
HEAVY – 1
LIGHT – Ø
SOFT – Ø
RIGID – 3
BOXED or SQUARE — 6

FIGURE 13.4 **Summary Analysis, Page 3**

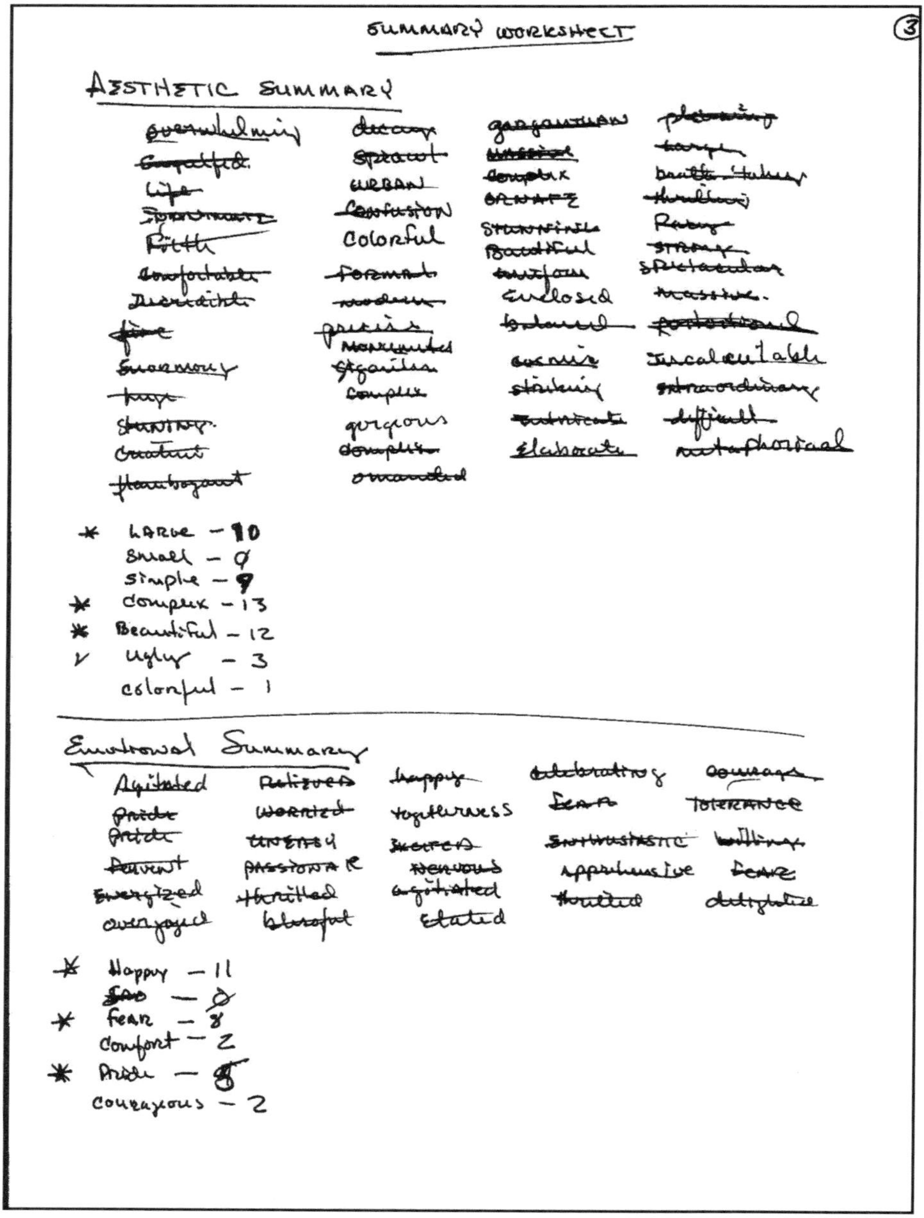

SUMMARY WORKSHEET

3

AESTHETIC SUMMARY

overwhelming
life
comfortable
flamboyant
decay
sprawl
URBAN
CONFUSION
Colorful
formal
modern
precise
monumental
complex
gorgeous
complex
ornamented
gargantuan
complex
Enclosed
balanced
striking
intricate
Elaborate
strange
spectacular
massive
incalculable
extraordinary
difficult
metaphorical

* LARGE – 10
SMALL – 0
simple – 9
* complex – 13
* Beautiful – 12
✓ ugly – 3
colorful – 1

Emotional Summary

Agitated
Pride
Fervent
Energized
overjoyed
WORRIED
UNEASY
PASSIONATE
thrilled
happy
togetherness
SCARED
NERVOUS
agitated
Elated
celebrating
FEAR
ENTHUSIASTIC
apprehensive
courage
TOLERANCE
FEAR

* Happy – 11
SAD – 0
* Fear – 8
Comfort – 2
* Pride – 5
courageous – 2

FIGURE 13.5 **Summary Analysis, Page 4**

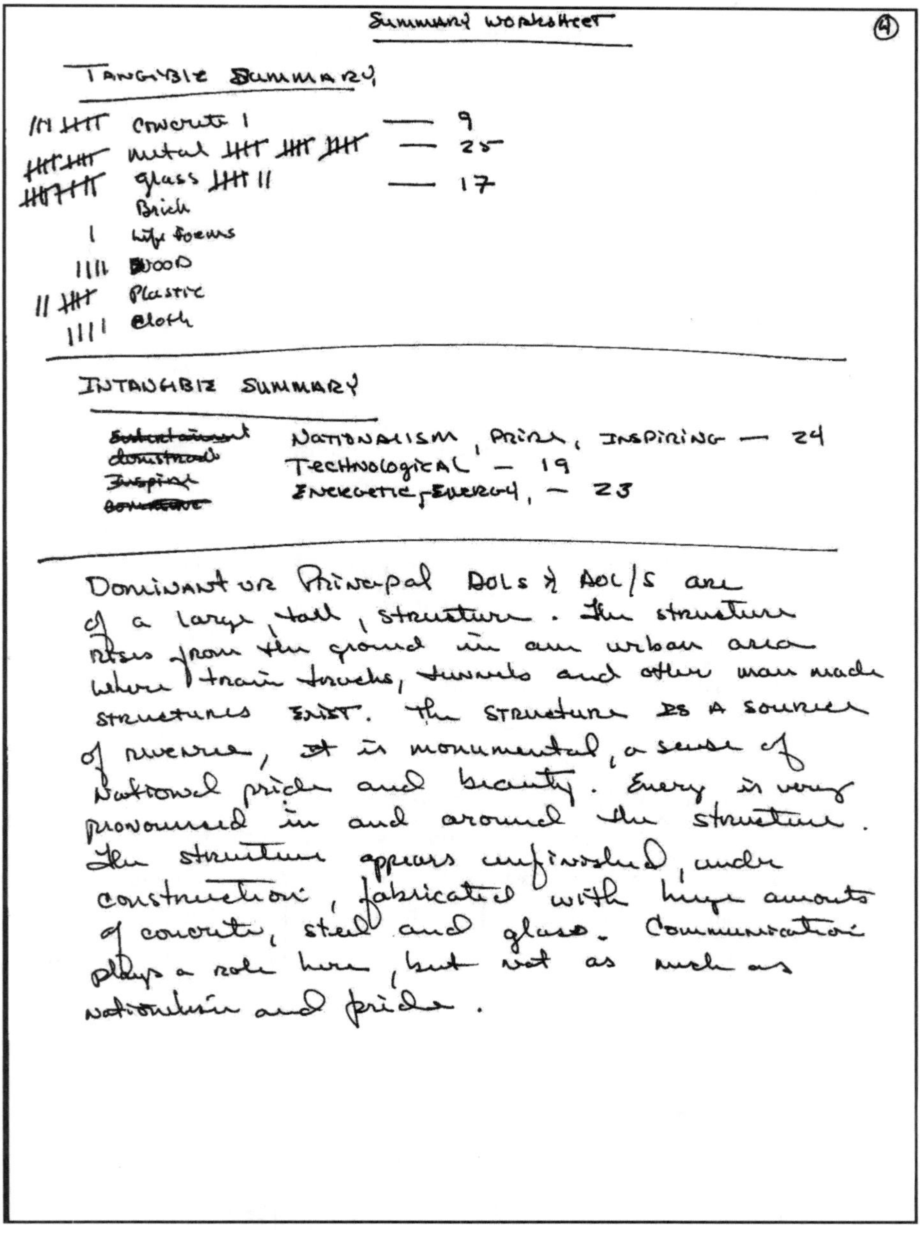

Summary Worksheet ④

TANGIBLE SUMMARY

IM HTT   Concrete 1   — 9
HTT HTT metal HTT HTT HTT   — 25
HTT HTT glass HTT II   — 17
         Brick
    I   Life forms
  IIII   Wood
 II HTT Plastic
  IIII   Cloth

INTANGIBLE SUMMARY

~~Entertainment~~   NATIONALISM, PRIDE, INSPIRING — 24
~~Consumed~~   TECHNOLOGICAL — 19
~~Inspire~~   ENERGETIC, ENERGY, — 23
~~Sourceive~~

Dominant or Principal DOLs & AOL/s are
of a large, tall, structure. The structure
rises from the ground in an urban area
where train tracks, tunnels and other man made
structures exist. The structure is a source
of revenue, it is monumental, a sense of
National pride and beauty. Energy is very
pronounced in and around the structure.
The structure appears unfinished, under
construction, fabricated with huge amounts
of concrete, steel and glass. Communication
plays a role here, but not as much as
nationalism and pride.

you can make every effort to be precise. The reason for all this effort is to make the writing of the summary easier and more complete. Instead of generating it all from pure memory, this process is deliberate and constructive, and new Viewers are often surprised at the sheer volume of data derived in a session.

SESSION SUMMARY FORMAT

The Summary Template serves as your guide for writing the actual session summary. You begin by naming the target coordinates, the Viewer, the date, and the start and end times.

Paragraph I

When you write Paragraph I, the analytic paragraph, write it out completely; don't just fill in the blanks on the template—see the Sample Session Summary on page 338 for an example. The reason for this is that data from the session will continue to develop during the summary process. Ending the session is analogous to turning off the water running through a garden hose at the spigot. When you do this, you know that water continues to flow through the hose. As I mentioned earlier, the same is true of data derived from signal line contact. You terminate the session, but as you work through the discipline of analyzing the session data and completing the summary format, you will find that, often, new data shows up.

For example, you may not have any olfactory elements of data from the session. However, while you are writing the first paragraph of the summary, you suddenly develop a sense of something, a "cooking food smell," not perceived during the session. Record it now, and understand that, unless someone is cooking a meal outside your window, any food smells are considered elements of data trickling in from the subconscious mind. It is the "ritual" of the summary process that prompts the release of this data, which is why the integrity of the session environment must be protected during the summary.

You address all the points in Paragraph I of the template, listing the major elements of data you discovered from the analysis process, and then move on to Paragraph II, the narrative.

Paragraph II

This is known as the narrative paragraph because it is used to formulate a "story," from start to finish, about your journey in the target. Include your perceptions and your experiences, such as AOLs and breaks, movements, and bi-locations. This is your opportunity to explain how the session flowed for you and to give an account of your adventure in the target site. Bear in mind, you must write this paragraph, tell this story, while trying not to label it, or "call the target." Do not distill an entire session down to what your conscious mind tells you it "thinks" the target is. This is a paragraph that relies heavily on the residual flow of data derived from the signal line following the termination of the session. It is also a canvas for creative verbal stitching of "overall" perceptions from the session.

You will craft a story by covering how you felt during the session from physical, emotional, and spiritual perspectives. List chronologically how the data developed and what you sensed that was pronounced. If you perceived aesthetics, emotional data, or abstract intangible data related to the session and the target site, you should include it here. If you experienced data bleed-through of these categories of data in Stages I through III, you mention that in the summary, indicating that they appeared early in the session, and include the stage in which they appeared. For example, "I felt emotionally drained in this session while I was working in Stage II. I felt like this was a politically dominant target with a great deal of institutional complexity; I felt like I was in the middle of some huge debate, and the energy there simply wore me out before I reached Stage VI."

At any time during the narrative portion of the summary, you may want to reference a sketch you made. For example, "I felt myself pinned against a very large object (see sketch on page 22)." You have indicated that the object was pronounced, that you interacted with it, and that you sketched the object on page 22. If you do this in your summary wherever possible, your summaries will grow to be thorough, complete, and illustrative accounts of your sessions.

AOL IN THE SUMMARY

If you have an overwhelming analytical overlay that indicates the target by name, for example, the Golden Gate Bridge, then you must objectify that AOL even in the summary, and you should clearly indicate that you know it is an AOL. For example, "During the session, on page 15, I sketched a large, suspended metal structure connecting two pieces of land. This sketch in combination with other verbal and visual sensory data developed a strong AOL that I was observing the Golden Gate Bridge."

This aspect of the target gestalt might actually be a large irrigation pipe suspended across a gorge, which, if you were able to control the AOL, may be written in this way: "During the session, on page 15, I sketched a large, suspended metal object that spanned two pieces of land. I felt water was associated with this object in some way; it either was under it or contained within it. However, I was unable to determine this to any reliable degree. Regardless, my sense was clearly that some manmade object connected these two elements of land and that this object was suspended in the air."

The latter description ultimately includes more data than the first, and it is the better description, yet it is the former we are more prone to write. With practice, this changes, and you will improve. The reason for this goes back to the conditioning concept, in that we have been training throughout life to be succinct, to think and to speak in brief, all-encompassing terms, to call it, to label it. Years ago, before I learned to see the world through different eyes, I might have defined "nature" as "anything outside, in the woods." I can assure you I would not have been elaborate. I hope you will adopt the process of expanding and not limiting. Your task as a Remote Viewer is not only to see the world through a different set of eyes (nonphysical eyes), but also to learn to describe it, to objectify it for us all, to remove your perceptions from the illusion of thought form, distilling them so that we may drink from your experience.

Therefore, in this narrative paragraph, you should focus on what you "feel" the target looks like, its purpose, who or what is there; speak in general terms to give yourself every opportunity not to overlay the summary process with your imagination. You should reference your major sketches, tying together the major elements of abstract intangible data. For instance, your perceptions may have identified the three principal elements of intangible data to be "monumental," "governmental," and "pride." You are responsible for assembling this data into usable narrative descriptors, for example:

> I developed a sense there was a governmental aspect to this target gestalt. This sense is primarily based on the several pieces of verbal data derived in Stage IV, indicating conflict, weapons, vehicles, and uniforms. Vehicles and uniforms were sketched on pages 27 and 32, respectively. However, I also had a sense that there was a monument present, both from my intangible impressions and from several sketches of large concrete objects, which appeared to be sitting alone in places

of prominence; see sketches on pages 36, 49, and 51. Overall, my sense from this target was one of great pride, not so much individual pride, but rather a collective, national pride in some distant accomplishment or sacrifice. Perhaps it was a competition, or it may have been a conflict; there was not enough data to indicate which.

SUMMARY TEMPLATE

Paragraph I

The Analysis Paragraph. To complete this paragraph, follow the example in this chapter that illustrates how to use analysis worksheets to harvest data from the pages of your session. In some cases, elements of data may be absent, meaning you did not detect it or it was not present. Do not be alarmed by missing elements of data; simply trust the process and write out the summary in paragraph form after filling in the blanks with the results of your analysis. If you do not have data for a particular category, be sure to indicate by writing, "No principal smells," or "No principal energetic data was perceived," or words to that effect.

- My perception of the target site is a: (B) _____ [1] (C) _____ [2]
- The gestalt contains the following principal colors: _____, _____, and _____.
- The primary textures present are _____, _____, and _____.
- The principal energetic data present are _____, _____, and _____.
- The principal sounds present are _____, _____, and _____.
- The principal smells present are _____, _____, and _____.
- The principal tastes present are _____, _____, and _____.
- The principal temperatures present are _____, _____, and _____.
- The principal dimensional data are _____, _____, and _____.
- The principal aesthetics are _____, _____, and _____.
- The principal elements of emotional data present are _____, _____, and _____.
- The principal elements of tangible data present are _____, _____, and _____.
- The principal elements of intangible data present are _____, _____, and _____.
- I selected the following intangible for Stage V, _____, and I produced _____ additional pieces of data during the Stage V process.

---

1. This space is used for listing the last "B" component you decoded prior to moving into Stage II. If you took the coordinates again somewhere during the session, then it will be the last taken, the last ideogram decoded, is the last place you were theoretically repositioned in the target site. Remember that each time you take the coordinates, you are repositioning yourself in the target gestalt: therefore, it is necessary to list your last position or your last "B" component decoded.

2. This space is reserved for the last "C" component decoded in the session—following the same reasoning as indicated in footnote 1 above.

Paragraph II

The Narrative Paragraph. This portion of the summary is designed for you to provide a narrative summary of the total session. For the first paragraph, you performed a simple analysis and summary of the session, extracting clustered data so that you could create a verbal mosaic of the target site. In this narrative paragraph, your task is to tell the story of your ninety-minute journey in the target, referencing sketches (visual sensory data) and constantly being on the watch not to begin naming what you think the target site is. You may begin this as follows:

My general sense of this target at this stage within the structure is

_____

_____

_____

_____

_____

_____

_____

_____

_____

_____

_____

_____

_____

_____

_____

_____

_____

_____

NOTE: This is your version of the session—what you "feel" the target looks like, its purpose, who is here or was here, and so on. Use this section of the summary to reference sketches and to tie together the major elements of the abstract intangible data. Think of this as a story about the target, your experience with the target, and what you feel the target site might represent. Describe, while refraining from conclusion or judgment.

TARGET COORDINATES: 3345/1291

Name: Mark
Date of Session: 06/27/04
Start Time: 1300
End Time: 1430

Paragraph I

My perception of the target site is a: (B) manmade (C) structure. The principal elements of the gestalt contain the following colors: grey, white, and red, with other colors, blue, black, and orange, being very prominent as well. The primary textures present are polished, grainy, and horizontally ribbed or striated (AOL ladder-like). The principal energetic data present are radiant, vibrating, and a sense of thermal energy. The principal sounds present are repetitive sounds, machine sounds, and energetic sounds (AOL electronic signals, waves—perceived, not well defined). The principal smells present are water-related smells, acrid, greasy smells followed by a sweet smell (AOL diesel smell, and AOL food smells). The principal tastes present are rotten, dirty (AOL urban decay), and wet tastes. The principal temperatures present are muggy (AOL a sense of high humidity) and some cool. The principal dimensional data are verticals (× 18), diagonals (× 14), and curves or circles (× 15). The principal aesthetics are complex, beautiful, and large (numerous AOLs on large, huge, and massive structures). The principal elements of emotional data present are descriptors of happiness, fear, and pride, with some elements of apprehension and agitation developed in Stage IV; however, in the Stage VI verbal data, the pattern changed to exhilaration, passion, and excitement. The principal elements of tangible data present are concrete, steel or metal, and glass (AOL concrete and glass structures). The principal elements of intangible data present are descriptors of nationalism, technology, and energy. I selected the following intangible for Stage V, "communication," and I produced 144 additional pieces of data during the Stage V process.

Paragraph II

(a) My initial sense of this target was that it was an urban area filled with multiple structures of varied heights and shapes. Also present were improved or paved roadways, railways, and waterfront areas that are associated with a large built-up area. The target gestalt seemed to be near a large body of water, although for much of the session, this was only brushed upon, and my perceptions never really drove me to anything prominent. I did have the perception of a marina early on, my first AOL, which I declared on page 1 during the "C"-component decoding process.

(b) Elements of sound data came quickly during the Stage II process on page 3, and all could be categorized as sounds associated with machinery of some type. There was also a strong development of energy early on in the session, on page 3, indicating a presence of rushing, vibrating, moving/swirling, thermal, and radiant energy. The sense of AOL machinery repeated itself on page 4, where the AOL was declared and sketched as "a greasy spinning piece of metal."

(c) On page 5, a strong sense of fluid associated with a natural water source was perceived (AOL sea smell), and a sketch indicating parallel lines of fluid movement. On page 6, data began to assimilate itself into indicators of dimension, beginning with squared, followed by a rigid, grey, concrete element, which was declared as an AOL of "a concrete sidewalk." This sidewalk was sketched on page 6. The indicator that this was an inhabited area was the presence of laughing, an AOL of "people laughing & talking" on page 6, at the bottom. Page 7 developed an AOL indicating diesel smoke, and the page ended with the first aesthetic-impact declaration that "I feel very put upon—agitated." In retrospect, I had a sense that I was being bombarded by something unseen, some form of energetic that developed further in the session.

(d) Page 8 produced the first "out of stage" intangible data, supporting the notion of "monumental" and "pride." A sketch on page 8 portrays a "white metal" structure with "fuzzy energy" emanating from it. The previous AI manifested again, and I was forced to declare an AI break after feeling engulfed in this very strong energetic. Still in Stage II, on page 9, I declared a confusion break because I felt I was all over the map in the session and could not lock on to any data.

(e) Other dimensional data began emerging, describing cubed, solid, and dense elements. A sketch on page 10 indicates an AOL of "stacked or formed concrete blocks," which I perceived to be quite massive and not the cement blocks used in wall construction. On page 11, the first sketch of an AOL, "a structure, tall and vertical," is present. There is also an AOL sketch of "stacked circles" or layered textures and substances, and on page 12, Stage II continued the development of data supporting a built-up or urban area.

(f) There is a sketch of an AOL of "a ladder-like structure," and even of an AOL of "a city skyline." On page 13, AOL elements of glass, brick, structures, and moving life forms required a break. A sketch gives perspective and proportion of the perceptions, and an AOL of "Chicago" was declared, possibly due to the AOL "a city skyline" being perceived next to "a body of water, windblown."

(g) Page 14 transitioned into Stage III, with several sketches indicating elements of some dimension, color, and fluid. Page 15 gives some indication that I was perceiving the target from above it; see the AI declaration "I am up high looking down—feels weird." Also on this page, a presence of AOL, "pattern in concrete," developed with a sketch.

(h) Page 16 has clear AOL sketches of a railroad yard with three or more sets of tracks and "tanker cars" present. There is, in the second AOL sketch, "a metal bridge over RR tracks." Stage III data further supports the notion that this target was an urban area, with "pipes overhead" and AOLs of "a chainlink fence," "an old, ornate bridge in urban area," and "graffiti words and signs." The S3½ indicates that I felt I was underground or near something underground. Page 18 contains a sketch of an AOL of "a concrete cylinder," and on page 19, the decision was made to progress forward into Stage II in order to purge a backlog of verbal sensory data.

(i) Page 20 developed smells and two pieces of additional Stage IV intangible data, indicating a strong sense of abstract elements bleeding through into the early session. I had a sense of AOL, "urban caves," and then decided to take the coordinates again in order to strengthen signal line contact. I again decoded "manmade structure" and moved into Stage II data with verbal indicators of dimension, "vertical" and steep. On page 21, I seemed to begin developing data indicative of being inside of something. I smelled "burnt" and "sweet," which became an AOL of "food smells." Sketches and supporting verbal data show an AOL of "auditorium or theatre seats," as well as of "glasses."

(j) On page 22, I moved forward to Stage III again, immediately producing two sketches of polished surfaces with verticals, curves, and horizontals. In the second sketch, a curved, partitioned element of data had clear sections, which now appears as an AOL of "glass windows or partitions." This same pattern of AOL, "glass and solid white metal," appears on the next page, page 23, in the upper sketch and again in the lower sketch, which depicts two lifeforms walking toward what maifests as AOLs, "an entrance to something" and most likely "a strcture." On page 24, the sketch depicts an AOL of "three metal escalators" and of "a red metal structure."

(k) Page 25 begins another portrayal of energy emanating from a hollow structure, with a sketch of an AOL of "a tower, a radio tower." Indicators on this page are "bouncing or rebounding waves of energy." Page 26 has several sketches depicting an AOL of "the concrete tower structure" and a new development of "a glass tunnel inside the structure." Page 27 has another S3½ declaring the target to be circular or to have large elements of dimensional data that are circular. A sketch on the same page shows an AOL of "a table & chair." Page 28 has a major sketch depicting an AOL of "a gathering of people looking out a set of windows" in a large room. On page 29, I felt the data was beginning to repeat significantly enough that I declared a movement to Stage IV.

(l) Stage IV began on page 30 with a minor sketch of a metal structure and an AOL of "a doorway or main entrance," which are not really supported by the string of S2 data in the Stage IV matrix. Significant, on page 31, is the declaration of "AOL electromagnetic energy associated with this structure." I feel this is significant only because of the large number of energetic verbal descriptors found in S2, S4, and S6 of this session. I continued the AOL drive of "the tower structure," and it required another break. On page 32, I declared another AOL break due to the reappearance of the metal and glass doorway. On page 33, a number of pieces of emotional data support a range of emotions, such as "agitated" and "worried," along with "relieved," "happy," "together," and "celebrating." This indicates to me that there was a wide range of human responsibility, interpretation, and involvement in this target. Again, there is an indication that I was viewing this target from a very high perspective.

(m) On page 34, the intangibles developed, indicating a range of concepts, which I felt linked them to some form of communication. However, the AOL drive of the radio tower appeared again, forcing another break. I challenged the image on page 35, trying to see if the imagery after the challenge would support being inside a structure. By all indications, it did, and I began decoding data relevant to the inside or the close outside elements of a "structure." AOLs of "turnstiles" and "binoculars" developed and were sketched. On page 36, there were AOLs of "a security guard or policeman" and "an electric motor." On page 37, the "white metal" structure appeared again and was sketched, but this time the AOL was of "a church steeple." Nothing significant developed on page 38, but on page 39, I perceived an AOL of an orange helicopter, and it was linked in a follow-on AOL of a "spired and horizontal metal structure." Page 42 has a string of intangibles addressing elements of what I feel are related to control and design, and then I sketched what developed into an AOL of "a communication tower."

(n) I took another AOL drive break since this was clearly related to the other tower complexes that were appearing in the session. An S4½ on page 43 indicates that I felt the target gestalt was linked to a large structure serving multiple purposes, such as "tourism, communications, national pride, and corporate interests." I immediately declared a bi-location break due to the presence of a very bad headache. When I resumed the session, I moved down to what I felt was the surface of the gestalt again. Sketches on page 44 depict a structure and people on the structure; I declared them as an AOL of "a deck or platform w/ a walkway."

(o) On the next three pages of the session, pages 45 through 47, nothing critical developed and the data began repeating itself despite several involuntary movements. Therefore, on page 47, I decided to select an intangible and begin the Stage V process. As I indicated in the first paragraph of the summary, the intangible I selected was "communication," and I developed another 144 pieces of data, ending Stage V on page 56, and beginning the verbal sensory matrix of Stage VI on page 57 and the visual sensory matrix on page 58.

(p) In Stage VI, I compiled seven pages of verbal data and eight pages of visual data. During the Stage VI process, the picture of the target site developed into one of a construction site, in which a large object was being assembled that carried with it great national pride and functioned with extremely high levels of energy. Because Stage VI is visually driven, I begin this summary focus with the rendering developed on page 58 of several pieces of heavy earth-moving equipment that appear to be working together, with tall buildings in the background. From what appears to be an elevated perspective, I observed a deep, cross-shaped depression in the earth—see page 58a—with a soft and muddy landscape, including what appear to be railroad tracks nearby. In addition, I perceived a hard-surface road (concrete or asphalt), two distinct linear objects on either side of the depression, and a structure that was under construction. I was not able to determine if a structure or structures were under construction. The rendering on page 58b shows another element of structure, as do pages 58c and 58d. The image on page 58e shows men working on something, stacking it, assembling it, and guiding or directing something, and my sense was that something was above them.

(q) Page 58f shows what I perceived to be above the men on the previous page. It is some sort of hook, again supporting the concept of construction and assembly. The angle of perception appears to be highly elevated, as the surrounding area is well below the hook and rope or cable suspended below it. I had a good sense of perspective in this rendering, and felt I could see forever.

(r) This final rendering, on page 58g, solidified much of the concept of the target for me. I had a sense of energy, powerful electric energy, present in this target. Even though this rendering shows what appears to be lightning and even produced an AOL, "lightning strikes," I feel the image is symbolic, as if energy is critical to this target, from the outside in or the inside out. Therefore, my final analysis of the session is that I perceive a large object, manmade, and perhaps still under construction. The object is a source of pride, but it is also a source of agitation or argument. However, power is a constant here, and I feel the power is not political, which was previously a sense in the session. Now, I feel strongly that the power associated with this target is constant, every day, and it is significant and necessary, and would be missed if interrupted or removed.

14

After the Summary—Target Feedback

The big question is whether you are going to be able
to say a hearty yes to your adventure.

Joseph Campbell

EVALUATING YOUR SESSION DATA

Target feedback is the packet of information compiled by the person who "created the target" and assigned the coordinates. This is in the form of photographs, written descriptions, and/or video of the actual target site. After you finish your summary, you may want to postpone looking at the feedback (this advice applies when you are working targets solo rather than in a group). Wait a few days, or even a week or two, and work another session, using the same target. Develop a complete summary, compare it with the previous one, and *then* look at the feedback. On the other hand, you may choose to review your session against the feedback immediately—it is your call. Postponing the feedback is a discipline that will pay big dividends in the mastering of structure. However, I realize it is not for everyone; do what is best for you.

When you complete your session, when you complete the summary, and finally look at the feedback, be very careful not to jump to conclusions about the session—stay in the observer role. This means, have courage, read the feedback, and look for similarities in your data. Look for parallels in subtle sketches and verbal indicators that match pieces of the feedback. Mine the positive from the session, look for the good, and do not dwell on what you missed. If you called the target by name, for example, "I think this is a rocket ship on a launch platform," and you now find it was not a rocket ship but a radio tower, ask yourself, "How much information did I receive that was correct?" After you reinforce the positive, you can be critical, as long as you are critical from a training perspective. This means asking yourself, "How much did I miss because I didn't think it was important, having allowed myself to settle on what I thought the target was? How much more data could I have developed had I let go of my desire to call the target?" Analysis is just that, analysis of the product: what I did well, or did not do well, and how I can do it better next time. If you keep this focus and attitude, you will succeed in developing your skill as a Remote Viewer.

Once you've looked at the feedback and reviewed your session against it, do not stop there. Read the feedback several more times, and look at your session again, circling anything you feel fits the target feedback that you might have missed in your initial analysis. Look at the photographs provided in the feedback, and see if you can match your verbal descriptors to anything in the photographs.

Go on the Internet, and look up photos of the target and descriptions of the target event that others have written. Do your homework by looking for every piece of evidence available about the target site and comparing your findings with that evidence—be complete in your work. Do not necessarily take the feedback at face value; you could be perceiving the target from many different angles, altitudes, and positions; it is critical to your training to look beyond each photograph and see what else is there. Do this, and you will rarely be disappointed with your session; however, if you adopt the belief that what is in a photograph is all you were supposed to see, you will often be disappointed. Reach beyond the image; study, investigate, reevaluate, and master this.

You already know that this process is not 100 percent accurate. Remember, you are beginning the process with an empty glass, with nothing but two sets of four numbers. When you consider what you begin with, the volume of data you produce is astounding. The bottom line in this analysis is to be kind to yourself, to look for areas in which you can improve. Think like an athlete. In order to maximize your potential, you must fine-tune your performance. Think carefully about the entire session, the flow, the interruptions, the AOL drive, and any other significant breaks or difficulties. Did the verbal data outweigh the visual, or vice versa? Know your session, know what happened in it, and consider what you will do next time—this is a productive analysis of the session.

If you decide you need to work on visuals, then practice nonanalytic sketching before you do another target. If you need work in the development of verbal data, you should practice. Practice and practice some more—you will get better.

Now take a look at the target feedback for the Sample Session used in this book.

TARGET FEEDBACK 3345/1291: CANADA'S NATIONAL TOWER

This target is an event in past time – the completion of Canada's National Tower by placing the last section of antenna on top of the tower. Known as the "CN Tower," it is located in the heart of the downtown entertainment district of Toronto and is considered to be the world's tallest freestanding structure on land, measuring 1,815 feet (553 meters) in height.

Originally owned by Canadian National Railway who conceived the project in 1968, its main purpose is to serve as a communications and broadcasting tower. At the time, Toronto was growing rapidly and the abundance of new skyscrapers blocked and reflected transmission of radio, television and communications signals. The solution was to raise an antenna above the buildings. Today, the tower services radio, TV, cell phone and pager providers and others.

In addition to its function as a communications tower, the CN Tower is a significant source of national pride. Construction of the tower was a major architectural and engineering feat and a symbol of the strength of Canadian industry. Today, it is a tourist destination and subject of *The Height of Excellence* a movie which documents the complexities of building this landmark.

The basic structure of the tower is a giant hollow hexagonal concrete column with the metal broadcast antenna on top. There are elevators, the world's tallest metal staircase and utility lines contained within the concrete structure

and two visitor "pods" located at 1,100 feet (330 meters) and 1,465 feet (447 meters) elevation. The main visitor pod is seven stories high with a large white donut-shaped radome at its base which houses a series of microwave antennas. Located at various levels of the main visitor pod are

the Glass Floor and Outdoor Observation Deck, Horizons Café and Indoor Observation Deck and the award-winning restaurant, 360, the floor of which rotates to give guests a 360 degree view of the city below. 360 is also credited with having the world's highest wine cellar.

The smaller Sky Pod is located just below the metal antenna and houses the highest public observation deck in the world. The hexagonal shape of the tower's central core is clearly visible between the top of the main visitor pod and the Sky Pod, however from the ground up to the base of the main visitor pod, there are three supports extending from the main column giving it the appearance of a tri-pod.

February of 1973 marked the beginning of construction. Installing the foundation required digging to a depth of 50 feet, removing tons of earth and replacing it with concrete, steel rebar and steel cable. Building the structure on top utilized a unique system of moveable slip forms into which concrete was continuously poured. As the concrete cured, the slip form

was hydraulically raised approximately 20 feet per day to position it as successively higher segments of the tower were poured.

Securing the antenna to the top of the tower was completed using a Sikorsky Skycrane helicopter, which lifted forty-four sections of the antenna, each weighing seven tons, to the top of the tower, one at a time. The helicopter was nicknamed Olga, and her flights became a local tourist attraction with the daily schedule printed in the newspaper.

Men positioned at the very top of the tower guided the sections into place and secured them with bolts. Conditions at the top were windy and cold, often comparable to an Arctic storm, and workers suffered from frostbitten faces. The fact that these high-riggers worked without safety harnesses made conditions even more perilous. They had to be free to jump out of the way if a piece of steel started swinging.

When the final section was in place on April 2, 1975, the CN Tower became the world's tallest free-standing structure. The editor of the *Guinness Book of World Records* was on hand to record this milestone. People of all ages crowded downtown Toronto to witness the event. Office workers took extended lunch breaks to watch from nearby windows, and traffic came to a halt on Gardiner Expressway (a major freeway passing near the structure). After three attempts, the final sec-

tion of antenna was lowered into place by Olga's helicopter crew and secured by iron worker Paul Mitchell shortly after 2:00 pm.

The *Toronto Star* reported that Mitchell's command to the helicopter pilot—"Cut her loose!"—was piped in to a celebration in the observation gallery of the fifty-six story

Toronto-Dominion Centre drawing cheers from the three hundred contractors, politicians, and other party guests. Mitchell celebrated by dancing a jig and setting off a red smoke bomb from the top of the tower. Olga's pilot took a victory lap and exuberant motorists responded by honking their horns.

Further information on the CN Tower is available at www.cntower.ca. To view video footage online, see "CN Tower Opens to the Public," the CBC Digital Archives Web Site, Canadian Broadcasting Corporation, http://archives.cbc.ca/IDC-1-69-204-1024/life_society/cn_tower_opens/clip1.

TARGET FEEDBACK AND SESSION WORK

When you look at the target feedback, I'm sure you recognize elements of data collected in the CRV Sample Session. What is often striking is how precisely the contours of sketches will match photographs of the target site. For example, the Stage II sketch on page 255 of the Sample Session is a match, complete with "fuzzy energy," for the antenna on top of the tower seen in the photos. On page 258, the Viewer was looking up at a structure labeled "rigid," and you can see how precisely it matches the view from the base of the tower. The sketch at the bottom of page 259 and the AOL "a city skyline" can clearly be seen in the first photo of the target feedback.

While all of this seems completely astounding, it should actually come as no surprise. Now you can understand that the Viewer was actually seeing, hearing, smelling, and feeling everything that he would have experienced at the target site. Perhaps he was positioned in the very same spot as the photographer who took the pictures. Perhaps he found his way to the position of a worker high up on the antenna.

Notice the assessment in the Session Summary of the aesthetic, emotional, and intangible aspects of this target and how they relate to the "massive" structure present. Note the emotions of "happiness" and "pride" that one would expect of tourists visiting a national landmark and celebrating the culmination of the construction of this architectural and engineering wonder. Also, "fear" and "apprehensive" are appropriate emotions for someone standing on an observation deck. Especially notice the aesthetic impact declared on page 262, "I am up high looking down—feels weird."

When the AOLs "Chicago" and "city skyline" appear next to the AOL "body of water, windblown," it makes perfect sense. Toronto *is* a city next to a wind-blown body of water, but it is not Chicago. You can see how inaccurate the rest of the session data would have been if the Viewer had latched on to Chicago as the target, negating any subsequent information that failed to match his notion of that particular city. Pay attention also to the Viewer's early AOL while decoding the "C" component. A marina is actually present at the target site, clearly visible in the target feedback photo of the view from the observation deck, but it is not the primary structure of this target. Along the same lines, this target is not the railroad yard sketched on page 263; however, if you research the CN Tower further, you'll discover that Union Station is nearby, and the original developer of the tower was Canadian National Railway—the tower's original name was actually Canadian National Tower. It is a strong historical aspect of this target.

The Viewer chose "communication" as the strongest intangible element, completely accurate, and he experienced bi-location related to a sensitivity to microwave radiation, which was clearly present at this target site. Even the mention of lightning on page 320 is relevant beyond the obvious correlation to strong radiant energy; further research reveals that the CN Tower is struck by lightning more than seventy-eight times per year.

Do you see now how important it is to include everything you perceive, even seemingly contradictory pieces of data? For instance, it is possible to be at this target site and detect elements present in a dining room full of people, a communications tower, and a construction site—seemingly unrelated environments until you understand the whole picture. Might you be tempted to censor your perceptions if, in one moment, you saw a pointy metal object with fuzzy energy and, in the next, a heavy concrete structure, and then huge glass windows with lots of people? Looking at the rich variety of highly accurate data objectified in this session by one Viewer, do you begin to see what is possible when session data from a group of Viewers is combined?

CONCLUSION

You must remember that nothing of quality in this life comes without some degree of effort on your part. The great minds of our time worked at becoming great and defining their greatness. The great performers, writers, poets, athletes, businesspeople—anyone who rises to the top—all do so with effort. *You* can do this. No matter where you are after your first session, the choice is always yours to move on or not. As poet Mary Oliver wrote, "What is it you plan to do / with your one wild and precious life?"

It is my prayer that you will do whatever it takes to know that you are more than the physical. I live my life in your service, because I want you to know that you are powerful, that you are omnipotent, omniscient, and omnipresent. I desire that you walk this life knowing that and, in so doing, you redefine who you are in this world. Believe in yourself, then come to know. Your whole life is but a point in time; enjoy it by living it on purpose. Author Martha Beck said, "Any transition serious enough to alter your definition of self will require not just small adjustments in your way of living and thinking but a full-on metamorphosis." Know that you are transforming; know that Remote Viewing is a tool that will facilitate this. In addition, as you become aware of the still small changes presenting themselves to you, live your life knowing that it will never be the same again.

Epilogue: What Is Next for You? Empowering Human Beings Through the Art and Science of Remote Viewing

Transformation literally means going beyond your form.

Wayne W. Dyer

I am reminded of the lyrics from a Don Henley song, "Everything Is Different Now," in which he is asked by the love of his life, "Will you stand here in this fire with me? Are you ready for another life?" The song is an invitation to transformation, as is this book. With this book, you have a ticket to see across a span of space-time, a tool to know that you are, and have always been, more than the physical world will allow. You should know that you came from the Source, and that the Source is you.

However, just because I wrote this book does not mean I have all the answers, and just because you've read this book does not mean you now know where you are going. The best way to know is to keep learning, to keep experiencing, to keep making the journey inward and beyond. This epilogue contains a practice for peace and knowing in life. It is my practice, and I share it with love. You will also find a number of course descriptions for your review. My intention is to make you aware of what is ahead for you, should you choose to follow this path further. The choice is always yours. I want you to know that there is iron in your soul. Discover it, and forge it into a new life.

THE SEVEN IMPERATIVES OF PEACE: A PRACTICE FOR LIFE

Deep within each of us dwells a slumbering power, a power that would astonish, a power most only dream of, a power each possesses yet ignores. Such a force can revolutionize an individual's life as well as our turbulent human condition. This force is as powerful as any human fury, needing only to be awakened, trained, and put into action. When misguided, this force becomes conflict, discord, un-happiness, and even the apex of all human fury: war on an ever-increasing scale of lethality and precision. Once guided and shaped, this force becomes our iden-tity, our manifest behavior, creating a physical, emotional, and spiritual life of peace in a world feeding on hatred and anger.

I want to give you the seven imperatives of peace to use as a practice in your personal life, a practice for how you might live an individual as well as a col-lective life of purpose and service. This practice will give every Remote Viewer the attainable state of a peaceful existence in a day-to-day exploration of belief systems, which have the power to create and destroy on an individual and a col-lective level. I would ask you to review your physical destiny, your emotional destiny, and your spiritual destiny, using the power of the moment and Remote Viewing as a path to fuel an inner peace in your life.

If you are to bring peace to any aspect of this human condition, then such peace must begin within. I know that it is easy to say this, that peace can prevail. Further, I know that this notion has been proposed countless times before. I am aware that the mechanics of a peaceful transformation are far more difficult to execute than to talk about—this practice can change all that. I am not a philoso-pher or a metaphysician, nor am I a spiritual leader, though some of my students would beg to differ. What I am is a warrior transformed by his own practice and vision, which I will share with you here. Know that, each day, I am living this same practice with you. Together we will make a difference.

Life can be difficult; I know that it was for me. I spent half a lifetime learn-ing and teaching the art and science of war—and then suddenly I was not. This practice I now share with you helped me in each moment to come to a new understanding of my place in this existence. I want to tell you how Remote Viewing and these practices helped me develop a path to personal awareness and power, making no pretense of enlightenment or spiritual knowledge; I simply offer these practical methods for developing an empowered condition. If you follow these basic principles, you will transform virtually anything in your life from chaos to opportunity, from hopelessness, anger, and hatred to love, compassion, and joy. I want you to know how to create a compelling future of promise and possibility.

We find ourselves on the threshold of the Fourth Turning of the global society—we stand mid-crossing, between a time of the unraveling of our collective objectives and a time of destruction. How may we live such that peace might prevail?

Originally I prepared this outline as a guided meditation and prayer, which was delivered before two thousand people participating in a rally in Toronto, Canada, to establish a new global paradigm for peace. When asked to deliver this message, I struggled at length over exactly what to say. I had spent eighteen years of my life as a special operations infantryman, and now, for the first time in my life, as an old warrior, I was asked to deliver a "prayer for peace," and I had no idea where to begin. Oddly, the thought came that I should ask my father for his views. One might not think of this as unusual, unless you knew my father. He was a twenty-four-year career military man who had fought in two wars, World War II and Korea, retiring from service only months before he was to ship out to Vietnam. He said he just could not take another war.

I asked my eighty-four-year-old father, "What would you say to a group of people in this day and age about peace?" My father looked down at his feet for a moment, thinking, and then raised his head with tears in his eyes and said, "Forgive." He went on to give me four of the eventual seven imperatives I now live by, and each came from him with perfect clarity and purpose. My father passed away in 2003, after enduring a stroke-induced coma that took him from me only a few short months after he spoke these words to me.

My father was not a Buddhist, a Christian, a Jew, or a Muslim, but neither was he an atheist. He was a man who believed in human goodness on an individual and a collective level, and it was this belief that he empowered me with. It was this belief that I now teach the world over. My father was an optimist.

The First Imperative: Forgive

Forgiveness must be a pure act of contrition. Such an act requires that you give up any notion of being right, and that you have no requirement for recompense. Above all, forgiveness must precede any dialogue—especially for peace. There can be no peace in you, in your relationships, in your work, or in your life situation without forgiveness. How can we expect peace to manifest itself into the human condition if it does not begin with our example? Forgiveness is paramount, and its order in relation to all other imperatives is nonnegotiable. If all acts, dialogue, and gestures are not first conditioned by forgiveness, then indeed they will be interpreted as acts of manipulation, aggression, control, anger, or fear. These perceptions will exclude the peaceful resolution of anything. Forgive—in your heart, in your mind, and in your word.

The Second Imperative: Have No Rage

Have no rage, whether in reaction to social injustice or to the insanity of world leaders or to those who would do harm and threaten. Rage fuels criticism, condemnation, complaint, judgment, and all other negative forces driving the human condition. Rage is a powerful energy that, with intense practice, can be transformed into a fierce compassion. Compassion defines your purpose, and purpose contains no rage, no fear, and no anger. Commit to live life and to transform this world without rage.

The Third Imperative: Disagree

It is okay to disagree with what is said, who is saying it, and what is happening—but do all you can to identify with those you disagree with. Everything has a root cause—everything—even the most terrible acts of human fury. We all believe we are right about what we believe, which is why beliefs are ultimately so absurd and costly to the human condition. You must know, and know how you know it, to make a difference.

The Fourth Imperative: Keep Moving Forward

Keep moving forward, always, no matter what life presents to you. Live each day, each hour, and each second of each moment with all the compassion and love you can carry. Nothing else matters but now. All else is an illusion of the conceptual mind, and we must seek to live nonconceptually. Move forward, no matter how terrible you think things are becoming. Just as the world keeps turning, keep moving in your life situation, and you will find peace within and without. Whatever the human condition brings to us individually or collectively, remember that anything is possible on the other side of the moment—but you are responsible for getting yourself there.

The Fifth Imperative: Be Against Nothing

It is counterproductive to involve yourself in the dualistic resistance of being against something. To be antiwar is to carry a double negative. It is important to remember how the language we use shapes our experience and our purpose. To refer to your efforts to secure peace as a "fight" for peace is to accept in your mind the notion that a war against war makes any sense at all—it does not. The peace movements of the world lack two things: common language and common purpose. Establishing these critical elements of any effort to present peace is the responsibility of the leaders, organizers, and believers. The language and the purpose of the movement must reflect the desire to promote peace, to bring peace, to introduce peace to the world. You should never use the words "we fought against something and won (or lost)." This is the language of war, not peace.

In the language of peace, the concept of being against nothing is akin to Gandhi's *ahimsa*, a Sanskrit word commonly translated as "nonviolence" and, more accurately, "harmlessness" and reverence for all life. In its comprehensive meaning, *ahimsa* means entire abstinence from causing any pain or harm whatsoever to any living creature, either by thought, word, or deed. *Ahimsa* was the basis of Gandhi's successful movement to free India from British rule, expressed by Gandhi himself when he wrote, "My love of the British is equal to that of my own people. I claim no merit for it, for I have equal love for all mankind without exception. It demands no reciprocity. I own no enemy on earth. That is my creed."

The Sixth Imperative: Do Not Let Others Define Your Reality

Let no one define your reality or falsely limit your possibilities. You are an empowered being, empowered with the full knowledge of the Matrix, capable of manifesting any reality for yourself and the world. Stay informed by watching the world—but stop listening when you feel the quest for knowledge is taking energy from you. The most destructive waves moving within the electrostatic field of the planet are those of fear and hatred. Turn off the television; turn away from the radio show, the newspaper, or the magazine that would serve only to make you feel bad about yourself and the world. Read inspiring works, meditate, dance in the Matrix, or simply write your feelings in a journal. Own how you feel—and do not give your power away.

The Seventh Imperative: Find Your Purpose in This Life

Find your purpose in this life by finding a new way of seeing and working in the world. Forge yourself a new soul by transforming your path, finding your true purpose in this life—I did. Forge a new soul for yourself, and work toward forging a new soul for humanity. Things in this life are what we feel they are.

How long have you known this? How long have you known this without yet knowing it in practice? The way to a better, more peaceful world is for us to begin feeling and seeing one. Do this, and then go one step further—know it is possible!

Live by example, in the moment, to see people as they are and for what they are in the eyes of the Matrix. Forever be aware of our common humanity. Vow to end anger, aggression, and fear within yourself. Once this agreement is made, you will know your purpose, and through the defining of your personal mythology, you will act on your purpose to serve truth, never asking that it serve you. Finally, you will know your duty to humanity.

YOU ARE NOT FINISHED, YOU HAVE ONLY JUST BEGUN

Can we change our personal or collective destiny? I believe the answer is yes. In my four-part series of evolutionary workshops, we focus more closely on the paradigm shift taking place in human societal evolution and the role that Remote Viewing will play in expanding conscious, pure awareness in the global society of the new millennium. The following course descriptions will introduce you to the opportunities for further Remote Viewing training.

Coordinate Remote Viewing: The Residential Course

Coordinate Remote Viewing is defined by the U.S. Department of Defense as "the learned ability to transcend time and space, to view people, places, and things remote in time and space, and to gather information on the same." Both Phases I and II have been the subject of this book.

Phase I, Basic Coordinate Remote Viewing, is the foundational core of Remote Viewing training. Approximately thirty-five hours of training, Phase I is information-based and introduces students to the basic protocols of Stages I, II, and III of Coordinate Remote Viewing.

Phase I students learn to enter an altered state of consciousness, receive a set of encrypted coordinates, produce an ideogram (the first graphic representation of the target site), and decode the ideogram. Further, students learn to perceive textures, sounds, colors, tastes, smells, temperatures, energetic data, and dimensional data from across a chasm of space-time. Using their new and developing "nonphysical eyes," students perceive the target and sketch visual snapshots of distant and fleeting images.

Phase II, Intermediate Coordinate Remote Viewing, completes CRV training and serves to open a new door into the CRV student's soul. The protocols and structure of Phase I are carried forward into Phase II of CRV, which also requires roughly thirty-five hours of training. The structure is expanded to include the sensory perceptions of aesthetics, emotional data, tangibles, and intangibles, and even the process of recognizing one's own conscious imagination. Sketches become detailed perspective drawings called *renderings*, and students often feel they are actually physically present in the target site. Before moving forward to Extended Remote Viewing, intermediate students will be tasked to do a CRV session called an Open Search Inward, in which they will discover something unique and precise about themselves.

Extended Remote Viewing

Phase III, Basic Extended Remote Viewing (approximately sixty hours of training), is designed to guide students through the application of a hybrid form of Remote Viewing. It is knowledge-based instruction; the Basic ERV student has moved to a new level of understanding about the Matrix of all creation, accepting one's concepts as being knowledge-based and not merely belief-based. ERV is the course that experienced Remote Viewing students call "learning to fly" because of the overwhelming sensation of free flight and movement felt during the session.

Without the structure of CRV, the ERV session environment differs substantially. Students are taught to traverse the alpha brain-wave state used in CRV and enter the theta brain-wave state called *ultradeep* in the lexicon of the Remote Viewer. Students are calibrated on measurable targets before being sent to view other civilizations, worlds, and dimensions, and report back as a class on their collective observations.

The Master Class

Phase IV, Master Extended Remote Viewing (approximately sixty hours of training), is the culmination of the Remote Viewing training series. The instruction is wisdom-based, focusing on issues regarding the whole of humanity, as well as those of self.

The Master ERV course refines the skills taught in the preceding RV courses, while shifting the Viewer's principal focus toward an ultimate and eternal goal. As in all previous RV courses, Master ERV students will be calibrated. They will collectively select questions that relate to the physical, emotional, and spiritual needs of the human condition.

Once prepared, Master ERV students embark on multiple journeys into other dimensions, seeking other beings, asking specific questions, and returning to the physical world with answers, revelations, and truth, which will be shared and interpreted as a class. The myriad of perspectives and clarity of vision the class presents simply defy language. You must experience it to understand it.

The Explorer Group—To the Edge of Knowledge and Beyond

You will join your friends once again as we collectively journey into the Matrix of all creation to seek truth, find knowledge, and become wisdom. The Explorer Group is an annual summit reserved exclusively for graduates of the Master Class, Phase IV of Remote Viewing training. The purpose of this exciting retreat is to unite those who have made the commitment in the Master Class to live their lives in such a way as to make a positive difference in the individual and collective outcomes of human destiny. This unique conference assembles dedicated Remote Viewers and powerful thinkers from around the world for seven days of intensive Remote Viewing, dialogue with friends, and strategic planning.

These highly advanced Remote Viewers will continue the exploration of the 128 targets identified as known other-world targets compiled from the thousands of open searches into the Matrix from the military Remote Viewing unit, as well as from other advanced classes throughout the years. These targets exist so that we might learn what is needed for us on the return to the eternal. These targets exist on the edge of knowledge—it is our purpose now to go there and beyond.

The Explorer Group will work with open-frame techniques to define the Remote Viewer's efforts toward enhanced human performance potentials and the altering of human destiny.

Embracing the Shadow Self—Discover Who You Truly Are

This course focuses on the *shadow self*, which is a Jungian term for that part of ourselves we would prefer not to possess or recognize. It is this part, or several parts, of ourselves that we want to get rid of or hide deep in the dark recesses of our being. This shadow self may also be a form of us we have previously identified but have not yet embraced. The shadow self can be a beautiful and precious part of us deep within, but when we were children, we were afraid to bring it into the world. Regardless, we must go through our shadow self in order to reach our higher spiritual self. If not embraced, our shadow self tethers us to the past and limits our spiritual unfolding.

Discover who you truly are. It is difficult, if not impossible, to mature spiritually if we neglect the shadow self. In order to grow spiritually, we must learn to travel into darkness, taking with us everything that we are, even those parts of us we would prefer not to have. This course is designed to help students do just that, to use the tools of Remote Viewing to identify shadow events. These shadow events prompt emotions (shadow emotions), and these emotions beget beliefs, which in turn prompt an identity fed by actions. We will develop more than one identity in this existence, and each identity carries with it a manifest behavior to support the identity. You will learn to break the cycle of behavior supporting four identities, and you will learn a process for releasing and embracing each.

You need to know that something extraordinary is possible in your life—and with this course, it absolutely is. Described by many of my students as the "finest course you offer," this course is for those of you who have started on your journey, moving ever more rapidly toward the psychospiritual transformation we so often speak of in class. If you want to take a deeper look at the personal issues that percolate from the Matrix of all creation, this class is for you.

What is inhibiting you or preventing you from experiencing life fully? It is all within your grasp. This course is an opportunity to look deeply into yourself to discover who you truly are and determine the experiences you will bring with you on your path toward wisdom. When you discover and reexperience the significant aspects of your eternal past, then you may become truly healed or transformed, feeling more alive and happy than you ever thought possible. Learn to live a life of promise and possibility.

Appendix A:
How to Make Practice Targets

Practice is everything.

Periander

Practice targets are a critical piece of your training regime. Once you have finished this book, you will need to make some decisions regarding your training schedule and materials. First, know that practice targets are available from a variety of sources—for example, the Internet, eBay, and Remote Viewing clubs, teachers, and individuals. You can purchase them ready-made from my company, or you can learn to make them and trade them with other Remote Viewers. If it is your intention to get better at Remote Viewing, and if you are willing to commit to a practice schedule, there is no shortage of places to obtain materials for practice.

However, you should be aware that there are some issues with practice targets. Purchasing targets ready-made over the Internet or going to various open-source websites to practice can be dangerous. A great deal of care must go into the selection of training targets and the concept behind the assignment of the coordinates. Many third-, fourth-, and fifth-generation Remote Viewers were not taught this, and as a result, little thought is put into their selection of training targets. In fact, many of the targets selected are inappropriate and unsafe, emotionally and spiritually. Not everyone has your best interests in mind. And not everyone knows how to select targets and hold a concept of them while assigning coordinates.

Periodically, my staff receives phone calls from frantic individuals who have some horrible story to tell about using one of these open-source formats. These individuals call when they receive their feedback and find out the coordinates were for a murder scene or the execution of some fanatical world leader. Ask yourself, do you really want to step into the energy of something like this? When you do step blindly into this kind of energy, know that there is a cumulative negative effect, and everyone has a breaking point no matter how you think you might shield yourself. You step into the process like a child, innocent and pure, only to find that you have been asked to explore "for practice" something horrible—it is not right. I caution all my students to be wary of the open-source availability of practice targets.

You are responsible for your experience, as only you can decide where you will obtain your training materials. I will say this: If you are looking for practice websites, the closer you stay to the original military-trained Remote Viewers (the first generation), the better off you will be. Several of my students are developing targets and selling them on eBay. The problem is, even I cannot tell who is who within this system, and therefore I cannot recommend a name or a particular set of targets.

You can purchase target packs from my office. We have hundreds of targets that have been prepared with scrupulous professional integrity. If you elect to purchase targets from our publisher, Sounds True, know that we make the targets on their behalf, so you can also trust their content implicitly.

CREATE TARGETS TO EXCHANGE WITH OTHER REMOTE VIEWERS

The ideal situation is to develop a working relationship with another Remote Viewer, or with a group of Remote Viewers, and swap targets with one another. Make ten or fifteen targets and mail them to an RV friend, who in turn makes ten or fifteen targets and mails them to you. You each then have clean targets to work.

Many Viewers take great pride in the development of their practice targets and derive much pleasure from exchanging targets with other Remote Viewers. In doing this yourself, you will learn how to make quality targets, and you will practice your ability to hold the concept of the target while assigning the coordinates. If you have the time to put into it, this is absolutely the best way to continue your practice efforts. However, if time is at a premium, rather than not practice at all, you should purchase practice targets and keep up your training schedule.

This appendix discusses the proper selection of target material, the assignment of coordinates, and the proper handling of what you create. The creation of practice targets is a critical skill you must understand and master in order to continue your Remote Viewing development. Creating practice targets can be fun and satisfying if you follow a few simple guidelines.

CREATING PRACTICE TARGETS

In order to create a practice target, you'll need to choose a target, create a target feedback packet, and assign coordinates to your target.

Step 1: Identify Sources for Potential Target Feedback

When choosing practice targets, you will be limited by the availability of material to use for target feedback. You are looking for comprehensive, verifiable feedback, such as photographs, reports, or descriptive articles in books, newspapers, or magazines. The more complete the feedback, the better a Remote Viewer will be able to compare the session summary and Remote Viewing experience with the actual target and all its identifiable attributes: the physical site, items present, colors, sounds, activities, historical or spiritual significance, and so on. You begin by identifying a source for potential targets. If you are on a budget, check with your local library, which may sell out-of-date periodicals such as *National Geographic* or assorted travel magazines for a nominal price. These magazines prove useful in the selection of targets like historical sites or major international landmarks. However, if you cannot find an inexpensive source for them, the Internet is a very useful resource as well. Used-book stores often sell older periodicals and travel magazines, and finally, many new-book stores carry a very wide variety of suitable resource materials.

Step 2: Select an Appropriate Target

Review the contents of these source documents, and select targets that are authentic and not staged photographs from advertisements or cartoons, since the events they portray are not likely to be real. You want to look for portrayals of events, such as coronations, wedding ceremonies, and those of significant collective human accomplishment. Look for photographs and stories about places of interest, places that are spiritually significant or transformational, historical, and wondrous. Select natural or manmade landmarks. Look for stories on artifacts and objects, familiar and unfamiliar. Look into questions of science with feedback available so that you are not exploring in the blind with no feedback. Essentially, you are looking for places, things, events, and collective human efforts that have empirical evidence you can use in the development of the feedback.

Select significant targets that carry all the elements of a complex gestalt. Use photographs of real targets: actual persons, places, events, and objects. Do not use graphic-arts representations of a place or object; instead, search until you find an actual photograph of the target. Do not use paintings or cartoons representing some event, person, or place—they are renderings produced by another person, and they will carry that energetic imprint. In general, use common sense. If it does not seem like it should be used as a target, it probably should not be. Keep it basic and simple.

Selecting targets that are nebulous, vague, or too simplistic—a fire hydrant, a ball in a box, a map with an X marking the spot of something—is asking for trouble. You enjoy the luxury of having been trained on extremely difficult and complex target gestalts. And you have been trained to view the target in real time or at a specified time in history, and not simply via the feedback. Do not cheat your training and skill level by selecting targets that are frivolous.

I said you should make sure that you have conclusive feedback for each of the targets; this is critical at this stage of your learning process. Do not build a practice target for which you have no feedback or limited feedback at best. Take the Kennedy assassination, for example. First, I cannot tell you how many times students have asked me why we do not use this as a target in class. My answer is this: Why would I want to spend time sending students backward to see something I cannot prove or disprove, that I cannot substantiate or negate in their findings? All I have available to me in the way of feedback is what the world provides, and that, at best, is speculation. Hence, I have no real definitive feedback, and as such, this would not be an acceptable training target—nor is it a good practice target. It may well be a good operational target for advanced Viewers who want to spend the time to look backward and marry their findings to the available evidence—but that is another situation altogether. Keep it simple and pure, and you will be much happier in your endeavor.

Step 3: Assemble Your Target Feedback

Once you have identified a potential target, collect photographs and capture written explanations about the target. These narratives should include dates, details, and facts about the target, including its history to the present. You can scan these and print them; you can take them from the Internet, being careful in all cases not to violate any copyright laws regarding photographs or text. In most cases, if you e-mail the website to let them know what you want to use the photos for, you will be granted permission to use low-resolution images for reference purposes. If you are designing these for sale, other conditions of approval will apply.

Carefully cut out photos and text and paste them onto a clean white sheet of standard 8½-x-11-inch paper. Remember that you are striving for an all-inclusive target packet. This information will be sealed in an envelope and will provide richly detailed feedback for whoever works the target during a Remote Viewing session.

Step 4: Write a List of Known Attributes

After you have developed the written data to support the target feedback, but before you seal it in the envelope, remember that you can further expand the feedback by including a list of known attributes for this target. To do this, simply look at the target in relation to the Stage II and Stage III categories of data: colors, textures, smells, tastes, sounds, temperatures, energetic data, dimensional data, aesthetic data, emotional data, and so forth. Using your own words, compile a list of fifty or so of these attributes, and include them as part of the feedback. The Viewer can look at this list and compare the session results, checking off everything that was perceived in the session. This will allow the Viewer to calculate the percentage of accurate data in the session, which is not *critical* to anything, but it is of interest as the Viewer's skill level increases.

Step 5: The Target Packet

When you feel you have provided as much information about the target site as you can, place everything inside an envelope. Leave the envelope open for now.

Step 6: Assign the Coordinates

Now you must assign a set of coordinates to the target. This consists of identifying the concept of the target in your mind, objectifying the concept, and generating eight (two sets of four) random digits to represent the concept of the target.

First, you must be able to hold an accurate concept of the target in your mind as you assign the coordinates. To do this, you may want to look at the target feedback again, consider the photographs that are part of the feedback, and perhaps even look on the Internet to see the target from another perspective.

When you have a clear idea of what you would like a Remote Viewer to see in this target, write a tasking statement. A tasking statement is an objectification of the concept of the target—essentially locking the concept into two-dimensional form.

For example, for a session in which the target was the *Titanic* disaster, the concept was "ice on metal contact." I wrote that down as a statement before I assigned the coordinates to the target. I held in my mind an image of this concept as I wrote the tasking; after the tasking was objectified, I held the same image in my mind as I assigned the coordinates. You should do the same, or you will run the risk of mentally wandering in the concept. Remember, if you wander in the concept, the Viewer will wander in the session. Write the tasking statement, and then assign the coordinates while you hold the image and as much of the feedback as you can in your memory.

Next, you will generate two sets of four random digits to represent the concept of the target. Remember that the random nature of the coordinates relates to the inability of the Remote Viewer taking the coordinates to assign any meaning to the nature of the target based upon the sequence of the numbers. For example, if I assigned the coordinates 2001/0911, what might happen to a group of Viewers taking these coordinates? Obviously, a significant number of them would immediately link them to the World Trade Center towers and the events of September 11, 2001. The Viewers would be instantly front-loaded, and the ability to develop data would be driven by the conscious mind. Therefore, the random nature of the coordinate process is for the benefit of the Viewer and nothing else. If my concept of the target mentioned above had these coordinates assigned, 2004/5761, you would have no idea what the target was, would you? Thus, you could only follow the structure, detecting and decoding the pure data that came to you in the session. This is why we consider the coordinates encrypted, encoded, or randomly assigned.

To help you with the assignment of the two four-digit numbers, I suggest you create the first four digits of the coordinates by starting with the current year.

Write this number on the outside of the envelope. This process is the one we use in our classes because it allows us to keep track of which targets we have used and in what years we have used them. Every year, you will make new practice targets, and over time, you will have a bunch of them that you have not yet used. Marking each envelope with the year the target was developed may prove helpful in five or ten years. We still have practice targets around the office that we made in 1997 and 1998. Knowing what year we made them allows us to decide if we will use them, or if we will discard them because newer ones come with better feedback. There are any number of reasons for doing it this way; the bottom line is that assigning the year works for me, and it will work for you as well.

The next step in assigning the coordinates is to assign the number 1 as the last digit of the second coordinate, for example, 2004/_ _ _ 1. Remember that this last digit is the number 1 not because it has to be, but because it is easiest to develop a rapid and reflexive ideogram as you leave the number 1. Therefore, years ago, I decided to make every second coordinate end in the number 1, and I found that my students no longer struggled with the early development of ideograms. Write this number on the envelope.

This leaves only three more digits to assign to the target concept. As you think about the concept of the target, you assign the next three numbers that come into your head, for example, the numbers 3, 1, and 5. Thus, the coordinates for the target are 2004/3151.

If you struggle with the random generation of the last three digits—and some people do—use this method as an alternative: for the last three digits, use the day of the month and the time of day. For example, 2004/_ _ _ 1 becomes 2004/12 _ 1 when it is the twelfth day of the month, or 2004/03_1 if it is the third day of the month. For the third digit, use the hour of the day: 1 for one o'clock, 2 for two o'clock, and so on. If it is ten, eleven, or twelve o'clock, then use the first number of the hour, which is the number 1. However you choose these three digits of the coordinates, write them on the envelope. This completes the assignment of coordinates.

Clearly, this process can be easy or slightly more complicated, but you should be clear on the whole nature of encryption, encoding, and random numbers. You should understand that the random nature of the coordinates is really for the Remote Viewer and not for the person assigning the coordinates or other onlookers. You should have some idea how to assign the coordinates, keeping in mind that you must leave no clue as to the nature of the target within the numbers. You can use this method, or you can just make the numbers up off the top of your head—it will not violate any protocol as long as they are random.

Step 7: Write Coordinates on the Outside of the Envelope and Seal It

You now have encrypted coordinates for your target, in this example, 2006/3151. Once you have written these on the outside of the envelope, you can seal it.

SHARE TARGETS WITH A FRIEND

This next point is crucial: don't frustrate yourself by trying to keep this target for your use. Obviously, you know what the target is, so you will be front-loaded if you try to work it—do not waste your time. Remember that your conscious mind will plague you every time you are front-loaded, which is the very reason for the random coordinate process. Some people justify making their own targets, claiming that if they make fifty targets, how can they possibly know which is which? I assure you that even with fifty targets, every time you work a target from the pile, your conscious mind, working at the speed of thought, will inventory the remaining targets. With this mental inventory in place, each new session will increase in intensity and anxiety as your conscious mind tries to determine which of the remaining targets this one is. This is a reality, so why needlessly punish yourself? Instead, send the target to a friend to work! You should only work targets of which you have no knowledge—you must be working in the blind.

Appendix B:
Recommended Reading

*I suggest that the only books that influence us are those
for which we are ready, and which have gone a little farther
down our particular path than we have yet gone ourselves.*

E. M. Forster[1]

If you are truly interested in becoming a skilled Remote Viewer—if you really want to understand it—you must read and develop a level of comprehension about a multitude of topics, including classical physics, quantum physics, theosophy, philosophy, psychology, personal health, biophysics, biology, scientific theory and process, cosmology, and metaphysics. The books and articles I have listed here form an adequate starting point for those serious about the art and science of Remote Viewing. I know the list is significant, and as such, you should select from it as the quote above implies: what you are ready for, and nothing more. In the reading list, an asterisk next to a title indicates one I highly recommend, but this list is by no means all-inclusive. My staff and I routinely suggest additional authors and titles during lectures and seminars.

To help you sort through this extensive list, I have divided it into several major categories, and I have listed the categories in what I feel is a realistic order of priority. Follow the guideline above; that is, look to each category, find what you feel you are ready for, and leave the rest for some other time, perhaps as your Remote Viewing dotage books to be read far into the future. My intention is to provide references as adjunct information, so that you can develop a deeper understanding of the mechanism and science behind this endeavor.

Learning Remote Viewing can be likened to learning the game of golf. What you need to know to hit the ball you can learn in a few lessons, augmented by several hours of hitting buckets of practice balls on a driving range. However, developing a degree of skill necessary to play eighteen holes in a foursome requires a great deal more instruction, practice, and research. Bad golfers drag their clubs out of the garage once a month and play a round with friends, only to spend the time (usually) complaining about how badly they are playing. Well, what do you expect? Good golfers practice regularly, even if they cannot play regularly; they research the game by watching others play, by reading about techniques and equipment, and so on. In general, good golfers are serious about doing more than simply maintaining the status quo. Great golfers adhere to a practice and play schedule. They employ a second set of eyes (called a coach) to oversee and evaluate the technical aspects of their swing, their approach, their follow-through, every aspect of their game. Great golfers study the game and every nuance of it. Most great golfers know the history of the sport, the evolution of it, the present technology, and the potential rising out of the future. They work their brains and bodies in order to perfect their play and stamina. They do all of this and still live their lives.

Since you have invested so much time in this book and this phenomenon, it is my hope that you will take the process further, that you will explore with your mind all that science and spirit have discovered about your human potential, and that you will use this information to sustain your efforts and thereby recognize that you have the ability to be a great Remote Viewer. You have no limitations save those you assign to yourself.

BACKGROUND SCIENCE FOR UNDERSTANDING REMOTE VIEWING

Barrow, John D. *The Origin of the Universe.* New York: Basic Books, 1994.

Bentov, Itzhak. *Stalking the Wild Pendulum: On the Mechanics of Consciousness.* Rochester, VT: Destiny Books, reprint 1988.

Bohm, D., and B. J. Hiley. "On the Intuitive Understanding of Nonlocality as Implied by Quantum Theory." *Foundations of Physics* 5 (1975): 93–109.

Feynman, Richard P., with introduction by Paul Davies. *Six Easy Pieces: Essentials of Physics Explained by Its Most Brilliant Teacher.* New York: Perseus Books, 1996.

Gamow, George. *One Two Three . . . Infinity: Facts and Speculations of Science.* New York: Dover Publications, 1988.

Grof, Stanislav, with Hal Zina Bennett. *The Holotropic Mind: Three Levels of Human Consciousness and How They Shape Our Lives.* San Francisco: HarperSanFrancisco, 1993.

Gruber, Elmar R. *The Psychic War: Parapsychology in Espionage—and Beyond.* New York: Blandford Publishing, 1999.

Leadbeater, C. W., and Annie Besant. *Occult Chemistry: Investigations by Clairvoyant Magnification into the Structure of the Atoms of the Periodic Table and Some Compounds.* Whitefish, MT: Kessinger Publishing, 1997.

Ostrander, Sheila, and Lynn Schroeder. *Psychic Discoveries behind the Iron Curtain.* New York: Prentice-Hall, 1984.

Walker, E. H. "Foundations of Paraphysical and Parapsychological Phenomena." In *Quantum Physics and Parapsychology*, edited by Laura Oteri, 1–53. New York: Parapsychological Association, Inc., 1975.

Wheeler, John Archibald, with Ken Ford. *Geons, Black Holes & Quantum Foam: A Life in Physics.* New York: W. W. Norton, 2000.

White, John. *The Meeting of Science and Spirit: Guidelines for a New Age.* New York: Paragon House Publishers, 1990.

Wolf, Fred Alan. *Parallel Universes: The Search for Other Worlds.* New York: Simon & Schuster, 1990.

THE SCIENTIFIC HISTORY OF REMOTE VIEWING (CIRCA 1972–1993)

Puthoff, Harold E., and Russell Targ. "Information Transmission Under Conditions of Sensory Shielding." *Proceedings of the IEEE* (January 1975): 12–19.

Puthoff, Harold E., and Russell Targ. "Perceptual Augmentation Techniques: Part Two—Research Report." *Stanford Research Institute Final Report* (December 1, 1975).

Puthoff, Harold E., and Russell Targ. "A Perceptual Channel for Information Transfer over Kilometer Distances: Historical Perspective and Recent Research." *Proceedings of the IEEE* (March 1976): 329–354.

Targ, Russell, and Keith Harary. *The Mind Race: Understanding and Using Psychic Abilities.* New York: Ballantine Books, 1985.

Targ, Russell, and Jane Katra. *Miracles of Mind: Exploring Nonlocal Consciousness and Spiritual Healing.* Novato, CA: New World Library, 1999.

Targ, Russell, and Harold Puthoff. *Mind-Reach: Scientists Look at Psychic Abilities.* New York: Delacorte Press, 1977.

Tart, Charles T., Harold E. Puthoff, and Russell Targ, eds. *Mind at Large: IEEE Symposia on the Nature of Extrasensory Perception.* Charlottesville, VA: Hampton Roads Publishing Company, 2002.

THE SCIENTIFIC HISTORY OF REMOTE VIEWING
(CIRCA 1994 TO PRESENT)

Since I wrote *Psychic Warrior,* which was the first book about the highly classified CIA/DIA Remote Viewing espionage program, the door has been opened for any number of individuals to release information about their involvement in this program, be it from the research perspective, the analyst perspective, the management perspective, the evaluator perspective, the monitor perspective, and, of course, the Remote Viewer perspective. I can only speak from the perspective of the Remote Viewer, since this is what I was trained to be. However, there may come a time when you will want to explore further and witness the opinions, interpretations, egos, and indeed the critical perspectives of everyone who was ever involved in the espionage application of Remote Viewing. If I were to list all their papers, articles, and books, I am afraid the list would go on indefinitely. Therefore, I am listing several websites that I think are excellent, presenting solid science, historical data, and new research. Try to remember that everything is just another version, including the information contained in these Web pages.

http://lfr.org: The Laboratories for Fundamental Research Cognitive Sciences Laboratory. The principal is Dr. Edwin C. May.

http://anson.ucdavis.edu/~utts: University of California, Davis, Department of Statistics. The principal is Professor Jessica Utts, who is currently serving as the interim director of the Davis HonorsChallenge. Among other studies, Professor Utts is interested in applied statistics and has published most extensively on the use of statistics in parapsychology. I shared an interview with her many years ago for the television show *Sightings,* and I can tell you she is well worth reading—a stellar researcher and leader in her field.

http://www.irva.org: International Remote Viewing Association. The principal will vary annually by election or appointment. This is the largest collection of trained and untrained Remote Viewers in the world. Many of my former colleagues are founding members of this organization, and I recommend it as an ongoing source of information and networking. Visit the website for membership information and a conference schedule.

http://www.scientificexploration.org: Society for Scientific Exploration. Founded in 1982 by a committee of fourteen scientists and scholars who foster the study of all questions that are amenable to scientific investigation without restriction. The society has eight hundred members and associates from more than forty-five countries, holds annual meetings, and publishes a quarterly peer-reviewed journal. You can become an associate, a member, or a supporter of this society or simply subscribe to the *Journal of Scientific Exploration*. The principal is Peter Sturrock, of Stanford University.

http://www.parapsych.org: Parapsychological Association. An international organization of scientists and scholars engaged in the study of psychic experiences, such as telepathy, clairvoyance, psychokinetics, psychic healing, and precognition.

http://www.espresearch.com: Russell Targ. The principal is a physicist and author who was a pioneer in the development of the laser and cofounder of the Stanford Research Institute's investigation into psychic abilities in the 1970s and 1980s.

http://www.paradigm-sys.com: Charles T. Tart. The principal is a core faculty member of the Institute of Transpersonal Psychology in Palo Alto, California. Dr. Tart is internationally known for his psychological work on the nature of consciousness (particularly altered states of consciousness), as one of the founders of the field of transpersonal psychology, and for his research in scientific parapsychology.

SCIENTIFIC AND TECHNICAL RESOURCES AND REFERENCES

Bem, Daryl J., and Charles Honorton. "Does PSI Exist? Replicable Evidence for an Anomalous Process of Information Transfer." *Psychological Bulletin* 115 (1994): 4–18.

Bierman, Dick J. "The Amsterdam Ganzfeld Series III & IV: Target Clip Emotionality, Effect Sizes, and Openness." In *Proceedings of Presented Papers: The 38th Annual Parapsychological Association Convention,* edited by N. L. Zingrone, 27–37. Petaluma, CA: Parapsychological Association, Inc., 1995.

Broughton, Richard, and Cheryl Alexander. "Autoganzfeld II: The First 100 Sessions." In *Proceedings of Presented Papers: The 38th Annual Parapsychological Association Convention,* edited by N. L. Zingrone, 53–61. Petaluma, CA:Parapsychological Association, Inc., 1975.

May, Edwin C. "AC Technical Trials: Inspiration for the Target Entropy Concept." *SAIC Technical Report* (May 26, 1995).

May, Edwin C., Nevin D. Lantz, and Tom Piantineda. "Feedback Considerations in Anomalous Cognition Experiments." *Cognitive Sciences Laboratory Technical Report* (November 29, 1994).

May, Edwin C., J. M. Utts, V. V. Trask, W. W. Luke, T. J. Frivold, and B.

S. Humphrey. "Review of the Psychoenergetic Research Conducted at SRI International (1973–1988)." *SRI International Technical Report* (March 1989).

Morris, Robert L., Kathy Dalton, Deborah Delanoy, and Caroline Watt. "Comparison of the Sender/No Sender Condition in the Ganzfeld." In *Proceedings of Presented Papers: The 38th Annual Parapsychological Association Convention,* edited by N. L. Zingrone, 244–259. Petaluma, CA: Parapsychological Association, Inc., 1995.

Puthoff, Harold E., and Russell Targ. "Perceptual Augmentation Techniques: Part Two—Research Report." *Stanford Research Institute Final Report* (December 1, 1975).

THE ART AND SCIENCE OF REMOTE VIEWING

This list includes the work of other members of the Remote Viewing unit, which I believe you should read when you are finished with this book. From these selections, you will pick up additional techniques perhaps not covered in this text. Each of these individuals is telling their version of the Remote Viewing world, and you should know what those versions are. What is fascinating is that each of us worked in the same place day to day, was given the same categories of targets, good and bad, yet has a different perspective on how the unit functioned, what we learned, how we experienced the phenomenon of Remote Viewing, and what we consider to be the lessons learned from RV. Remain the observer, and understand that each of us can only paint the picture as it is perceived through our personal lens. My key recommendation here is for you to read about the art and science of Remote Viewing, the science and the history behind it, and to avoid reading those works composed entirely of gossip and opinion. In order to become a better Remote Viewer, you need not read heavily about Remote Viewing per se, especially since most of what has been written about it thus far is pure opinion, speculation, or at best, a person's version of the facts—and this includes my book *Psychic Warrior*. Read *Psychic Warrior* if you want to read a story of transformation, sacrifice, and a family's courage, but do not read it to learn how to Remote View. It was never intended to fulfill that purpose. *Psychic Warrior* is the story of my life and my experience in the military and beyond. The following list should be held to the same understanding: these are not how-to books; they are samples, examples, and stories, but they are not manuals designed to teach you the protocols of Remote Viewing.

Remote Viewing Accounts

Buchanan, Lyn. *The Seventh Sense: The Secrets of Remote Viewing as Told by a "Psychic Spy" for the U.S. Military.* New York: Paraview Pocket Books, 2003.

McMoneagle, Joseph. *The Stargate Chronicles: Memoirs of a Psychic Spy.* Charlottesville, VA: Hampton Roads Publishing Company, 2002.

McMoneagle, Joseph. *Mind Trek: Exploring Consciousness, Time, and Space Through Remote Viewing.* Charlottesville, VA: Hampton Roads Publishing Company, 1993, 1997.

McMoneagle, Joseph. *The Ultimate Time Machine: A Remote Viewer's Perception of Time, and Predictions for the New Millennium.* Charlottesville, VA: Hampton Roads Publishing Company, 1998.

Morehouse, David. *Psychic Warrior: Inside the CIA's Stargate Program: The True Story of a Soldier's Espionage and Awakening.* New York: St. Martin's Press, 1996.

Rifat, Tim. *Remote Viewing: What It Is, Who Uses It, and How to Do It.* London: Vision Paperbacks, 2003.

Schnabel, Jim. *Remote Viewers: The Secret History of America's Psychic Spies.* New York: Dell Publishing, 1997. [This book is probably the most definitive chronological work to date. If you want a version of the history of Remote Viewing from inception to the alleged decline in 1996, this would be the book. It is written by a CIA "strategic writer," and it serves its purpose, including an attack on me. That said, I cannot in good conscience steer you away from it. It includes the names, places, and missions of just about every aspect of RV through the 1970s, 1980s, and early 1990s.]

Meditation

Anh-Huong, Nguyen, and Thich Nhat Hanh. *Walking Meditation.* Boulder, CO: Sounds True, 2006.

Kornfield, Jack. *Meditation for Beginners: Six Guided Meditations for Insight, Inner Clarity, and Cultivating a Compassionate Heart.* Boulder, CO: Sounds True, 2004.

Lama Surya Das. *Natural Radiance: Awakening to Your Great Perfection.* Boulder, CO: Sounds True, 2005.

Miller, Richard. *Yoga Nidra: Awaken to Unqualified Presence through Traditional Mind-Body Practices.* Boulder, CO: Sounds True, 2005.

Rinpoche, Tenzin Wangyal. *The Tibetan Yogas of Dream and Sleep*. New York: Snow Lion Publications, 1998.

St. Ruth, Diana. *Sitting: A Guide to Buddhist Meditation*. New York: Penguin Group, 1998.

Suzuki, Shunryu. *Zen Mind, Beginner's Mind: Informal Talks on Zen Meditation and Practice*. New York: John Weatherhill, 1970.

Thornton, Mark. *Meditation in a New York Minute: Super Calm for the Super Busy*. Boulder, CO: Sounds True, 2006.

Trungpa, Chögyam. *Shambhala: The Sacred Path of the Warrior*. Boston: Shambhala Publications, 1984.

GENERAL READING FOR REMOTE VIEWERS

Bell, J. S. "On the Problem of Hidden Variables in Quantum Theory." *Reviews of Modern Physics* 38 (1966): 447–452.

Brennan, J. H. *Time Travel: A New Perspective*. St. Paul, MN: Llewellyn Publications, 1997.

Capra, Fritjof. *The Tao of Physics*. Boston: Shambhala Publications, 1984, 1999.

Carter, Rita. *Mapping the Mind*. Berkeley: University of California Press, 1998.

Conlan, Roberta, ed. *States of Mind: New Discoveries about How Our Brains Make Us Who We Are*. New York: John Wiley & Sons, 2001.

Davies, Paul. *About Time: Einstein's Unfinished Revolution*. New York: Simon & Schuster, 1996.

Davies, Paul. *The 5th Miracle: The Search for the Origin and Meaning of Life*. New York: Simon & Schuster, 2000.

Davies, Paul. *The Last Three Minutes: Conjectures about the Ultimate Fate of the Universe*. New York: Perseus Books, 1994.

Davies, Paul. *The Mind of God: The Scientific Basis for a Rational World*. New York: Simon & Schuster, 1993.

Dean, D., J. Mihalasky, S. Ostrander, and L. Schroeder, *Executive ESP*. New York: Prentice-Hall, 1974.

Duffy, Bruce. *The World as I Found It*. Boston: Houghton Mifflin, 1988.

Edelman, Gerald M., and Giulio Tononi. *A Universe of Consciousness: How Matter Becomes Imagination*. New York: Basic Books, 2000.

Edwards, Betty. *Drawing on the Right Side of the Brain*. New York: St. Martin's Press, 1979.

Festinger, Leon. *A Theory of Cognitive Dissonance*. Palo Alto, CA: Stanford University Press, 1957.

Gardner, Howard. *The Mind's New Science: A History of the Cognitive Revolution*. New York: Basic Books, 1987.

Gazzaniga, Michael S. *Nature's Mind: The Biological Roots of Thinking, Emotions, Sexuality, Language, and Intelligence*. New York: Basic Books, 1994.

Gladwell, Malcolm. *The Tipping Point: How Little Things Can Make a Big Difference*. New York: Little, Brown and Company, 2000.

Grof, Stanislav. *When the Impossible Happens: Adventures in Non-ordinary Realities*. Boulder, CO: Sounds True, 2006.

Hawking, Stephen. *A Brief History of Time*. New York: Bantam Books, 1988.

Hawking, Stephen. *The Universe in a Nutshell*. New York: Bantam Books, 2001.

Hobson, J. Allan. *Dreaming as Delirium: How the Brain Goes Out of Its Mind*. Cambridge, MA: MIT Press, 1999.

Horvitz, Leslie Alan. *Eureka! Scientific Breakthroughs That Changed the World*. New York: John Wiley & Sons, 2002.

Hubble, Edwin. *The Realm of the Nebulae*. New Haven, CT: Yale University Press, 1935, reissue 1983.

Jahn, Robert G., and Brenda J. Dunne. *Margins of Reality: The Role of Consciousness in the Physical World*. New York: Harvest Books, 1989.

Johnson, George. *In the Palaces of Memory: How We Build the Worlds Inside Our Heads*. New York: Alfred A. Knopf, 1991.

Karow, Alice Louise. *Cook from Your Heart: Recipes for Transformation*. Philadelphia: XLibris, 2006.

Lark, Susan M., and James A. Richards. *The Chemistry of Success: 6 Secrets of Peak Performance*. Berkeley, CA: Bay Books, 1999.

Lloyd, D. H. "Objective Events in the Brain Correlating with Psychic Phenomena." *New Horizons* 1 (1973): 69–75.

Lorimer, David, ed. *The Spirit of Science: From Experiment to Experience*. Edinburgh: Floris Books, 1998.

Lynch, Gary. *Synapses, Circuits, and the Beginnings of Memory*. Cambridge, MA: MIT Press, 1986.

Magueijo, João. *Faster Than the Speed of Light: The Story of a Scientific Speculation*. New York: Perseus Books, 2004.

Maor, Eli. *To Infinity and Beyond: A Cultural History of the Infinite*. Princeton, NJ: Princeton University Press, 1991.

Marshall, Colonel S. L. A. *Men Against Fire: The Problem of Battle Command in Future War.* Gloucester, MA: Peter Smith Books, 1978.

McCulloch, Warren S. *Embodiments of Mind.* Cambridge, MA: MIT Press, 1988.

McTaggart, Lynne. *The Field: The Quest for the Secret Force of the Universe.* New York: HarperCollins, 2002.

Monod, Jacques. *Chance and Necessity: An Essay on the Natural Philosophy of Modern Biology.* New York: Alfred A. Knopf, 1971.

Morris, Richard. *The Nature of Reality: The Universe After Einstein.* New York: Noonday Press, 1988.

Overbye, Dennis. *Lonely Hearts of the Cosmos: The Story of the Scientific Quest for the Secret of the Universe.* London: Pan Macmillan, 1991.

Peat, F. David. *Synchronicity: The Bridge Between Matter and Mind.* New York: Bantam Books, 1987.

Phillips, Stephen M. "Extrasensory Perception of Subatomic Particles: Historical Evidence." *Journal of Scientific Exploration 9* (1995): 489–525.

Planck, Max. *Where Is Science Going?* Woodbridge, CT: Ox Bow Press, 1981.

Radin, Dean. *The Conscious Universe: The Scientific Truth of Psychic Phenomena.* San Francisco: HarperSanFrancisco, 1997.

Rees, Martin J. "The Ultimate Fate of the Universe: An Eschatological Study." *The Observatory* 89 (1969): 193.

Rhine, Louisa E. *Hidden Channels of the Mind.* New York: Warner Books, 1989.

Roland, Paul. *Revelations: Wisdom of the Ages: Prophetic Visions and Secret Knowledge to Guide Us into the Millennium.* Berkeley, CA: Ulysses Press, 1995.

Searle, John. *Minds, Brains, and Science.* Cambridge, MA: Harvard University Press, 1986.

Shapiro, Deb. *Your Body Speaks Your Mind: Decoding the Emotional, Psychological, and Spiritual Messages That Underlie Illness.* Boulder, CO: Sounds True, 2006.

Siler, Todd. *Breaking the Mind Barrier.* New York: Simon & Schuster, 1997.

Sinclair, Upton. *Mental Radio.* New York: Warner Books, 1991.

Soal, S. G., and F. Bateman. *Modern Experiments in Telepathy.* London: Faber & Faber, 1954.

Strauss, William, and Neil Howe. *The Fourth Turning: An American Prophecy.* New York: Broadway Books, 1998.

Surowiecki, James. *The Wisdom of Crowds: Why the Many Are Smarter Than* the Few and How Collective Wisdom Shapes Business, Economies, Societies, and Nations. New York: Doubleday, 2004.

Talbot, Michael. *The Holographic Universe.* New York: Harper Perennial, 1992.

Tolle, Eckhart. *The Power of Now: A Guide to Spiritual Enlightenment.* Vancouver: Namaste Publishing, 1999.

Weil, Andrew. *Dr. Andrew Weil's Mind-Body Tool Kit.* Boulder, CO: Sounds True, 2006.

Wilber, Ken. *Quantum Questions: Mystical Writings of the World's Great Physicists.* Boston: Shambhala Publications, 1984.

Wilber, Ken. *The Integral Operating System.* Boulder, CO: Sounds True, 2005.

Wilkins, Sir Hubert, and Harold M. Sherman. *Thoughts through Space: A Remarkable Adventure in the Realm of Mind.* Charlottesville, VA: Hampton Roads Publishing Company, 2004.

Yates, Frances A. *The Art of Memory.* Chicago: University of Chicago Press, 1974.

Zukav, Gary. *The Seat of the Soul.* New York: Simon & Schuster, 1989.

CHILDREN AND PSYCHIC ABILITY

Carroll, Lee, and Jan Tober. *The Indigo Children: The New Kids Have Arrived.* Carlsbad, CA: Hay House, 1999.

Curtis, Chara M. *All I See Is Part of Me.* Bellevue, WA: Illumination Arts Publishing Company, 1994.

Virtue, Doreen. *The Care and Feeding of Indigo Children.* Carlsbad, CA: Hay House, 2001.

Virtue, Doreen. *The Crystal Children: A Guide to the Newest Generation of Psychic and Sensitive Children.* Carlsbad, CA: Hay House, 2003.

ADDITIONAL RESOURCES AND REFERENCES

I also highly recommend the following authors as people who have inspired me to live a life of promise and possibility. I consider them friends and colleagues.

Deepak Chopra, M.D.

Wayne Dyer, Ph.D.

Don Miguel Ruiz

Marianne Williamson

For more information about my work:

www.davidmorehouse.com

info@davidmorehouse.com

Index

biology, 210

Bohr, Niels, 59

brain, the biological, 212–213, *213*. *See also* mind, the

brain-wave states, 361

breaks, 93, 132–138, 229
AOL breaks, 136, 156–158
confusion breaks, 134, 137, *137*
missed breaks, 133, *133*
too-much breaks, *137*, 137–138

C

"C" components, 93, *125*, 125–128, *127*, 136, 137–138. *See also* A/B/C component process

capacitors, 76

Capra, Fritjof, 58

Cartesian systems, 17–18

CD, 44

Center Lane Program, 24

Central Intelligence Agency (CIA), 20–23, 26–28, 32–33, 102

Chadwick, James, 75

challenges, 129

change, 72

Channon, James B., 23

choice, 2

Chomsky, Noam, 221

Chopra, Deepak, 62, 211

CIA. *See* Central Intelligence Agency (CIA)

coding, 93–94

cognitron data, 94, 212–216, 229–230. *See also* cognitron formations

cognitron formations, 212–216, *215*, *216*, 228. *See also* cognitron data

coherent light, 77–78

Cold War, the, 23

collective unconscious, the, 15, 35, 55, 111, 211

Committee for the Scientific Investigation of Claims of the Paranormal (CSICOP), 25

communication, 229–230, 231

communication objects, 230, 231

conceptual illusion, 10, 32, 54–55, 69, 71, 72, 73, 146

conscious mind, the, 60–61, 66, 94, 120

consciousness, Freudian model of, 120

constructive wave interference, *63*

continuous creation, *73*

cooldown, 94, 109–110

cooldown mask, 43

Coordinate Remote Viewing (CRV), 15, 17–18, 26, 37, 100, 101, 102, 169–189. *See also* Remote Viewing (RV)
definition of, 10
lexicon of, 60–66, 75–79, 91–105
moving forward by going back, 184–186
optimum learning environment, 42–47, *46*
Phase II of training, 41, 42
Phase I of training, 41, 42
protocol, 107–141
residential course, 360–361
ritual of, 111
six stages of, 41
Stage I, 107–141
Stage II, 138–139, 143–167, 184–186, 199–200
Stage III, 164, 166–167, 169–189
Stage IV, 161, 162, 187–189, 191–207, *193*, *195*
Stage V, 138, 206–207, 209–232
Stage VI, 233–245

structure of the process, 46–47
training program, 42–43
coordinates, 94
    assigning, 369–372
    recording, 372
    retaking, 132–138
    taking, 115–117
cosmology, 95
creation, continuous, *73*
Cruise, Tom, 205
crystals, 77, 78
CSICOP. *See* Committee for the
    Scientific Investigation of Claims of
    the Paranormal (CSICOP)
cuing position, 115–117, *116*

D

D&ST. *See* Directorate of Science and
    Technology (D&ST)
data, 10–11, 61–62
    aesthetic data (AD), 92, 162, 191,
        201–202, 241
    cognitron data, 94, 212–216,
        229–230
    data bleed-through, 95, 160–162,
        161
    data clusters, 95
    data strings, 95
    dimensional data (D), 96, 151–152,
        200–201
    emotional data (ED), 96–97, 162,
        191, 202–203
    intangible data (I), 98–99,
        151–152, 191, 194, 204
    mind, the, 145–146
    raw viewing data, 12
    sensory data, 11–12, 143–144,
        150–151, 225
    tangible data (T), 104, 203–204
    verbal data, 10–11
    in verbal data, 145–151, 199–200,

235–236
    in visual data, 152–154, 171, 172,
        173–174, 235–236
    waveform data, 10–11, 15, 54–55,
        61, 66, 68, 79, 109, 191–192
data bleed-through, 95, 160–162
data clusters, 95
data strings, 95
data bleed-through, *161*
decoding, 93–96, 120, 145, 172–173,
    179–180, 191–192, 194. *See also*
    pure Viewing
Defense Intelligence Agency (DIA), 19,
    26–27, 22, 102. *See also* Department
    of Defense
delta function, *69*
Department of Defense, 9, 22–23, 26,
    360. *See also* Defense Intelligence
    Agency; military intelligence
destructive wave interference, *64*
detecting, 96, 120, 145, 172–173,
    191–192
DIA. *See* Defense Intelligence Agency
    (DIA)
diagonal, 96
dialectics, 76
Didion, Joan, 145–146
digital modality, 100
dimensional data (D), 96, 151–152,
    200–201
Dirac, Paul, 59, 68, *69*
Directorate of Science and Technology
    (D&ST), 26–27
disagreement, 358
discomfort. *See* personal inclemency
drawing. *See* rendering; sketching
dreams, 72
drugs, 53–55
dualistic awareness, 36–37

E

Edwards, Betty, 174

ego, letting go of, 48–49, 50, 56

eight dimensional space, 211

eight-dimensional space. *See also under* waveform data

Einstein, Albert, 38, 59, 68

electron, the, 76

electrostatic field of the terrestrial plane, *77*

emotional data (ED), 96–97, 162, 191, 202–203

emotional impact (EI), 97, 171, 236, 163

emotional stress. *See* personal inclemency

empirical knowledge, 36, 38

encoding, 93–94

energy, 51, 55, *63*, *64*, 73
    food and, 52
    positive, 51
    quantum physics and, 70
    time and, 70
    waveform and, 62–65

environmental inclemency, 115

ether, the, 75, 97

evaluator cycle, *31*, 31–32

event arcs, 108

evoking, 97

exercise, 52

"experience Rolodex", 178–179

Explorer Group, 37, 362

Extended Remote Viewing (ERV), 37, 97, 100, 102, 192, 220, 361

extremely low frequency (ELF) electromagnetic radiation, 115

F

feedback, 97

Feynman, Richard, 59

First Earth Battalion, 23

food, 52

forgiveness, 357–358

four-dimensional space. *See also* four-dimensional thought form

four-dimensional thought form, 10, 11, 66, 68, 109

four-dimensional space, 211

Franck, Frederick, 174

free association, *218*

Frege, Friedrich Ludwig Gottlob, 212

Freud, Sigmund, 217

front loading, 97–98, 15, 18

function, 227, 228

future, the, 69, 71, 72–73, *73*, 74. *See also* time

G

Gaius Sallustius Crispus (Sallust), 4

Gandhi, Mohandas Karamchand (Mahatma), 359

Gauvin, Fernand, 2–3

Gestalt, the, 28, 98, 104, *118*

glial cells, 213, 216

global mind, the, 35, 55, 111, 211

global society, 36, 38
    evolution of the, *89*
    four turnings of the, 86–87

God, mind of, 34, 35, 39, 61, 211

Golden Sphere Concept, 23

Gottlieb, Sidney, 21

Grid Mercator system. *See* Universal Transverse Mercator (UTM) Grid System

Grill Flame, 22

gustatory modality, 100

H

half stages, 183–184
Henley, Don, 355
holigraphic universe, the, 35
holograms, 78–79
Holographic Matrix Field, the, 78–86, *80–81, 82–83, 84, 85. See also* Matrix Field, the
Horney, Karen, 217
Howe, Neil, 86
"hundredth monkey effect", 55
Huxley, Aldous, 59
hydration, 52

I

I/A/B/C sequence, 98
ideograms, 98, 120–128, 136, 137. *See also* rendering; sketching
    developing the, *118*, 118–120
    split ideogram, 134
image, challenging the, 181–183
imagination, 179
Imperial College, England, 58–59
inclemency, 98
    environmental, 115
    personal, 113–115
inexpressible knowledge. *See* spiritual knowledge
infinite, the, 75
inner dialogue, 48
INSCOM. *See* Intelligence and Security Command (INSCOM)
intangible data (I), 98–99, 151–152, 191, 194, 204. *See also* intangibles
intangibles, 213, 215, 222–226, *224, 226. See also* intangible data (I)
Intelligence and Security Command (INSCOM), 24, 23–24

intention, *31*, 31–32, 99, 228–229, 230
intuitive knowledge, 36, 37–38
ionosphere, 76
isomorphism, 28

K

Kant, Immanuel, 28, 211
Kinesthetic Modality, 100
King, Larry, 27
knowing, 36–38, 72
    vs. believing, 35–36
    empirical knowledge, 36, 38
    intuitive knowledge, 36, 37–38
    spiritual knowledge, 36
Koppel, Ted, 27

L

labeling, 153–154, 172–173
language, 145–151, 212, 217–222. *See also* verbal data
language exercises, 149–151
laser cavities, 77
lasers, 77–78
latitude, 17–18
layers, seeing in, 192
learning environment, 42–47, *46*
Lichtenberg, Georg Christoph, 35
light
    coherent, 77–78
    monochromatic light, 76–77, 78
light waves, 11–12
liminality, 99
longitude, 17–18

M

Machu Picchu, 148

Remote Viewers. *See also* Remote
Viewing (RV)
  age of, 34
  becoming a Remote Viewer, 29–40
  Coordinate Remote Viewers, 37
  Extended Remote Viewers, 37
  Master Extended Remote Viewers,
    37
  spirituality and, 34–36
  transformation of, 38–40
  vocation and, 34
Remote Viewing (RV), 102. *See also*
Coordinate Remote Viewing (CRV)
  accuracy of, 16
  alcohol and, 53
  ancient practices of, 20
  on the battlefield, 47
  Coordinate Remote Viewing, 10, 15
  definition of, 9–14
  ego and, 56
  exercise and, 52
  food and, 52
  history of, 19–28
  illlicit drugs and, 53–54
  learning, 41–56
  meat and, 52
  in the media, 27
  method for successful performance,
    51
  practice of, 51–55
  self-doubt and, 56
  self-judgment and, 47–51
  skepticism about, 24–25
  sleep and, 52
  spirituality and, 39
  stimulants and, 52–53
  as a team effort, 16
  terms of reference, 91–105
  three rules of, 15–16
  as a tool, 38
  water and, 52
Remote Sensing, 22
rendering, 102, 103, 235, 242–244,

361. *See also* sketching
residential course, 360–361
ritual, 111
Ruiz Delgado, Jorge, 148
Russell, Bertrand, 212
Rutherford, Ernest, 75

S

Sakamura, Ken, 214
sample session, 43, 46, *327–331*,
  247–321
Schrödinger, Erwin, 74, 210
Schrödinger's probability density
  equation, 74
science
  spirit and, 57–59
  technology and, 210
scientism, 25
self-doubt, 50, 56
self-judgment, 47–51
sense. *See* perception; sensory data
sensory data, 11–12, 143–144,
  150–151, 152–154, 225. *See also*
  perception
sensory perception. *See* perception
sensory journaling, 149–150
session feedback, 97
session, timing the, 109
session analysis, 323–343, *327–331*
session heading, the, 111–112, *112*
session summary, 323–343
  analytical overlay (AOL) in,
    333–335
  format of, 332–333
  sample of, 338–343
  summary template, 336–337
setup, 228–229
shadow self, the, 362–363

About the Author

David Morehouse, Ph.D. is a former U.S. Army Ranger Commander and Special Operations Officer. After suffering a gunshot wound to the head in the kingdom of Jordan in 1987, he was recruited and trained in Remote Viewing in a top-secret CIA program code-named Project Star Gate, as described in his international bestseller, *Psychic Warrior: Inside the CIA's Star Gate Program.* Since his departure and honorable discharge from the military he has devoted his life to empowering others so that they might shift from the mere belief that they are more than the physical to actually knowing it through the practice and application of any number of dutiful paths—Remote Viewing being one of those paths.

His commitment to human excellence, promise, and possibility has taken him across the globe, teaching and lecturing; he has lectured by invitation at venues including the Mikhail Gorbachev State of the World Forum, the Alliance for a New Humanity, The Global Sciences Foundation, and several United Nations functions in Montreal, Canada, as well as Stanford University's graduate business program. He has taught alongside Deepak Chopra and Don Miguel Ruíz.

His Remote Viewing story and teaching have enthralled millions on the Discovery, History, and Sci-Fi channels. In his Remote Viewing seminars, he has taught over 23,000 students in sixteen countries. He is the author of *Nonlethal Weapons: War Without Death*, *Psychic Warrior*, and *The Deceivers*.

Also Available on Audio from David Morehouse

To order or request more information, call 800-333-9185 or visit www.soundstrue.com.

The Remote Viewing Training Course
Principles and Techniques of Coordinate Remote Viewing

An unprecedented home study course for Coordinate Remote Viewing from David Morehouse—the most complete self-training program available for unlocking your innate ability to see across space and time. Includes 21 CDs, a 284-page illustrated workbook, eye mask, and 3 practice targets.

The Remote Viewing Training Course
ISBN 978-1-59179-101-0 / U.S. $249.00

Remote Viewing
An Introduction to Coordinate Remote Viewing

Get your first taste of your unlimited potential with this introductory audio course by David Morehouse. Includes 4 CDs of instruction and 3 practice sessions on DVD.

Remote Viewing: An Introduction to Coordinate Remote Viewing
ISBN 978-1-59179-240-6 / U.S. $29.95

SOUNDS TRUE was founded in 1985 with a clear vision: to disseminate spiritual wisdom. Located in Boulder, Colorado, Sounds True publishes teaching programs that are designed to educate, uplift, and inspire. We work with many of the leading spiritual teachers, thinkers, healers, and visionary artists of our time.

To receive a free catalog of tools and teachings for personal and spiritual transformation, please visit www.soundstrue.com, call toll-free 800-333-9185, or write to us at the address below.

The Sounds True Catalog
PO Box 8010
Boulder, CO 80306